SPACE TRAVEL
A Technological Frontier

SPACE TRAVEL

A Technological Frontier

Alan R. De Old, Ed.D.
Bloomfield High School, Bloomfield, NJ

Joseph W. Judge, MEEE.
The Aerospace Corporation, Los Angeles, CA

Teri-Lynn Judge, MSEE.
Martin Marietta Space Systems, Long Beach, CA

Davis Publications, Inc.
Worcester, Massachusetts

Copyright ©1989
Davis Publications, Inc.
Worcester, Massachusetts, U.S.A.

All rights reserved. No part of this publication may be reproduced or transmitted in any form or by any means, electronic or mechanical, including photocopying, recording, or any storage and retrieval system now known or to be invented, except by a reviewer who wishes to quote brief passages in connection with a review written for inclusion in a magazine, newspaper, or broadcast.

Design: Penny Darras-Maxwell

Cover Illustration: Tom Norton

Frontis: The Orbital Maneuvering Vehicle will play an important part in Space Station operations.
P.J. Weisgerber, TRW Corp.

Printed in the United States of America

ISBN: 0-87192-206-1

Acknowledgements

This textbook was written with advice and information from many people at research centers, government agencies, and companies concerned with space technology.

We extend special thanks to:

Bart Barthelemy, Wright-Patterson Air Force Base
Fred Brown, TRW Space and Technology Group
John Cooke, McDonnell Douglas Corporation
Robert Davis, The Aerospace Corporation
Allen Frew, TRW Space and Technology Group
Mark Hess, NASA Office of Space Station
Marcia Smith, Library of Congress
S.F. Bogodyaj, Glavkosmos

We are also indebted to the following organizations for their assistance with information and illustrations:

Arianespace
British Aerospace
MBB, Space Systems Group, ERNO-USA, Incorporated
McDonnell Douglas Corporation
Morton Thiokol Incorporated
National Aeronautics and Space Administration (NASA)
    Marshall Space Flight Center
    Goddard Space Flight Center
    Johnson Space Center
    Office of Space Station
Rockwell International, Rocketdyne Division
Salamander Books Limited
TRW Incorporated
Central Administration of Space Technology Development, Moscow

Much of the background information for this book comes from: *Transportation: The Technology of Moving People and Products* by Alan De Old, Everett Sheets and William Alexander; 1986, Davis Publications, Inc. It is cited in the text as: De Old, 1986.

CONTENTS

Preface   6
Introduction   7

Part One   TO EARTH ORBIT   9
Chapter 1   **Expendable Launch Vehicles**   10
Chapter 2   **Space Shuttles**   26
Chapter 3   **Aerospace Planes**   66

Part Two   WITHIN EARTH ORBIT   81
Chapter 4   **Orbital Maneuvering Vehicle**   82
Chapter 5   **Manned Maneuvering Unit**   102
Chapter 6   **Space Stations**   114

Glossary   140
Index   142

PREFACE

As humans we are unique in our ability to invent and use technology for the betterment of life on Earth. Central to this process is our capacity to dream — to look to the future.

In the 1930s, a cartoon character named Buck Rogers captured the imagination of all who read about his adventures in space. In the 1950s, the television program entitled *Captain Video* took us into space in rocket ships to explore and investigate new worlds. More recently television and movies have extended these journeys in such shows as *Star Trek*, *Star Wars*, and *Battlestar Galactica*. Science fiction has expanded the human experience, encouraging us "to go where no one has gone before."

Movies and television make extraordinary technology look routine: with blinding speed, spaceships range through the universe; at the flick of a switch, people are transported, or beamed, from one place to another. In the 1930s, you would have had a difficult time convincing people that this was anything but fiction. Today, aerospace technology has transformed some of this fiction into reality.

We invite you to read this book and examine the technology of space transportation of today and the technology of the immediate future. This world presents tremendous challenges in things yet to come. You can play a part in shaping that future by understanding and contributing to technology.

INTRODUCTION

Space, the last frontier, differs from the many other frontiers encountered during human history. When the descendants of the original Siberian migrants reached the tip of South America, they could travel no farther. When Columbus landed in the West Indies, he reached the end of his journey. When the westward expansion across North America took place, it ended at the Pacific Ocean. But when we entered space, we opened a door that seemingly has no end. We have traveled in Earth orbit, reached the moon and sent unmanned probes out to explore the planets of our solar system. And what of the other space frontiers ahead? Beyond our solar system, there is the entire Milky Way Galaxy. Beyond our galaxy, there are other galaxies containing more stars, solar systems, and possibly other inhabited worlds.

Millions of years passed between the beginnings of human technical means and an important day in 1957 when Sputnik became the first artificial satellite in orbit around the Earth. Since then, we have taken the first steps in exploring space. With each new step, we have needed to develop new technologies. Certain developments, including expendable launch vehicles, the space shuttle, and the aerospace plane, bring people and payloads into orbit around the Earth. Other developments, such as the Space Station, Manned Maneuvering Vehicle and Orbital Maneuvering Vehicle, are specifically for working in space. Many different technologies make these types of space transportation possible. The following chapters describe these space vehicles and their technologies.

When reading this book, remember that these vehicles are, like science fiction, the result of imagination. We must first picture in our minds what we want. But, unlike science fiction, we must justify the idea by proving that it can work properly, safely, reliably, on time and at a reasonable cost. Arriving at the best design involves trade offs until a compromise is reached that will satisfy everyone. Many good ideas fail when they cannot be proven possible or worthwhile. Finally, a supreme effort must go into building and using the vehicle. Technological ideas which have survived this succession are presented in this book.

PART ONE

TO EARTH ORBIT

Why do we transport people and products into orbit around the Earth? Most reasons fall into three categories: scientific, commercial, or military. Scientific missions in orbit include photographing the Earth below and space above, as well as measuring space radiation. Another type of scientific mission takes place on space stations in orbit around the Earth. There, scientists investigate many technologies and find out how humans can live in the weightlessness of space. A typical commercial mission involves placing a communication satellite into orbit. The military also places satellites into orbit. These missions include navigation, communication, early warning and surveillance.

Putting objects into orbit requires a great deal of energy. The farther out the object must be, the more energy is needed to place it in its orbit. These large amounts of energy are needed to overcome the gravity of the Earth. To overcome gravity, launch vehicles are used. These vehicles accelerate up through the atmosphere and into the vacuum of space. Such vehicles are either expendable or reusable. Most missiles and rockets are expendable since they are only used once. These expendable launch vehicles launch straight up and then slowly turn to accelerate into orbit above the Earth. They are "used up" when their missions are completed. Once finished, they fall back to Earth and splash down into the ocean.

Reusable launchers include space shuttles and aerospace planes. In the shuttle space transportation system, both the shuttle itself and the solid rocket boosters are refurbished after every mission. Only the liquid-fuel tank is not reused. Every part of an aerospace plane will be designed to be reused. It will probably require less refurbishing than the shuttle and may someday take-off from airports to soar into space.

These vehicles exhibit some of the most impressive technology created by the people of our modern world. Some of this technology will be explained in the following chapters. Because these vehicles are so complex, explanations will be given of the parts, or subsystems, which together make up the whole vehicle or system. Here then, are some technological systems which bring us to Earth orbit: Expendable Launch Vehicles, Space Shuttles, and Aerospace Planes.

Boosters such as the Atlas, originally used for military use, have now found more peaceful uses.

The Saturn V, the largest ELV ever built in the U.S., enabled humans to reach the moon. It has not been used since the end of the Apollo space program.

Chapter 1

EXPENDABLE LAUNCH VEHICLES

Large rockets are used to launch satellites and people into space. They are called expendable launch vehicles (ELVs) because they can only be used once, as opposed to the space shuttle which is reusable.

Scientists first started experimenting with small rockets in the early 1900s. During this time they discovered many of the principles of rocketry. In the 1940s and 1950s, most rocketry research was directed at producing long-range bombs, such as the Intercontinental Ballistic Missile (ICBM). However, this emphasis changed drastically in 1957 when the Soviet Union launched the first human-made satellite, Sputnik. The "Race for Space" became a scientific and commercial as well as military venture. For a long time, only the United States and the Soviet Union could explore space. However, many nations are now sending their own rockets into space.

After years of successful launches, placing people and satellites in space became routine to the general public. The performance and reliability of rockets was taken for granted. This attitude changed after the 1986 space shuttle *Challenger* explosion. It was a tragic reminder that rockets are huge, complicated machines filled with powerful chemicals. It takes a thorough understanding of the ELV's technology to safely harness its power.

Historical Development

Early science fiction inspired many to think about traveling in space. People such as H. G. Wells and Jules Verne wrote stories of rocket flights and alien invaders. However, one man wrote serious proposals for rocket flights into space. Konstantin Eduardovich Tsiolkovsky (1857–1935), considered an eccentric dreamer, lived in Kaluga, a small Russian town outside Moscow. He wrote many articles between 1880 and 1930 about rocket flight and space travel. He explained the principles by which rockets could fly in the vacuum of space. Many scientists at the time did not think this was possible.

TO EARTH ORBIT

Tsiolkovsky was the first person to propose liquid-propellant rockets, multi-stage boosters, gimbaled engine guidance, and gyroscopic stabilization — concepts explained later in the chapter. He even proposed techniques for life-support systems and space station construction. His ideas inspired many future rocket scientists.

In the United States, Robert H. Goddard (1882–1945) first proved one of Tsiolkovsky's ideas. In 1912, Goddard showed that rockets could work in the vacuum of space. He was one of our first scientists to experiment with liquid-propellant rockets. Because of his pioneering efforts, the National Aeronautics and Space Administration (NASA) named one of their research facilities after him.

Two other names stand out prominently among the ranks of rocket scientists: Werhner von Braun (1912–1977) and Sergei P. Korolev (1906–1966). Korolev was the father of rocketry in the Soviet Union. His missile design made the Sputnik launch possible.

Werhner von Braun led the team that developed rockets for the Nazi German Army during World War II. After the war, he came to the United States to work as a rocket scientist. In the 1960s, he was instrumental in developing the Saturn V booster for the trips to the moon.

Getting Into Orbit

Launch vehicles provide the energy required for an object to escape Earth's gravity and achieve orbit. In the 1950s, military rockets such as ICBMs were built to briefly shoot up above the atmosphere into space. However, these missiles were not designed to put their payloads into orbit. Earth's gravity eventually pulled them down. The technology of putting satellites into orbit was first demonstrated by the Soviet Union with the 1957 launch of Sputnik. They used an ICBM with extra fuel to place Sputnik into orbit. Sputnik was an 83.6 kilogram aluminum sphere which housed a radio and some other electronics. Larger and more powerful boosters were soon developed. In 1969, the Apollo Saturn V booster put more than 60,000 kilograms into orbit.

A booster's thrust at lift-off must be greater than its weight in order to lift-off from the Earth. This means that the upward force, or thrust, of the rocket must be greater than the pull of gravity on the booster. The upward force created by the rocket exhaust is called the thrust. It is described by Newton's Third Law, which states that for every action there is an equal and opposite reaction. The rocket exhaust is the action in Newton's law, while the reaction is thrust. When rocket fuel burns, it releases great amounts of energy. This energy is in the form of hot, high-pressure gas and combustion products. Rockets use a throat followed by a nozzle to convert this heat and pressure energy into kinetic energy. Kinetic energy is the energy of a moving object. The amount of kinetic energy depends on both the mass and the speed of the object. Hot gases and combustion products move at very high speeds and have very large kinetic energies. Therefore, the action of rocket

EXPENDABLE LAUNCH VEHICLES

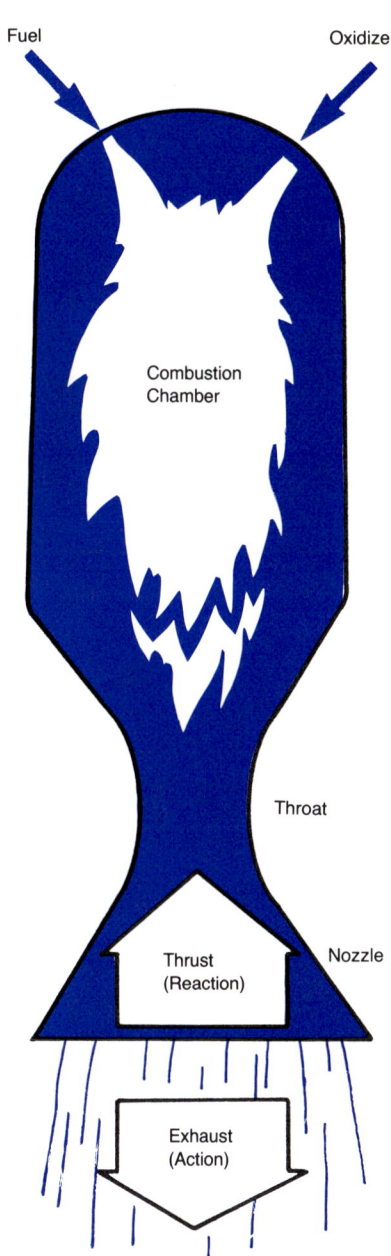

Heated gases expand at very high velocities in all directions. The design of the rocket motor directs those gases to expand into one direction. The resulting force propels the rocket in the opposite direction.

exhaust blasting downward will produce the thrust reaction force pushing upward on the booster.

Boosters are often built in stages. A first stage usually fires, or burns for one or two minutes. Sometimes extra strap-on boosters are attached to the first stage to assist with more thrust during lift-off. When a stage is finished firing, it is separated from the remainder of the vehicle above it. It then usually falls back to Earth. Smaller second or third stages later fire and propel the satellite into its proper orbit. These extra stages are called upper stages. Boosters can usually use different upper stages, depending on the mission. Powerful upper stages are used to send probes to the planets, people to the moon, or very large satellites to Earth orbits. Smaller upper stages are used to put smaller satellites into Earth orbits.

To get a satellite into orbit, a booster must place it outside of the atmosphere. If it were not out of the atmosphere, friction caused by the air would slow it down. Gravity would then pull it back down to Earth. Once in space, the satellite must continue to fight gravity by moving horizontally at a high speed. This large horizontal velocity is called the orbital velocity. This is the satellite principle. Orbital velocity depends on altitude. For example, the orbital velocity at a 320 kilometer altitude orbit is about 28,000 kilometers per hour in a horizontal direction. This velocity is needed at that altitude whether the satellite is traveling around the equator or around the North and South Poles. The orbital velocity is only 11,063 kilometers per hour for an orbit 35,880 kilometers above the Earth.

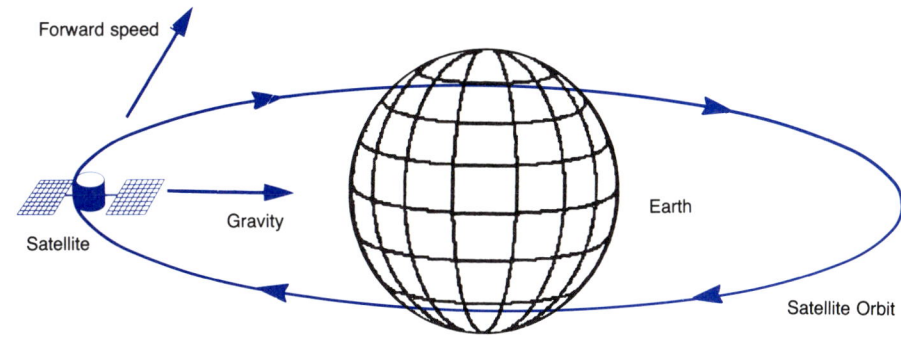

Horizontal (tangential) velocity is needed to keep the satellite from falling to Earth. Altitude affects this velocity.

13

Upper Stages

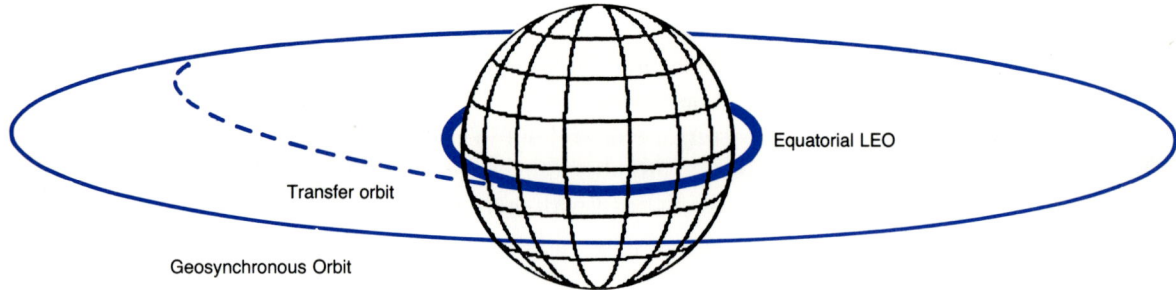

ELVs almost always have more than one stage, or rocket. Each stage fires and burns to produce thrust, one after the other. When each stage runs out of fuel, it is disconnected from the booster. Then the next stage fires.

The term "upper stage" usually refers to the small rocket attached directly to the payload. It sits inside of the ELV, waiting for its turn to fire. A typical upper stage pushes a satellite from LEO to geosynchronous orbit. It takes a curved path, called a transfer orbit. The upper stage is then jettisoned when the payload reaches the desired orbit.

Orbits

Low-Earth orbit (LEO) occupies altitudes between 100 kilometers and 1000 kilometers. Equatorial LEO satellites travel around the planet above the equator; polar LEO satellites travel over the poles. Many weather satellites fly in polar orbits. An inclined LEO is between polar and equatorial orbits. LEO velocities are so great that it takes only an hour or two for satellites to travel around the planet. A satellite in geosynchronous orbit, however, takes exactly 24 hours to travel around the planet. This only happens in orbits 35,880 kilometers above the surface of the Earth. If a satellite is in an equatorial orbit at this altitude, it will travel around the planet at the exact same rate as the Earth rotates. Therefore, to someone standing on the equator, this satellite will appear to stay directly overhead at all times. This is very useful for communication satellites.

The altitude and orientation of satellite orbits satisfies earth-bound demands in different ways. Communications are best handled by satellites with high altitude geo-synchronous orbits. Weather observation is best served by low altitude, rapidly moving satellites.

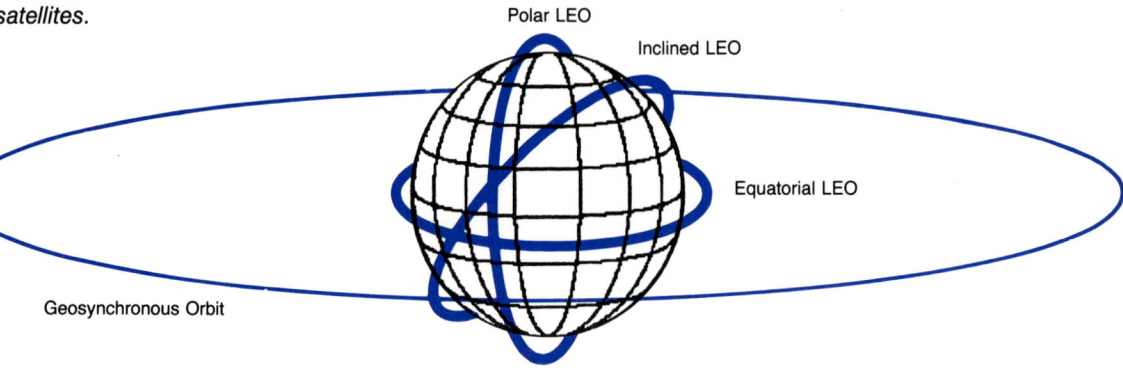

EXPENDABLE LAUNCH VEHICLES

Booster Rocket Technology

Booster rockets are very complicated vehicles. They contain tanks of chemicals, piping, pumps, motors, electronics, computers, and radios. All of this equipment must work reliably during the entire launch. The most important subsystems include the propulsion and guidance equipment.

Propulsion

Propulsion systems require chemical propellants to produce thrust. These propellants may be liquid, solid, or gas. However liquid and solid chemical propellants are most important to the booster industry. These forms permit a rocket to carry more chemical energy. This chemical energy is released in combustion (burning). The combustion products are accelerated by the released energy to produce thrust. The burning process usually involves a fuel and oxidizer reacting chemically to produce high-temperature, high-pressure gases.

Liquid-propellant rockets
The term "liquid propellant" refers to any of the liquid chemicals used in a rocket engine. Normally, these chemicals include an oxidizer and a fuel. However, they may also include additives that improve burning or thrust. Generally, liquid propellants permit longer burning time than solid propellants. Another advantage of liquid-propellant rockets is that combustion can be stopped and started by controlling the flow of propellants.

Liquid propellants can be classified as monopropellants, bipropellants, or tripropellants. A monopropellant contains a fuel and oxidizer combined in one substance. Monopropellant rockets are simple since they need only one propellant tank with its associated equipment. The most common monopropellant system uses hydrazine. A bipropellant is a combination of fuel and oxidizer that is not mixed until after the propellants have been injected into the combustion chamber. Presently, most liquid rockets use bipropellants. A tripropellant has a third chemical that improves performance.

Liquid propellants are commonly classified as either cryogenic or storable. A cryogenic propellant must be kept very cold or it will boil and evaporate away. For example, liquid oxygen boils at $-183°$ Celsius and liquid hydrogen at $-253°$ Celsius. Personnel at the launch site load these propellants into a rocket as near to launch time as possible in order to reduce losses from vaporization and to minimize problems caused by their low temperatures. A storable propellant will remain liquid at temperatures and pressures normal to humans and may be left in a rocket for days, months, or even years. For example, hydrazine boils at $113°$ Celsius.

In a bipropellant system, fuel and oxidizer are kept in separate tanks. They are kept well insulated if cryogenic propellants are used. These tanks are pressurized by an inert gas, such as nitrogen, to force the propellant into

TO EARTH ORBIT

Although the principle behind two-propellent rockets is easy to grasp, the mechanical realities are such that equipment must be designed and built to handle both very low temperature fuels and very high temperature reactions — and survive!

the rocket engine pumps. The pumps push the propellants into the combustion chamber. The pumps require rotational energy which comes from a turbine. The turbine and pumps are often built as a single piece of machinery, called a turbopump. These turbopumps are very difficult to design. The turbine is driven by the combustion energy of the propellants from a gas generator. The temperature of these gases can reach 816° Celsius. At the same time, the pump sections of the turbopump must pump liquids at temperatures as low as −253° Celsius. After the propellants leave their pumps, they flow through valves on their way to the combustion chamber. These valves allow the rocket to be stopped and started. The fuel propellant then flows through tubes which cool the walls of the nozzle and combustion

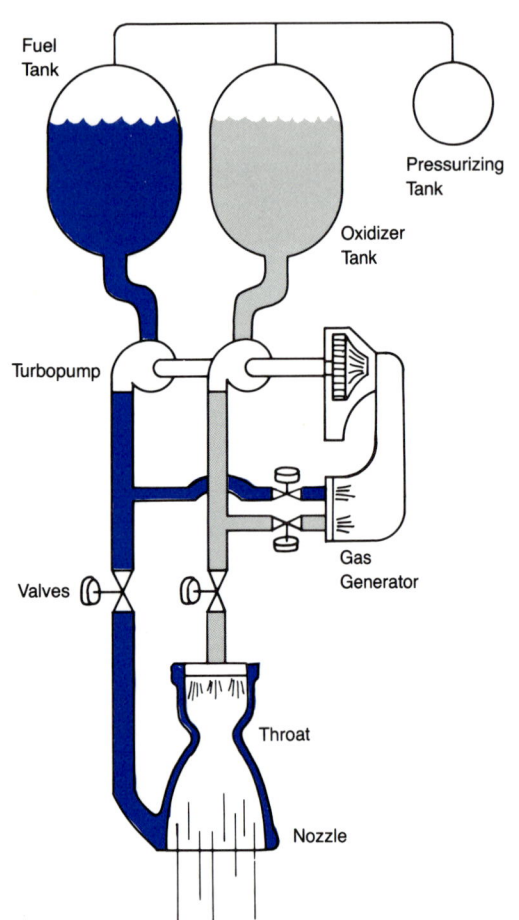

The reliable R.S.27 liquid-propellant rocket powers the Delta booster, a design that survives the vast temperature differences.

EXPENDABLE LAUNCH VEHICLES

Solid Cylinder

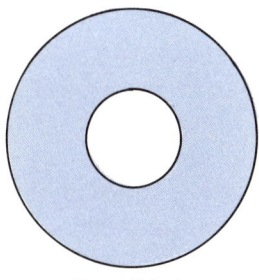

Bored Cylinder

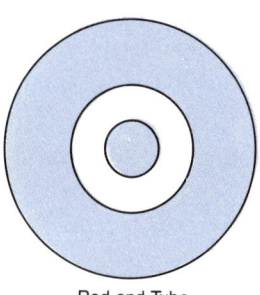

Rod and Tube

Internal Star

These cross sections of solid rockets show the exposed burning surfaces. Which will produce constant thrust, decreasing thrust, increasing thrust?

chamber. If this were not done, the walls might melt. Injectors guide the propellants into contact with each other in the combustion chamber. Then, the high energy combustion products blast out of the throat and nozzle to create thrust.

Solid-propellant rockets
Since the Chinese discovery of gunpowder in the eleventh century, solid propellants have been used to launch rockets. The solid-propellant rocket is rather simple compared to liquid-propellant rockets. The major components are the case, which holds the propellants and serves as the combustion chamber; the igniter; and the throat and nozzle. Because of its simplicity, the solid rocket is more reliable and less expensive than the liquid rocket. However, it is not as powerful.

The solid propellants used in modern rockets burn on their exposed surfaces to produce hot gases. These solids contain all the substances needed to sustain combustion. They do not need air or a separate supply of oxidizer to burn. One type of solid propellant consists of a mixture of both fuel and oxidizer which does not burn until it is exposed to a certain temperature. Another type, such as nitroglycerin, is a single chemical that has both fuel and oxidizer qualities. Both types normally use an igniter to begin burning. Once started, it is difficult to turn them off.

Solid propellants are often molded into shape inside the rocket cylinder. It is poured in as a muddy liquid around a mandrel and cools in a molded shape called a "grain". The mandrel is then removed, leaving a core where the combustion occurs. The shape of the grain determines how the rocket produces thrust over time. For example, a bored cylinder grain produces more and more thrust over time during a launch. A rod and tube grain produces constant thrust over time. A solid cylinder grain has thrust which decreases over time.

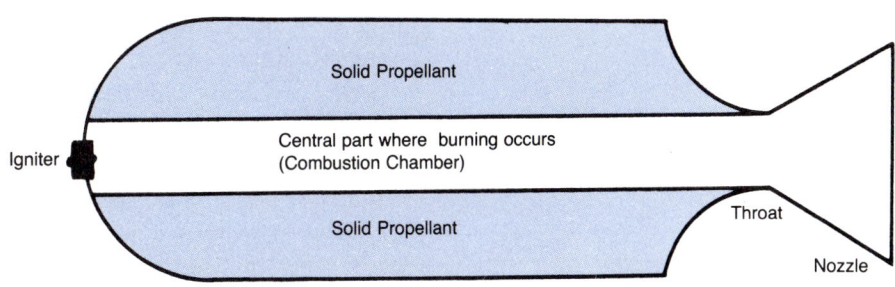

Although less powerful, the solid rocket affords a simplicity not achievable in the liquid fuelled rocket. With fewer sub-systems to break down, reliability is increased.

17

Guidance

Two very important tasks are required to guide boosters: sensing and controlling. Sensing the movement of the booster is done with precise instruments, called sensors, in the inertial navigation subsystem. These sensors are used along with computers to calculate where the booster is, how fast it is going, and in what direction it is going. Careful control of thrusters is necessary to make corrections.

Sensing position, velocity, and acceleration is done with accelerometers which measure acceleration. An accelerometer is really only a mass on a spring, though precisely manufactured. When the mass is moved on the spring, acceleration can be calculated. Sensing the direction of travel, or attitude, is done with gyros. The word gyro comes from the Latin word *gyrare*, which means to turn or whirl. These gyros are precisely constructed versions of the gyroscope. As the booster changes its direction, these gyros stay rotating in the same direction. Therefore, the attitude of the booster can be determined by the direction of rotation of the gyros. For example, imagine that you had a rotating gyroscope floating next to you inside the Space Shuttle. If the Shuttle turned one way or the other, the gyroscope would stay rotating in the original direction.

If computer calculations of the sensor signals show that the booster is exactly on course, signals are sent to the rocket controls to keep going as planned. If the calculations show that the rocket is slightly off course, signals are sent to change the direction of rocket thrust. This control is often done by mounting the rocket engine on a gimbal. A gimbal is a ball and socket bearing. The rocket is attached to the ball part and can be swivelled around in small angles. The direction of the rocket on the gimbal is accurately controlled by a hydraulic (liquid) or pneumatic (air) cylinder, similar to a service station automobile jack.

Reliability

During early missile and booster projects, the "fly and fix" philosophy predominated. Engineers built their design and flew it, hoping that it would work. Any problems which arose were fixed in the next version. However, this approach is now discouraged. The pressures of national prestige, national security, and cost are pushing the ELV industry to strive for boosters that work the first time and every time.

Reliability is a term that indicates the probability that equipment will perform its mission without failure. Designers use mathematics to estimate in advance the reliability of a booster. This reliability is most often stated as a probability, such as 0.999. This means that the probability of a successful launch is 99.9 percent; in other words, the ELV will probably launch 999 out of 1000 payloads successfully. Another measure of reliability is established

EXPENDABLE LAUNCH VEHICLES

Guidance

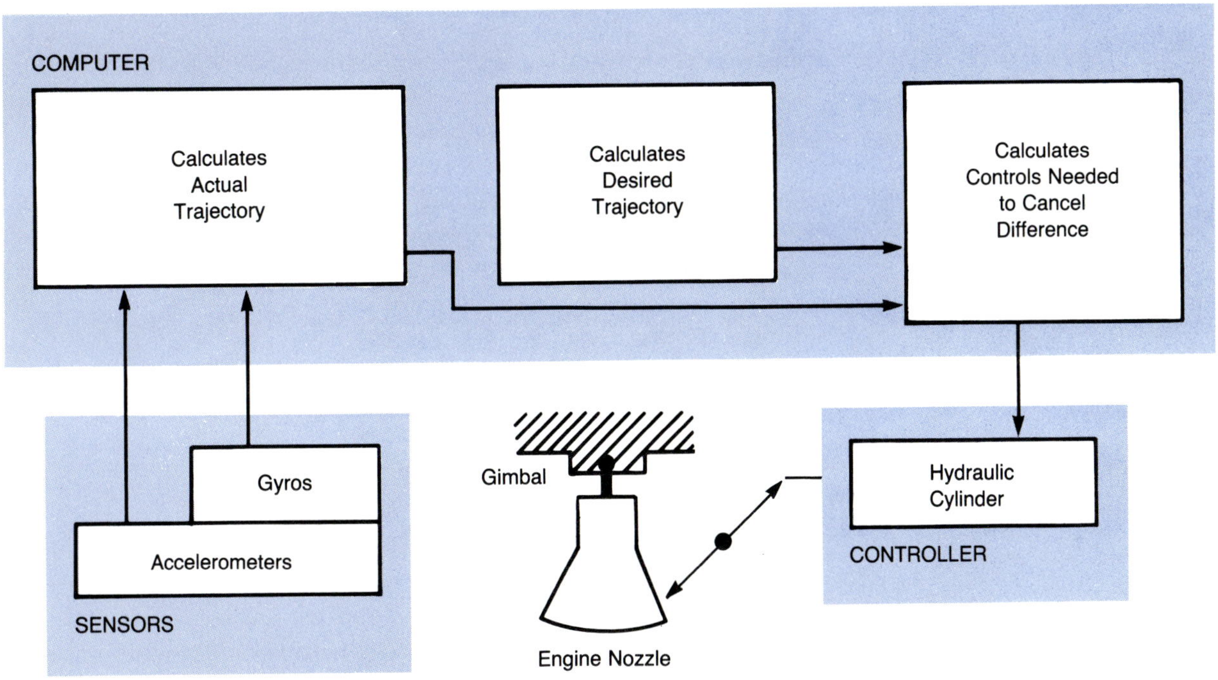

COMPUTER
- Calculates Actual Trajectory
- Calculates Desired Trajectory
- Calculates Controls Needed to Cancel Difference

SENSORS
- Gyros
- Accelerometers

Gimbal — Engine Nozzle

CONTROLLER
- Hydraulic Cylinder

To guide a rocket in a proper trajectory, the direction of the engines must be adjusted many times each second. The process that accomplishes this is similar to balancing an upside-down broom on your hand. You must constantly adjust the position of your hand to counteract any tipping of the broom.

Your eyes see the broom the same way that boosters use accelerometers and gyros to sense their trajectory. Your brain decides where to move your hand the same way that boosters use computers to calculate what changes are needed. Then you use your arm to change the position of your hand, the way that boosters use hydraulic cylinders to control the pointing of the engine nozzle. In both cases, as soon as the adjustment is made, the cycle must begin again.

by ELV performance. If 19 out of 20 launches are successful, then the reliability of the ELV is 0.95.

Manufacturers improve the reliability of their products using quality control and thorough testing. Quality control is the careful management of how devices are made and installed. It also includes carefully controlling design changes. Testing includes testing parts before they are installed. Extreme temperatures, pressures, vibrations and acoustics are applied to these parts. The most useful testing repeats many of these same tests on assembled subsystems and systems. An example of such testing would be if manufacturers tested satellite radios first by turning them on and shaking them for an hour. If they continued to work satisfactorily, they would then be installed in the satellite and the satellite would be shaken with the radio on. If the radio failed, the testing scheme successfully located a bad component.

Other methods to improve reliability are overbuilding and redundancy. Overbuilt systems are built to withstand test conditions which are tougher than they will experience in an actual mission. A redundant system includes spare components which take over when the original components fail. This allows the system to continue operating even though there are failures.

International Boosters

United States

The American ELVs include Scout, Atlas, Delta, and Titan. Scout is often launched from Wallops Island in Virginia. The rest of these boosters are launched from either Cape Canaveral in Florida or Vandenberg Air Force Base in California. Most of these boosters were originally designed as ICBMs. However, many space missions have been launched by them. Scout is often used to launch satellites which contain atmospheric experiments. Atlas was used in the early days of the Mercury manned space program. John Glenn became the first American to orbit the Earth after being launched by an Atlas. It is now often used to launch weather and communication satellites. Delta is typically used to launch communications satellites. It is considered the reliable workhorse of the NASA launch vehicles. Titans have been used with powerful upper stages to send probes, such as Voyager, to the planets.

Soviet Union

After more than thirty years of launching satellites into space, the Soviet Union has released very little information about their boosters. However, much information has been carefully pieced together by Western observers. Information gathering has been helped by the fact that there have been few completely new Soviet boosters. Developments have usually consisted of additions and changes to the original military missiles.

There are different ways of naming Soviet boosters. The most common set of names was established by Dr. Charles Sheldon of the Library of Congress. He assigned the letters A, B, C, D, F, and G to different boosters. He also used a number following the letter, such as D-1, to indicate how many upper stages were included. More than 700 of the A-2 boosters have been launched. This is the largest number of launches for any type of booster in the world.

EXPENDABLE LAUNCH VEHICLES

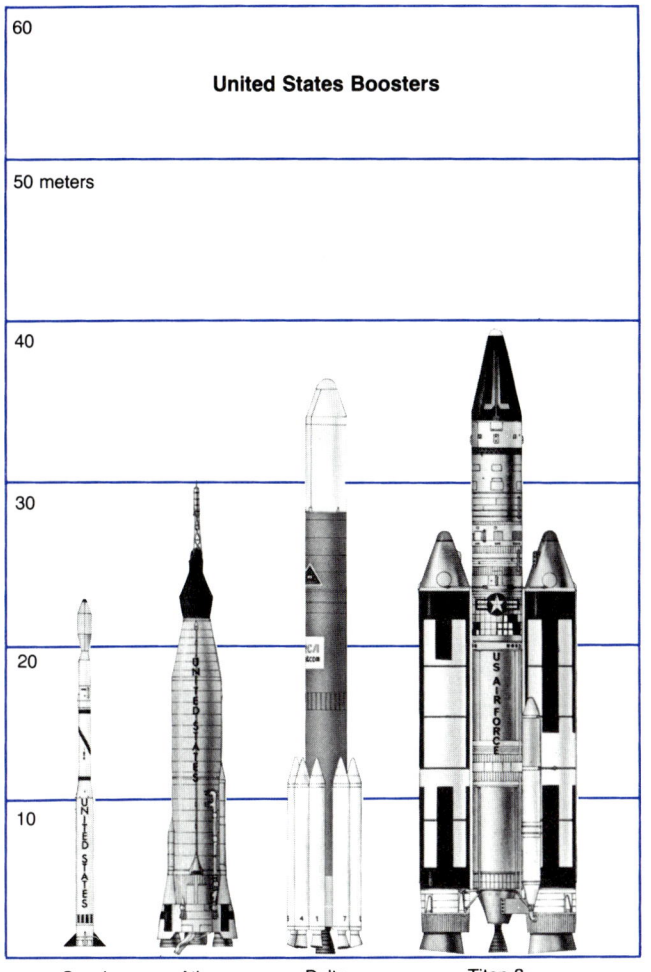
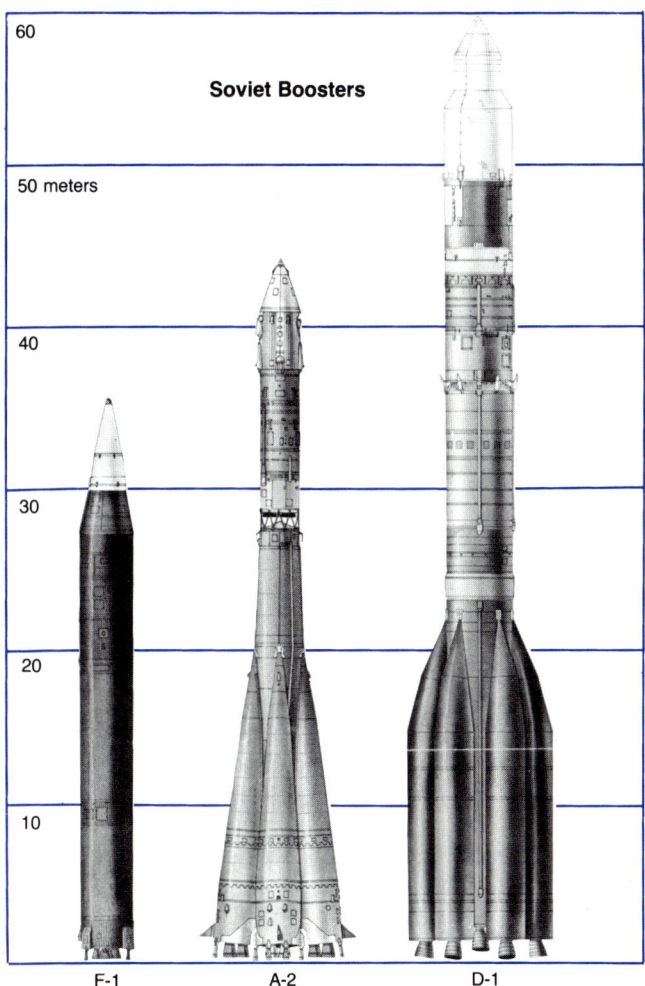

Not all rockets send men to the moon. Rocket sizes are geared to both the payload and the altitudes to which these loads must be delivered.

Country	Booster	Thrust (kilonewtons)	Payload (kilograms to LEO)
United States	Scout	480	177
United States	Atlas	1,725	2,200
United States	Delta	4,307	2,500
United States	Titan 3	12,832	13,425
Soviet Union	F-1	2,191	4,500
Soviet Union	A-2	4,929	6,600
Soviet Union	D-1	14,105	17,000
Europe	Ariane 1	2,400	2,500
China	CSL-2	2,738	1,900
Japan	N-1	1,450	1,200
India	SLV-3	422	40

TO EARTH ORBIT

Other Countries

Europe, China, Japan, and India are all developing ELVs. Most of their boosters are used for launching weather satellites and communication satellites. The remainder are for scientific experiments and military missions. In the 1980s they began to compete with the United States for launches. As a result of this, companies with satellites to launch can select between different boosters. There can be large differences in the cost and reliability of the many boosters available.

Europe, China, Japan and India have all developed expendable launch vehicles. They are now competing with the U.S. in providing reliable and cost-effective satellite placement services.

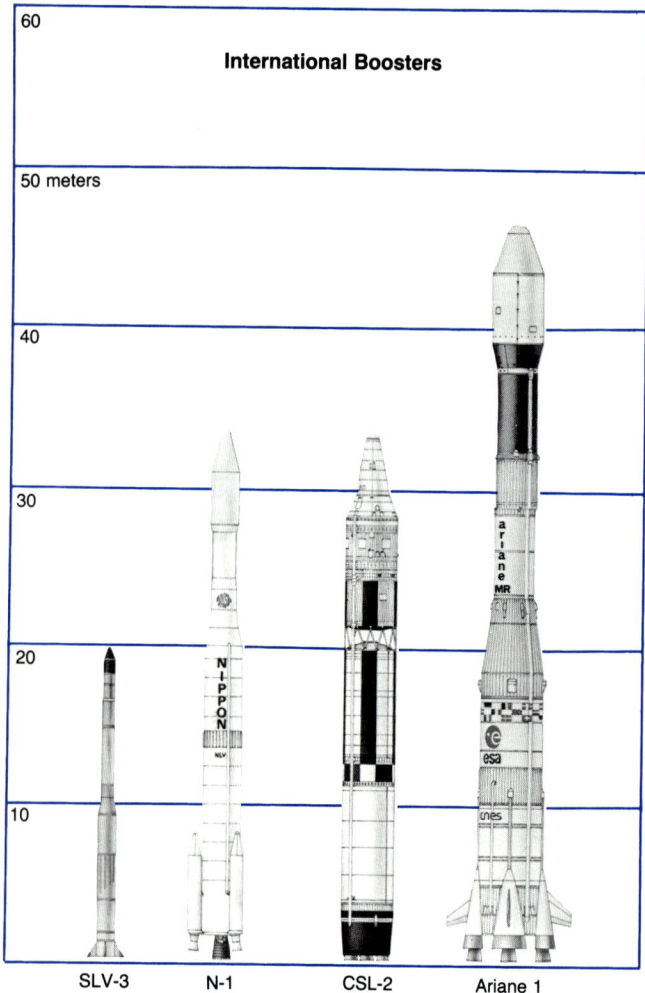

EXPENDABLE LAUNCH VEHICLES

Next-Generation Launch Vehicles

There are always improvements being made and new designs being proposed for bigger and better launch vehicles. Good examples of modifying existing boosters are the Delta 2 and the Titan 4 which were first launched in 1989. In the United States, concerns over the cost of putting payloads in space has prompted the creation of new booster design efforts. Examples include the Advanced Launch System for very large satellites and Pegasus for small satellites. Pegasus represents new technology since it has wings for lift and is dropped from an airplane.

A new Soviet booster, called Energia and labelled K-1, has been developed for putting huge payloads into space. It is two-thirds as powerful as the Saturn V booster developed in the 1960s for the American Apollo program. The K-1 is the first large Soviet booster to use liquid hydrogen fuel.

Europe is developing the Ariane 5, Japan is developing the H-2, and China is developing the CSL-3. All are planned to be bigger and better boosters for these countries. These national efforts are beginning to take on international significance. Most of these countries are beginning to offer their booster launches for sale. Launching satellites into space is becoming an internationally competitive business. Even though China and the Soviet Union are traditionally anti-capitalist, they are beginning to get involved in this new and profitable international business.

ELVs at Work

IMAGINE YOU ARE the president of a company called Reliable Communications. You are about to launch your first communication satellite. It will be put in a geosynchronous orbit above the Pacific Ocean. People will pay your company to have telephone and television signals sent to and from the Far East. Millions of dollars have been spent on the satellite, the booster and for NASA to launch the satellite. Your company hopes that the booster is as reliable as you say your satellite is.

A few hours before launch, everything has been disconnected from the Delta launch vehicle except the power wires and tubes for loading cryogenic propellants. The Cape Canaveral control room becomes quiet as the countdown continues. Shortly before ignition, the remaining wires and tubes are disconnected. At ignition, a great crackling roar is heard. Six of the nine strap-on, solid-fuel rockets have ignited. In the center of these, the liquid-propellant rocket has also ignited. The mission controllers carefully watch their consoles to see if anything is going wrong.

At 56 seconds into the launch, the six solid-propellant rockets burn out. Three seconds later the remaining three solid-propellant rockets are ignited. Shortly after this the six burned-out rockets are jettisoned from the main

A rocket launch (left) is a magnificent experience: sight, sensation and sound.

TO EARTH ORBIT

booster and fall away. At 118 seconds into the launch, the last three rockets burn out, are jettisoned, and begin also to fall back to Earth. At 256 seconds, the liquid main rocket is cutoff. Then this first stage separates from the rest of the vehicle and falls away.

The second stage rocket then ignites. The top of the rocket which covers and protects the satellite, called the fairing, separates into two pieces and is jettisoned from the rocket. At this point, the controller console reads, "FAIRING JETTISON NOMINAL". The inertial guidance system steers the satellite into orbit by controlling the second stage rocket gimbal. At about 687 seconds, the vehicle is in a 185 kilometer LEO and the second-stage rocket is purposely shut down. However, this orbit is not the equatorial LEO that you want; it is a slightly inclined LEO. To propel the satellite into a geosynchronous orbit, it is best to start from an equatorial LEO. Therefore, thrusters slowly propel the vehicle into an equatorial LEO. At about 1263 seconds, the second-stage rocket is re-started. At about 1286 seconds the second stage is shut down and jettisoned. After a 90 second coast, the third stage is ignited which places the satellite in its proper geosynchronous orbit. At 1576 seconds, the third stage is separated from the satellite.

The launch is a success. Most people in the launch control center breathe a sigh of relief. However, your work has only begun. The satellite must be tested and retested with your radio stations on the ground. You must be sure that the satellite will provide reliable service before it is used by paying customers.

Summary

Expendable launch vehicles are rockets used to put people or satellites into space. The thrust created by the rocket exhaust gases pushes, or accelerates, the vehicle into space. Satellites are placed in different orbits. These are typically low-Earth orbits (LEOs) and geosynchronous orbits. To stay in space, a satellite must move at the correct orbital velocity for its altitude.

Propulsion systems use combinations of solid-propellant and liquid-propellant rockets. The chemical energy of these materials is released during combustion and is transformed into kinetic energy in the form of fast moving gases. The action of this kinetic energy creates the thrust reaction to lift the vehicle. The guidance system senses acceleration and rotation of the booster. It then controls the direction of travel by steering the rocket exhausts. All subsystems within the booster must operate with a very high reliability. This means it must be highly probable that the mission will be a success.

EXPENDABLE LAUNCH VEHICLES

The United States and the Soviet Union have been launching satellites and people into space since the late 1950s. The most familiar uses of boosters are for launching weather and communication satellites. Other countries, such as those belonging to the European Space Agency, Japan, China and India have begun their own space programs. Some of these countries now offer their launch vehicles for hire.

Terms

accelerometer
ELV
fairing
geosynchronous orbit
gimbal
grain
gyro
ICBM

LEO
liquid propellant
orbital velocity
reliability
solid propellant
thrust
turbopump

Important People, Ideas, and Events

- Solid-propellant rockets came into existence soon after the discovery of gunpowder in China in the eleventh century.
- In the early 1900's, scientists began proving that liquid-propellant rockets could be used to reach outer space.
- The Soviet Union launched Sputnik, the first human-made satellite, on October 4, 1957. The United States soon followed with their first satellite, Explorer 1, on January 31, 1958.
- In the 1980's, countries other than the United States and the Soviet Union began to offer competing launch services.

Interesting Things to Do

1. Build a model of the Delta launch vehicle.
2. Build and launch a solid-propellant model rocket.
3. Request information from NASA and the European Space Agency (ESA) about their ELVs.
4. Decide which way is best to launch into orbit around the earth: with the direction of rotation, or against it.

Chapter 2   SPACE SHUTTLES

The space shuttle is a true aerospace vehicle: it is launched with a rocket, orbits the Earth like a spacecraft and lands like a conventional airplane. The American Space Shuttle is the major component of the United States Space Transportation System (STS). Designs for the shuttle were conceived in the early 1970s as part of the United States' plan for the development of space transportation. The plan called for a balance between manned and unmanned operations. The shuttle supports the manned operations of that plan.

The first shuttle flights began in April of 1981 and continued success was achieved during the first twenty four flights. A tragic disaster occurred on the twenty fifth flight when the shuttle *Challenger* exploded. The problem was traced to O-ring seals in the solid fuel rockets which were affected by unusually cold temperatures on the day of the launch. Despite warning from engineers, the launch was made — with disastrous results. The shuttle was immediately grounded and for almost two years additional research and testing took place to correct the problems. It was not until the fall of 1988 that shuttle flights were resumed.

Many situations arise in space that require solving unforeseen problems. The unique qualities of the human mind are the best tools for solving these problems. Space shuttle crews have met challenges on several occasions. On one Space Shuttle mission, an astronaut was sent outside the orbiter to retrieve a satellite which had not achieved its proper orbit. Because the satellite was tumbling, it was quickly determined that this method would be too dangerous. After assessing the situation, the astronauts maneuvered the Shuttle close to the satellite. They used its remote manipulator arm to capture the satellite and bring it back into the Shuttle cargo bay. After it was repaired, they redeployed the satellite so that it could boost itself into its proper orbit. This is but one of the many possible uses of the Shuttle.

Propelled by a total of five rocket motors, the Shuttle heads for orbit and a well-defined set of tasks.

TO EARTH ORBIT

The Space Shuttle can also be used to retrieve damaged satellites and return them to Earth for repair. It can take satellites into space and launch them into orbit. Its cargo bay can be used to take the European Spacelab into space so that scientific experiments can be carried out. It can also place large observatories in space, such as the Hubble Space Telescope. Plans for the 1990s call for using the Shuttle cargo bay to transport the basic elements of the structures for the Space Station which will be assembled in space.

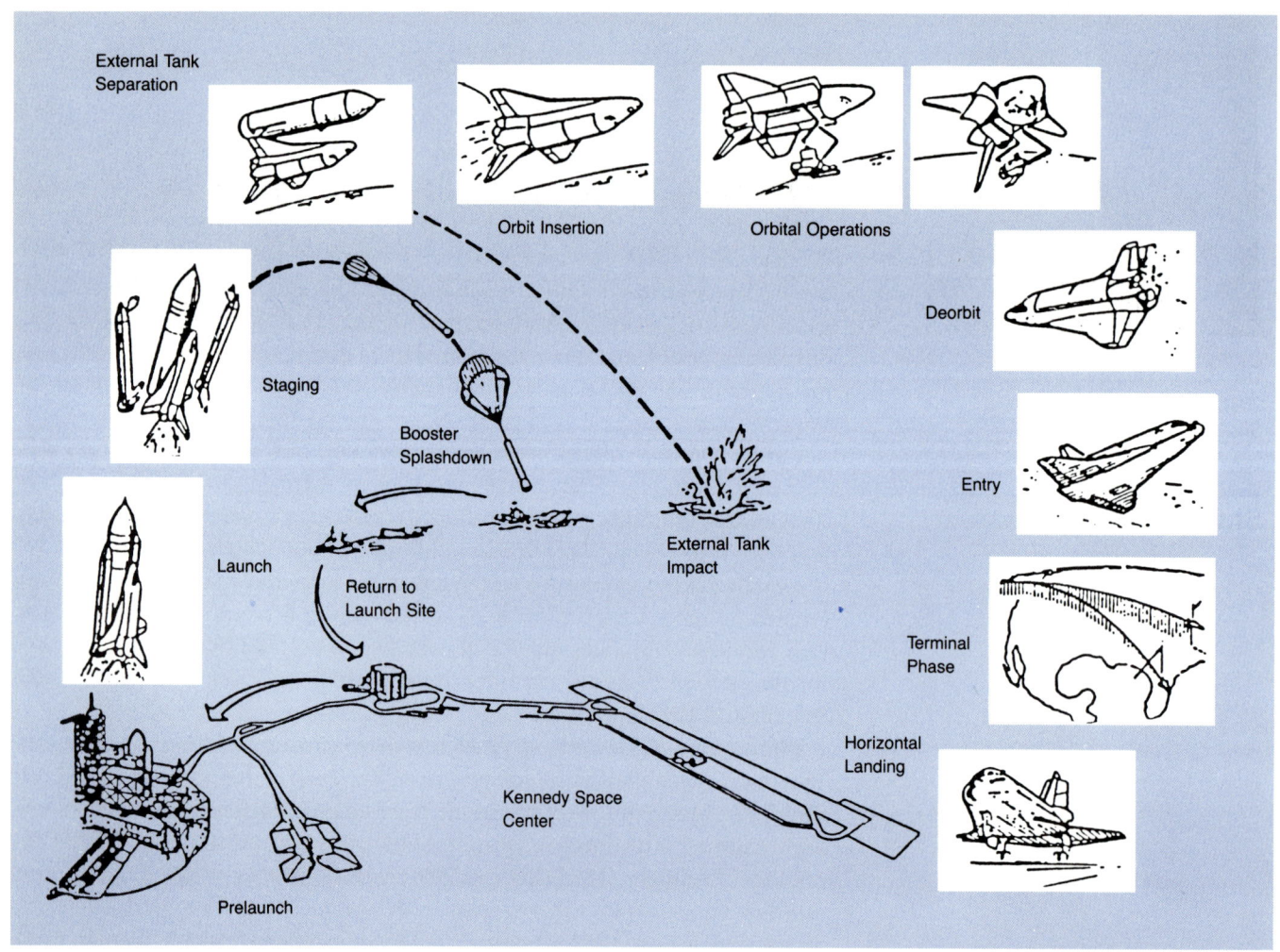

The Shuttle mission profile: a step-by-step listing of predictable events. How does this profile change when unpredictable events occur?

28

The European Space Agency has designed a laboratory that fits in the Shuttle's cargo bay.

Shuttle Mission Profile

5-4-3-2-1 IGNITION — orbiter main engines and solid rocket boosters — LIFT OFF — from Cape Canaveral in Florida. The initial phase of the launch continues for approximately two minutes when staging takes place as the solid rocket boosters are separated from the orbiter and external tank. The two rocket boosters parachute into the ocean where they are recovered for reuse. The orbiter continues into space "upside down." Just before achieving orbit, it jettisons the external fuel tank. The external fuel tank is the only portion of the Shuttle system that is not recovered because it breaks up during reentry into the atmosphere. The pieces splash down in the Indian Ocean. The orbiter achieves orbit altitude and utilizes its orbital maneuver- during reentry into the atmosphere. The pieces splash down in the Indian Ocean. The orbiter achieves orbit altitude and utilizes its orbital maneuvering system (OMS) to adjust its path. The orbiter and crew conduct on-orbit operations for up to 30 days, including research experiments, rendezvous and extra-vehicular activity.

Deorbit Burn
60 min to touchdown
175 miles
16,465 MPH

Blackout
25 min to touchdown
50 miles
16,700 MPH

Maximum Heating
20 min to touchdown
43.5 miles
15,045 MPH

Exit Blackout
12 min to touchdown
34 miles
8,275 MPH

Terminal Area
Energy Management
5.5 min to touchdown
83,130 FT
1,700 MPH

Autoland
86 sec to touchdown
13,365 FT
424 MPH

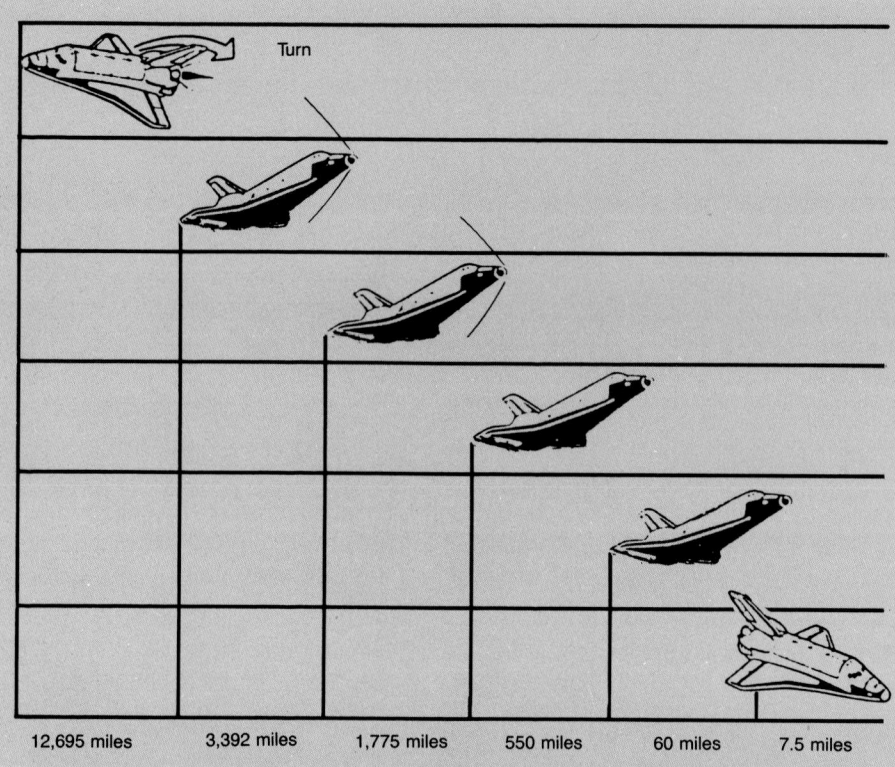

Autoland Interface
86 sec to touchdown
7.5 miles to runway
424 MPH
13,365 FT altitude

Initiate Preflare
32 sec to touchdown
2 miles to runway
358 MPH
1,725 FT altitude

Complete Preflare
17 sec to touchdown
2,540 FT to runway
308 MPH
135 FT altitude

Wheels Down
14 sec to touchdown
1,100 FT to runway
268 MPH
90 FT altitude

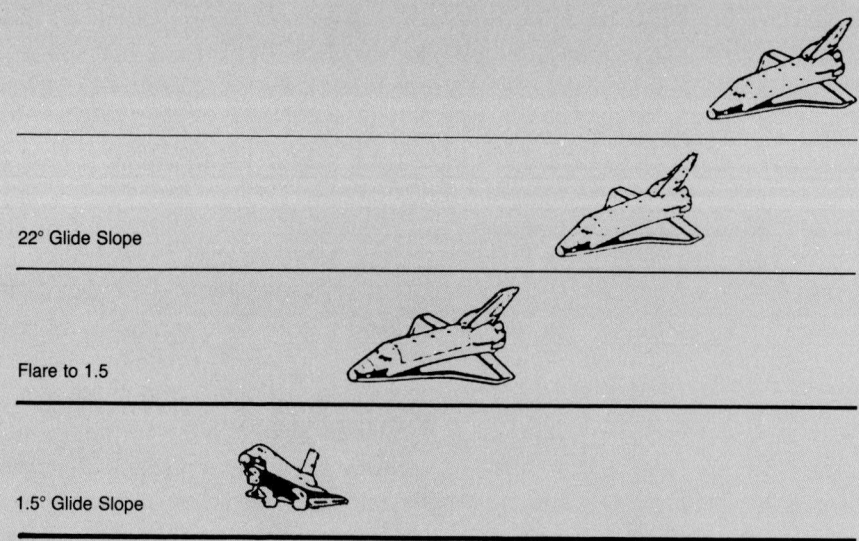

Touchdown
2,760 FT from end of runway
215 MPH

SPACE SHUTTLES

In order to reenter Earth's atmosphere, thrusters must slow the orbiter. Shields made from composite materials protect the Shuttle from the friction-induced heat. As the Orbiter slows, it becomes maneuverable, and ultimately lands like an airplane.

When the mission requirements have been met, the orbiter is prepared for reentry. The orbital maneuvering system propellants, monomethyl hydrazine and nitrogen tetroxide, are used in thrusters to slow the orbiter. These fuels, when mixed, ignite on contact. The orbiter slows and reenters the Earth's atmosphere. The heat shield on its underside protects the orbiter and crew by dissipating the heat generated by reentry. The orbiter has the ability to maneuver during this reentry phase. At approximately 12 kilometers altitude, the orbiter turns and lands like a conventional airplane at approximately 346 kilometers per hour. The Shuttle and solid rocket boosters are refurbished. Within two weeks it will have its new external fuel tank and be ready for another mission. The successful completion of this mission is a direct result of a tremendous amount of technology.

Shuttle Propulsion Systems

The Space Shuttle transportation system uses three major elements for propulsion: the Space Shuttle main engines, the solid rocket boosters and external fuel tank. Together they enable the launch and orbital maneuvering of the Shuttle.

Main Engines

The Space Shuttle's three main engines are clustered at the aft end. They operate using liquid hydrogen and liquid oxygen and can be controlled to limit the amount of thrust produced. During the initial phase of the launch, the three main engines operating together with the solid rocket boosters produce enough thrust to achieve orbit. The solid rocket boosters are used for about two minutes before they are staged. The main engines on the orbiter then use fuel from the external fuel tank to continue to operate for approximately eight and one half minutes. At this time the Shuttle's orbit is established.

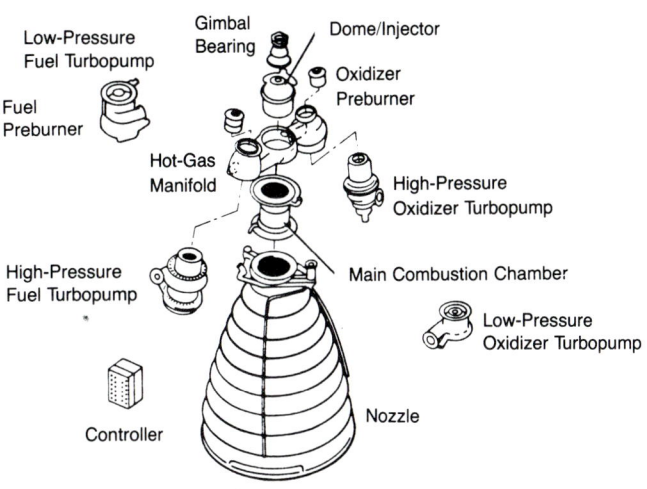

Major components of Space Shuttle Main Engines. The fuel supply for these engines is in the expendable external tank.

31

The supply of fuel for the main engines comes from the external tank (ET). Liquid hydrogen and liquid oxygen are mixed at a ratio of six to one which produces a thrust of approximately 1700 kilonewtons in earth's atmosphere. In the vacuum of space, these same engines generate approximately 2100 kilonewtons of thrust. The liquid hydrogen and liquid oxygen are restrained from entering the low pressure turbopumps (1 & 11) by prevalves which are located on the orbiter. This is done to insure that the cryogenic propellants have enough time to chill the engine to assure that the propellants remain liquid. The fuel then flows through the low pressure turbopump to the high pressure turbopumps (2 & 12) and then to the main fuel and oxidizer valves (3 & 13). On the liquid oxygen side the system fills the preburner valves (7 & 14). When the proper pressure and chill have been achieved, the start sequence is begun by an ignition command from the orbiter. On the hydrogen side the main fuel valve opens (3), which permits the hydrogen to flow into the coolant loop through nozzle tubes (5) and channels in the main combustion chamber (6). Part of this flow of hydrogen is diverted by a coolant control valve (4) to the preburners (8 & 15). The rest is routed back to the low pressure turbopump (1) to drive the turbine for that pump. After this flow passes through the turbine it is returned to the walls of the two preburners (8 & 15) where it cools the preburners, the hot gas manifold (9) and the main injector (10).

On the oxygen side the ignition command from the orbiter opens the main oxidizer valve (13) which allows the liquid oxygen to flow through two turbopumps (11 & 12) to the main injector (10). The liquid oxygen also goes through two valves (7 & 14) to the two preburners (8 & 15). Some of the oxygen is tapped off to drive the liquid turbine for low pressure turbopumps (11). The flow continues past the pump and reenters the circuit.

The engine is operated by a controller which includes a computer to interpret commands received from the orbiter. It monitors the engine before and during ignition, manages the redundancy features, receives or transmits data from the orbiter to the ground and operates the engine control valves. There are spark igniters in the dome of each of the preburners (8 & 15) and also in the main chamber (10). The preburners operate at a fuel mixture ratio of less than one part oxygen to one part hydrogen in order to produce a hot gas, or hydrogen rich steam, which is used to drive the turbines of the high pressure turbopumps (2 & 12) before entering the hot gas manifold (9). Here the hot, hydrogen-rich gas is mixed with additional liquid oxygen from the high pressure liquid oxidizer turbopump (12) for combustion. The combustion process utilizes a ratio of six parts oxygen to one part hydrogen to achieve the desired thrust. The liquid oxygen side of the engine also has a pogo suppressor (16) which absorbs any closed loop longitudinal dynamic oscillations that might be generated between the vehicle structure dynamics and the engine combustion process which could destroy the engine.

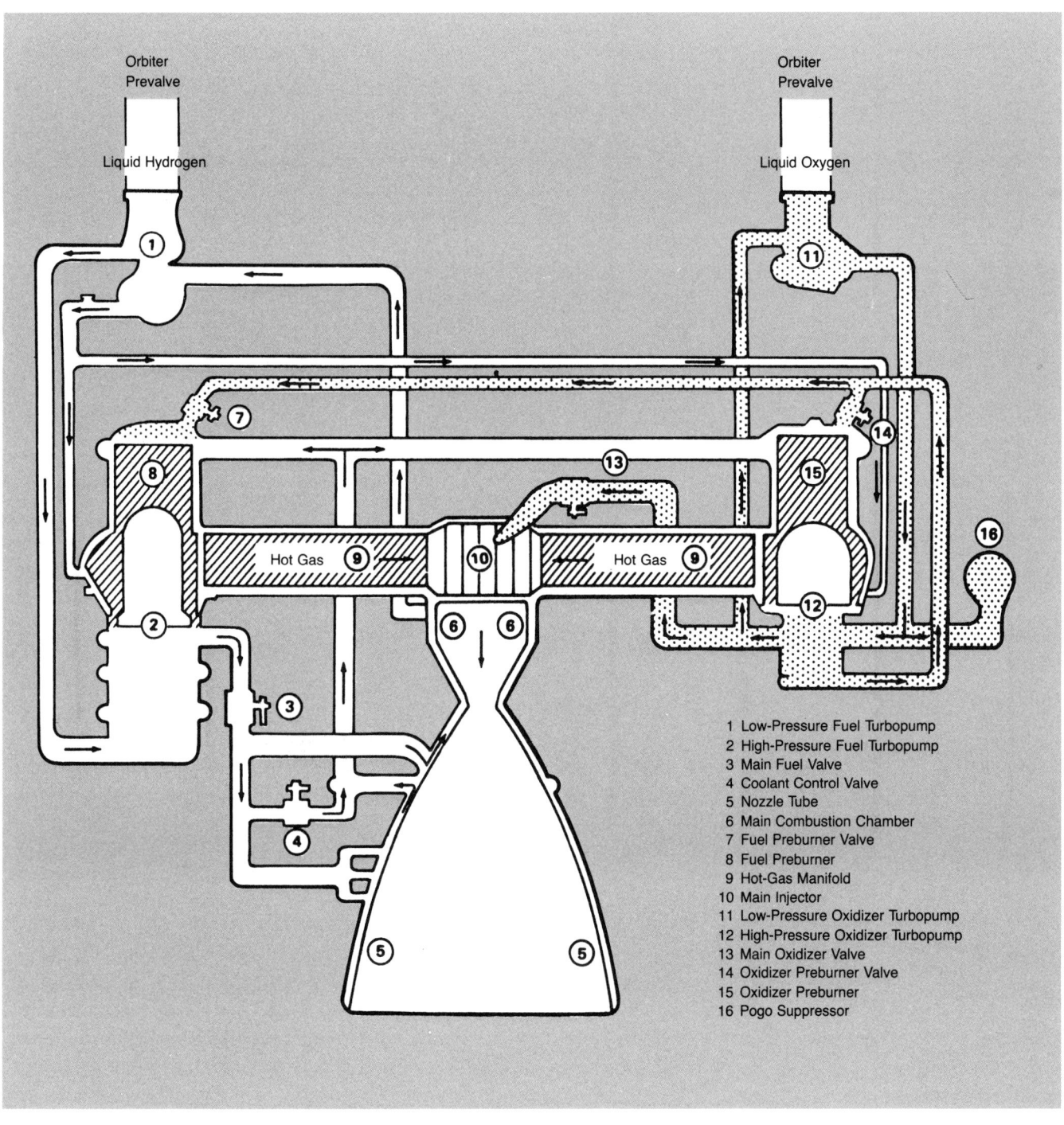

Main engine propellant flow.

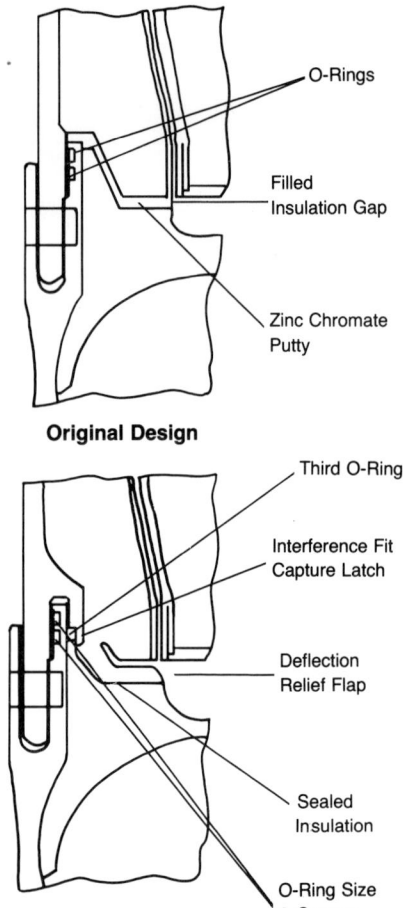

Original Design

- O-Rings
- Filled Insulation Gap
- Zinc Chromate Putty

New Design

- Third O-Ring
- Interference Fit Capture Latch
- Deflection Relief Flap
- Sealed Insulation
- O-Ring Size & Groove Change

O-ring joints were redesigned after their failure caused the 1986 Shuttle accident.

Solid Rocket Boosters

In order to escape the Earth's gravity the Space Shuttle needs more thrust than that provided by the main engines. Two solid rocket boosters augment the Space Shuttle main engines during the first two minutes of powered flight. Each solid rocket booster consists of several subsystems. They are the solid rocket motor, structural, thrust vector control, separation, recovery, and electrical and instrumentation subsystems.

The initial design of the solid rocket boosters used a rubber O-ring to seal the rocket segments. The solid rocket motor is made of eleven steel segments which are each held together by 177 high strength steel pins at each case segment joint. Three of these joints, called field joints have been redesigned by the manufacturer with a capture feature and three O-rings. These mating surfaces are bonded with an adhesive and also have a J-shaped deflection relief slot which reduces stresses and increases the sealing action of the bonded surfaces. In addition, joint heaters are mounted around the motor case at each field joint to maintain minimum temperatures for the O-rings.

The eleven segments of the solid rocket motor case include the forward dome segment, six cylindrical segments, the external tank attachment ring, two stiffener segments and the aft dome segment. The inside of the motor case is insulated to protect the case so it can be used twenty times. The propellant consists of PBAN (a binder), ammonium perchlorate (an oxidizing agent), powdered aluminum (a fuel) and some iron oxide to control the burning rate. After the propellant ingredients are mixed, the propellant is poured into the casting segments which have a mandrel in the center. After four days of curing, the propellant resembles a hard rubber eraser. The mandrel is then removed to create the burning cavity of the motor.

The ignition of the solid rocket booster begins with the firing of two NASA standard initiators (NSIs). They ignite a charge of boron potassium nitrate pellets which, in turn, start a small rocket motor called a pyrogen igniter, which is a motor within a motor. The first motor initiates ignition. The second motor provides the main ignition which starts the propellant burning at approximately 2900° Celsius. As the propellant burns, the hot gases are forced through the nozzle. The nozzle restricts the flow of the gases which creates pressure and produces thrust. As the gases pass through the narrow segment of the nozzle, they reach speeds of 9700 kilometers per hour as they pass out of the exit cone. There is also a flexible bearing which allows the nozzle to gimbal, which controls the direction of the rapidly moving gases. The high thrust during initial liftoff results from an eleven-point star configuration inside the cast propellant. After the star configuration burns out, thrust is reduced but gradually increases again due to the design of the burning cavity.

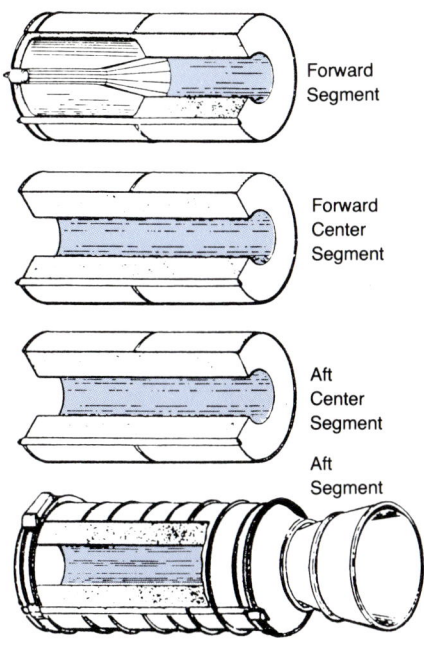

Space Shuttle Solid Rocket Motor. The motor is made of eleven segments joined end-to-end. The added thrust of two solid rocket boosters is needed to get the Shuttle aloft.

The solid rocket boosters are separated from the external tank after completing their burn. They coast a short distance before falling back to earth. A parachute recovery system, consisting of a pilot parachute, drogue parachute, and three main parachutes, is used to slow the descent of the boosters. The pilot parachute, which is stored in the nose cap, is deployed at an altitude of approximately 4700 meters by a barometric switch which ejects the nose cap. As soon as the pilot parachute is deployed and inflates, cutters release the drogue parachute pack. It instantly inflates sixty percent. Then a reefing line is cut to allow full inflation. At 2000 meters altitude a second signal from the barometric switch detonates a ring charge which separates the frustrum from the booster. The three main chutes then deploy out of the base. The drogue parachute continues the descent with the frustrum. The main chutes decelerate the boosters to approximately 100 kilometers per hour at splashdown. The solid rocket boosters are recovered and returned for refurbishment.

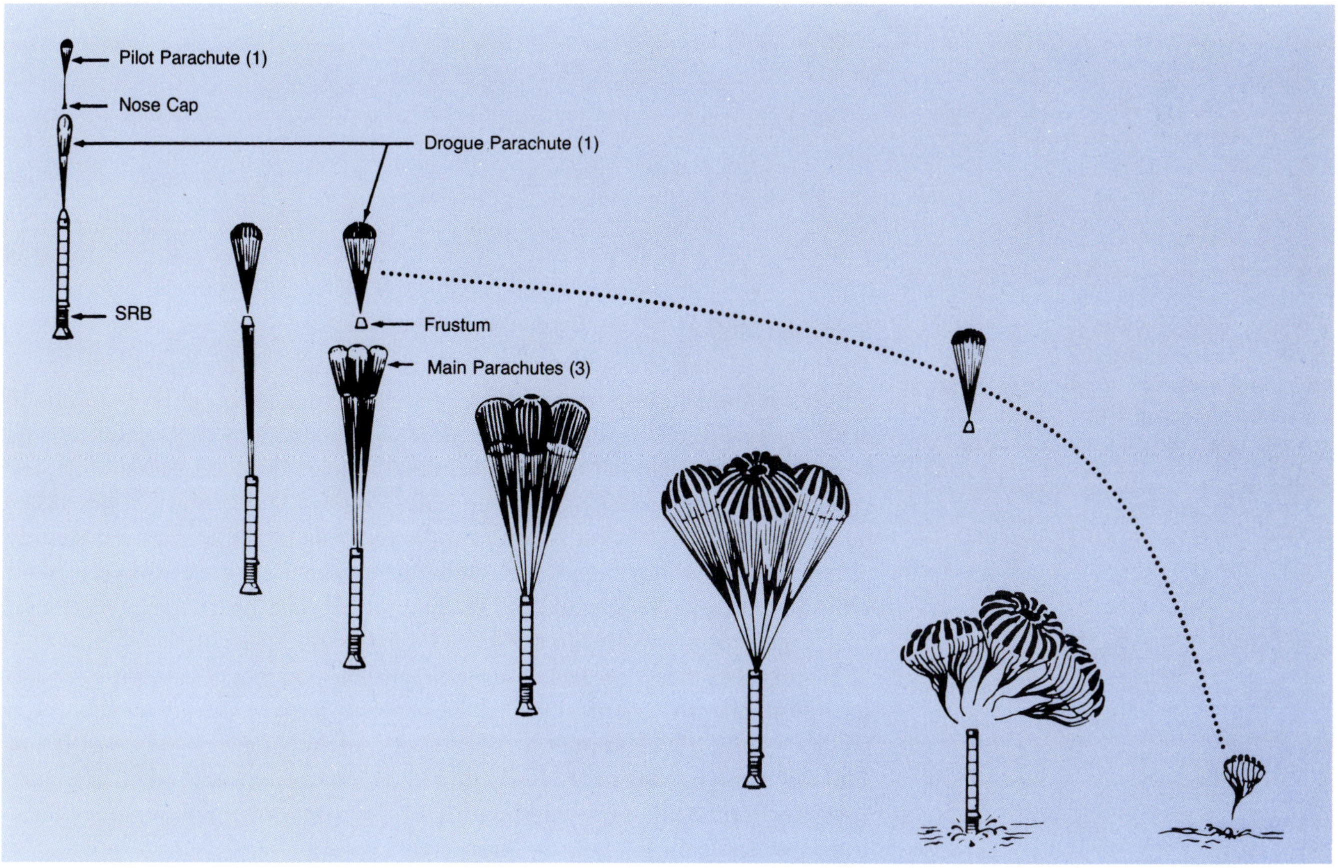

Parachutes slow the SRB so it can be recovered and reused.

TO EARTH ORBIT

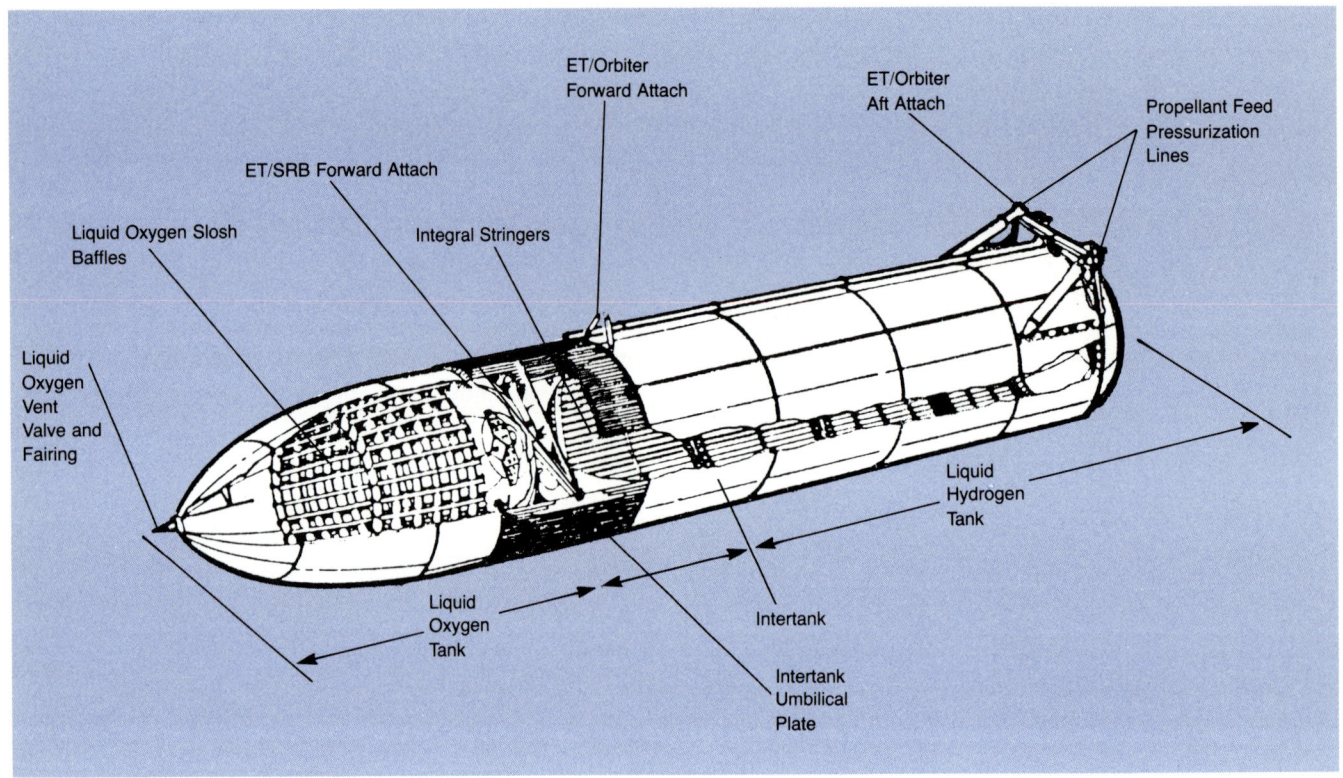

The external tank consists of three components: the oxygen tank (forward); the intertank (center) which houses instrumentation and processing equipment; and the hydrogen tank (aft). A high-efficiency insulating skin on the tank keeps the propellants at acceptable temperatures.

External Tank

The external tank of the Shuttle system contains the fuel for the three Space Shuttle engines. It also serves as the main structural element from launch to orbit because the two solid rocket boosters are attached to its sides as well as the orbiter. At launch the external tank absorbs the total thrust of 28,580 kilonewtons produced by the three main engines and the two solid rocket boosters. The solid rocket boosters separate at an altitude of approximately 50 kilometers while the orbiter with the external tank continues to near orbital velocity at an altitude of 113 kilometers. The nearly empty external tank separates and falls into the Indian Ocean.

The external tank consists of three major components. The oxygen tank is located in the forward position, the hydrogen tank in the aft position, and the intertank, which connects the two propellant tanks, is between them. The intertank houses instrumentation and processing equipment. The outside skin of the tank is insulated with a 2.54 centimeter-thick coating of polyisocyanurate foam to keep the propellants cold.

The liquid oxygen tank contains 541,452 liters of oxidizer at −183° Celsius. It is 16.3 meters in length and 8.4 meters in diameter. Since the liquid oxygen tank is the forward part of the external tank, it has its nose section curved to reduce aerodynamic drag. At the aft end of the liquid oxygen tank is a ring frame which contains a flange for joining the liquid oxygen tank to the intertank. Inside the liquid oxygen tank are slosh baffles that prevent sloshing of the oxidizer. Because liquid oxygen is twelve percent heavier than water, sloshing could throw the vehicle out of control. There are also anti-vortex baffles to minimize the rotating action of the oxygen as the propellant flows out of the bottom of the tank. Without them the propellant would tend to exit in a whirlpool action which could permit oxygen gas to enter the engine instead of the liquid oxygen.

The liquid hydrogen tank holds 1,449,905 liters of liquid hydrogen at −253° Celsius. It is made of four barrel sections, five main ring frames and two domes. It is 29.6 meters in length and 8.4 meters in diameter.

The intertank does not hold propellants, but serves as a connecting device between the liquid hydrogen and liquid oxygen tank. It is 6.9 meters long and houses instruments to link the external tank with ground instrumentation.

Space Shuttle Structure

The orbiter's structure is divided into five major components: the forward fuselage, the mid-fuselage, the aft fuselage, the wings, and the vertical stabilizer. Most of the structure is made of conventional aluminum.

Forward Fuselage

The forward fuselage follows conventional aircraft construction methods using aluminum alloy stringer panels, frames and bulkheads. It contains the crew module which is a 71.5 cubic meter area for working, living and storage.

The flight deck has the usual pilot arrangement which permits the craft to be piloted from either seat. The flight deck can seat four persons. There are more than 2000 separate displays and controls on the flight deck, which include toggle switches, circuit breakers, rotary switches, pushbuttons, thumbwheels, metered and mechanical readouts and indicator lights. All payload handling is controlled from the flight deck. Payloads can be manipulated, deployed, released or captured. There is a display area for rendezvous and docking control, as well as displays for mission operation and control. The flight deck also has six windshields to assist the astronauts in completing their work. In addition, there are two overhead windows, two rear view payload bay windows, and a window at the crew entrance and exit hatch.

TO EARTH ORBIT

The mid-deck contains provisions, storage facilities and sleep stations. It also contains the waste management system, the personal hygiene station and the work-dining table. Additional environmental control equipment and storage for trash is below the mid-deck in the lower deck.

The air lock, which provides access for extra-vehicular activity (EVA), can be located in one of several places. It can be inside the mid-deck of the crew module or outside the crew module in the payload area, depending on mission requirements. It can also be mounted on a tunnel adapter. The airlock is a cylinder with a diameter of 160 centimeters and a length of 211 centimeters. It allows for two crew members to change into spacesuits so they can perform extra-vehicular activity. The airlock is also used to transfer crew members from the crew module to the Spacelab through the spacelab tunnel. Another possible configuration would substitute a second docking module for the airlock to accommodate the docking of a second vehicle.

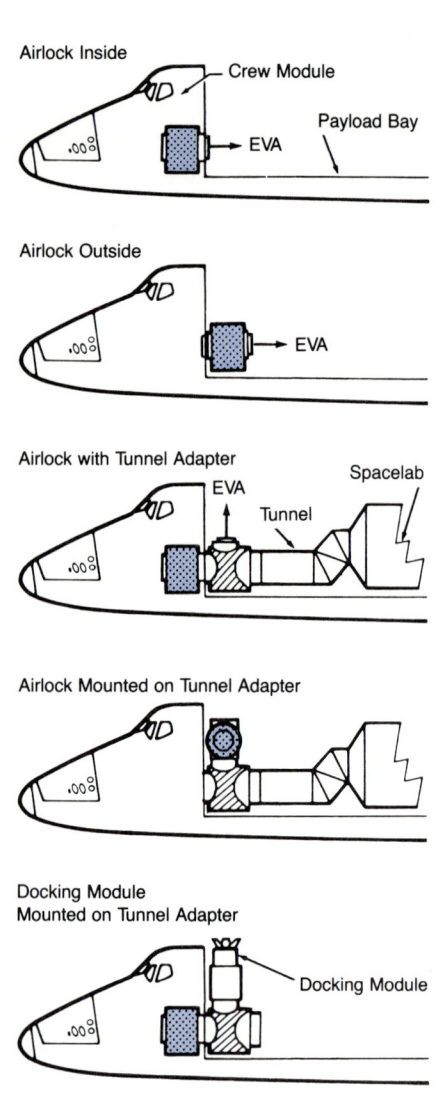

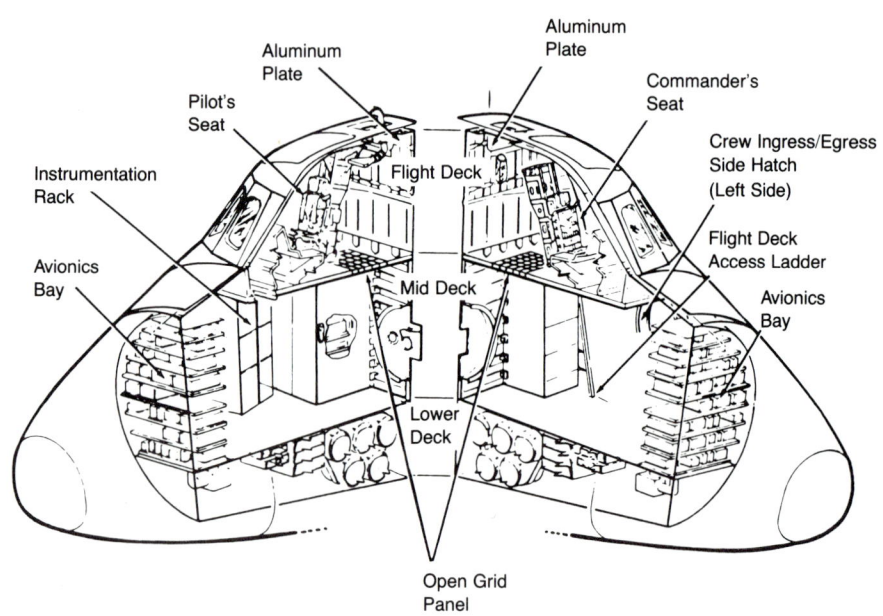

An airlock/tunnel adapter is a check-valve that allows humans to leave the safety of one area to reach the safety of another without jeopardizing the environment of either.

Living and working space is provided for the crew in the forward section of the orbiter.

SPACE SHUTTLES

Mid-Fuselage

The mid-fuselage forms the payload bay. It attaches to the forward and aft bulkheads. It is also the support structure for the payload doors and wing attachments. The mid-fuselage is 18.3 meters in length, 5.2 meters in width and 4 meters in height. There are 12 main frame assemblies that stabilize the structure and are the members to which the skin is attached. The main frames also support the side and door longerons which connect with the thirteen payload bay door hinges. The frames also support the weight of the payloads.

The mid-fuselage is built to maintain structural integrity and to provide the largest usable cargo space.

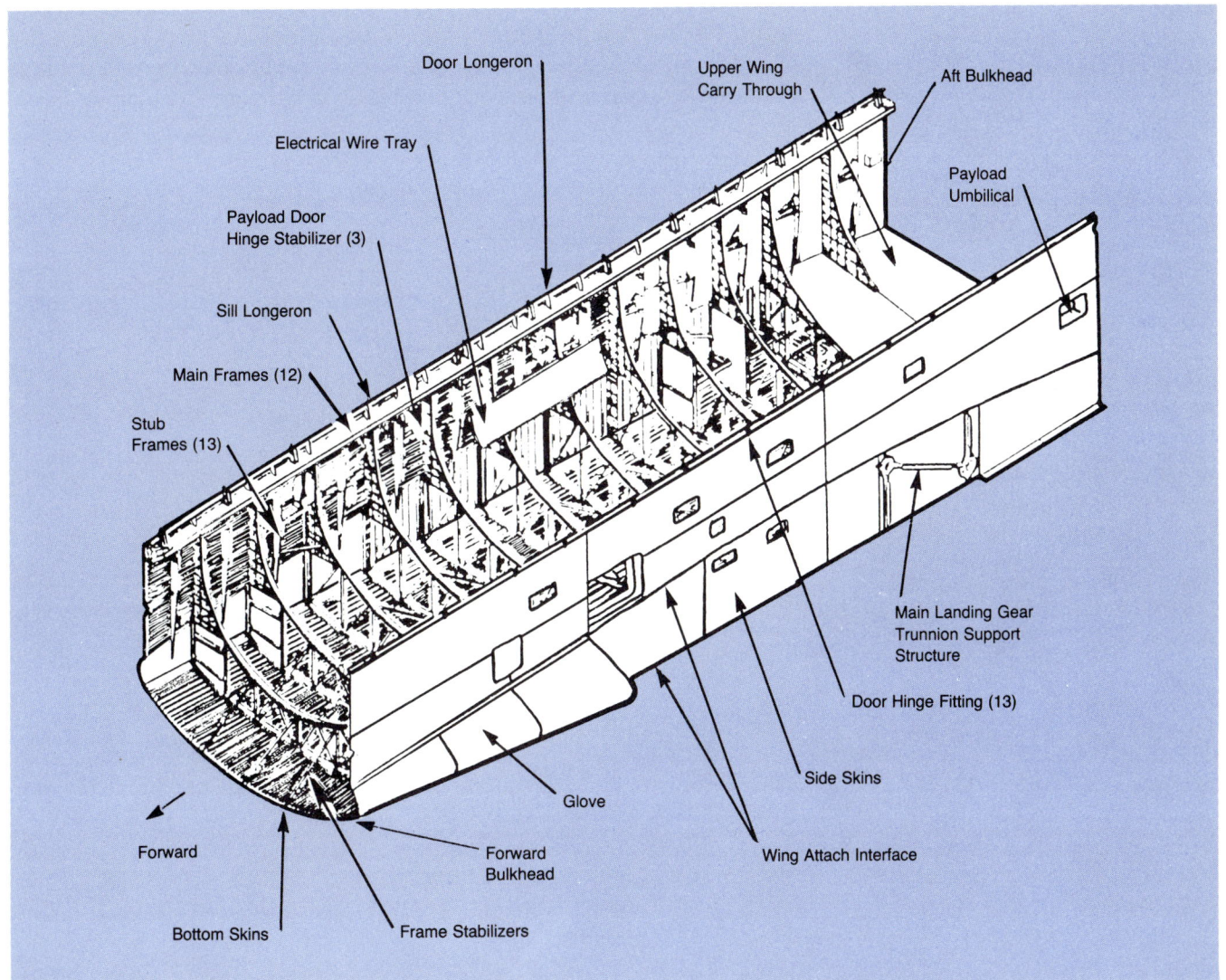

39

TO EARTH ORBIT

The payload bay doors are hinged at mid-fuselage and are 18.3 meters in length and 4.6 meters in diameter. They are constructed of a graphite epoxy material. This composite material expands and contracts less than conventional aluminum. This characteristic is necessary in dealing with the temperature extremes in space. The automatic and manual operating controls for the doors are located in the aft section of the flight deck. Inside the payload bay, which is not pressurized, there are structural attachment points. This has been planned in conjunction with the Spacelab and Spacelab Pallet. Another use of the cargo bay is for the Remote Manipulator System (RMS) which is a 15.2 meter articulating arm that is controlled from the flight deck. The arm resembles the structure of the human arm having a shoulder, elbow and wrist. The arm is operated from within the cabin, thus reducing the need for extra-vehicular activity. A television camera mounted on the arm permits the operator to see what his "hands" are doing.

The remote manipulation arm can maneuver cargo, or take TV pictures. Under what circumstances would the arm be most useful?

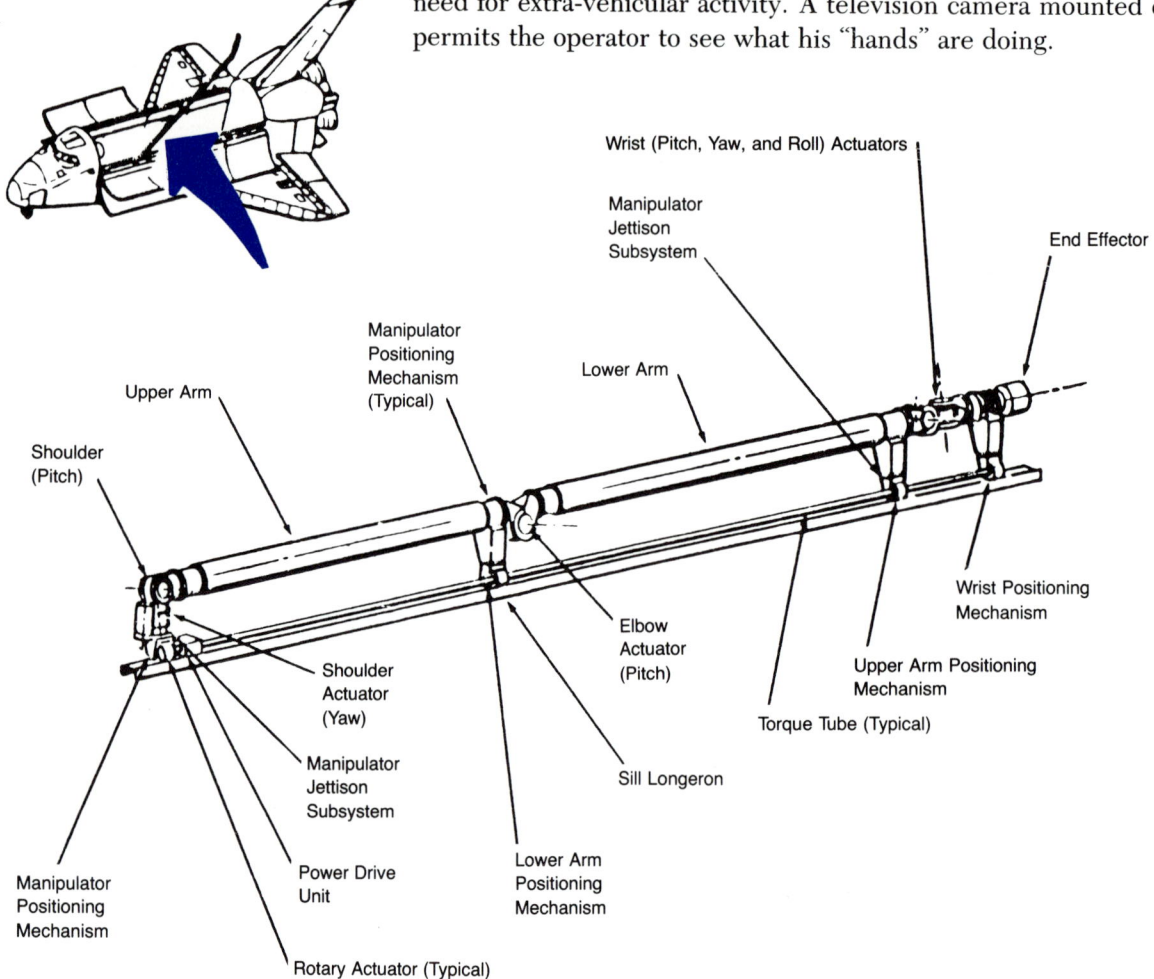

Robotics In Space

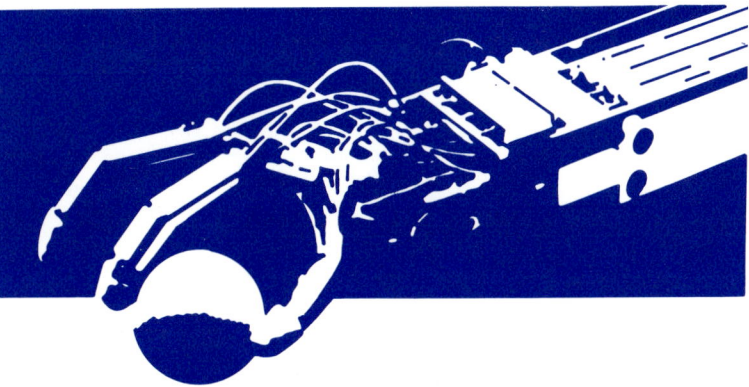

Robotics is a rapidly growing field which has played an important role in space work activities. A typical robot device consists of a manipulator (arm), end effectors (hands), a controller, actuators (power suppliers) and a possible array of sensors to provide environmental feedback.

The space shuttle makes use of a Remote Manipulator System (RMS) which resembles the human arm. It has six degrees of freedom (DOF) or independently operated joints. The shoulder has a pitch joint (up and down) and a yaw joint (left and right). The elbow has a pitch joint and the wrist has a pitch, yaw and roll action (rotation). The RMS has two closed circuit television cameras, one on the wrist and one on the elbow to enable the astronaut on the flight deck of the orbiter to see how the arm is moving. The end effectors have a three wire snare to grasp a grapple fixture which is part of every payload. The arm can be operated in several modes from fully manual to fully automatic.

Other robotic devices have been sent to Mars and Venus to study soil samples. After the spacecraft lands, an arm is unreeled from the spacecraft and digs a small trench. The soil is scooped up and dropped in a funnel on the top of the craft. The soil is passed through a screen and sent to a highly sophisticated laboratory in the craft to have the soil analyzed by sensors and the data sent back to Earth.

A benefit of improved robotics has been the development of artificial limbs for handicapped children. This limb can simulate the missing portion of the child's arm and hand. The hand has two working fingers (effectors) and a working thumb which enables the handicapped child to function in a normal manner.

TO EARTH ORBIT

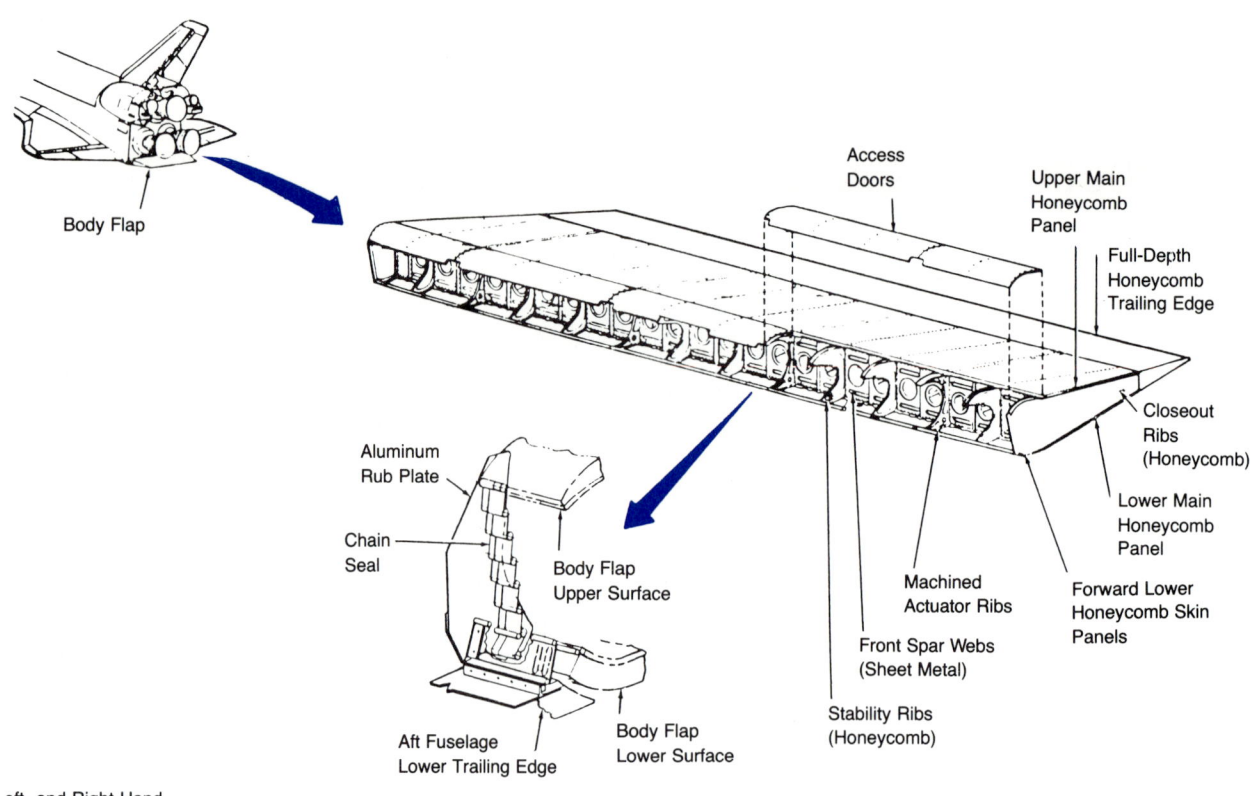

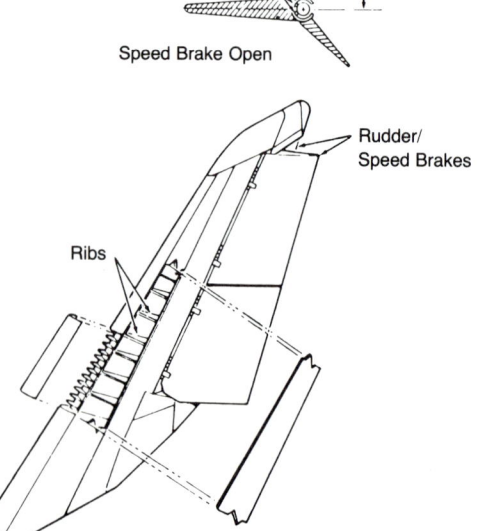

The vertical stabilizer provides both directional control and braking action — and only during the final stages of re-entry and landing.

Aft Fuselage

The aft fuselage is 5.3 meters long, 6.7 meters wide and 6.1 meters high. It contains parts of the orbital maneuvering system as well as the aft spar, the Space Shuttle main engines, the heat shield, and the body flap. It also supports the vertical stabilizer. Within the aft structure, the propulsion system thrust structure is used to absorb the intense forces generated by the main engines.

The body flap is an aluminum structure consisting of ribs, spars, skin panels and a trailing edge assembly. The flap utilizes a honeycomb structure to which the skin panels are attached. It is attached to the lower aft fuselage by four rotary actuators. Its purpose is to provide the Shuttle with pitch trim control as well as to provide a thermal shield for the engines during reentry.

Vertical Stabilizer

The vertical stabilizer is a vertical fin with rudder speed brakes. The construction of the fin includes a torque box of aluminum stringers, web ribs and machined aluminum spars covered with aluminum honeycomb skin. The rudder speed brakes are made of conventional aluminum ribs and spars with aluminum honeycomb skin panels. The braking action is accomplished by having the speed brake section split to each side.

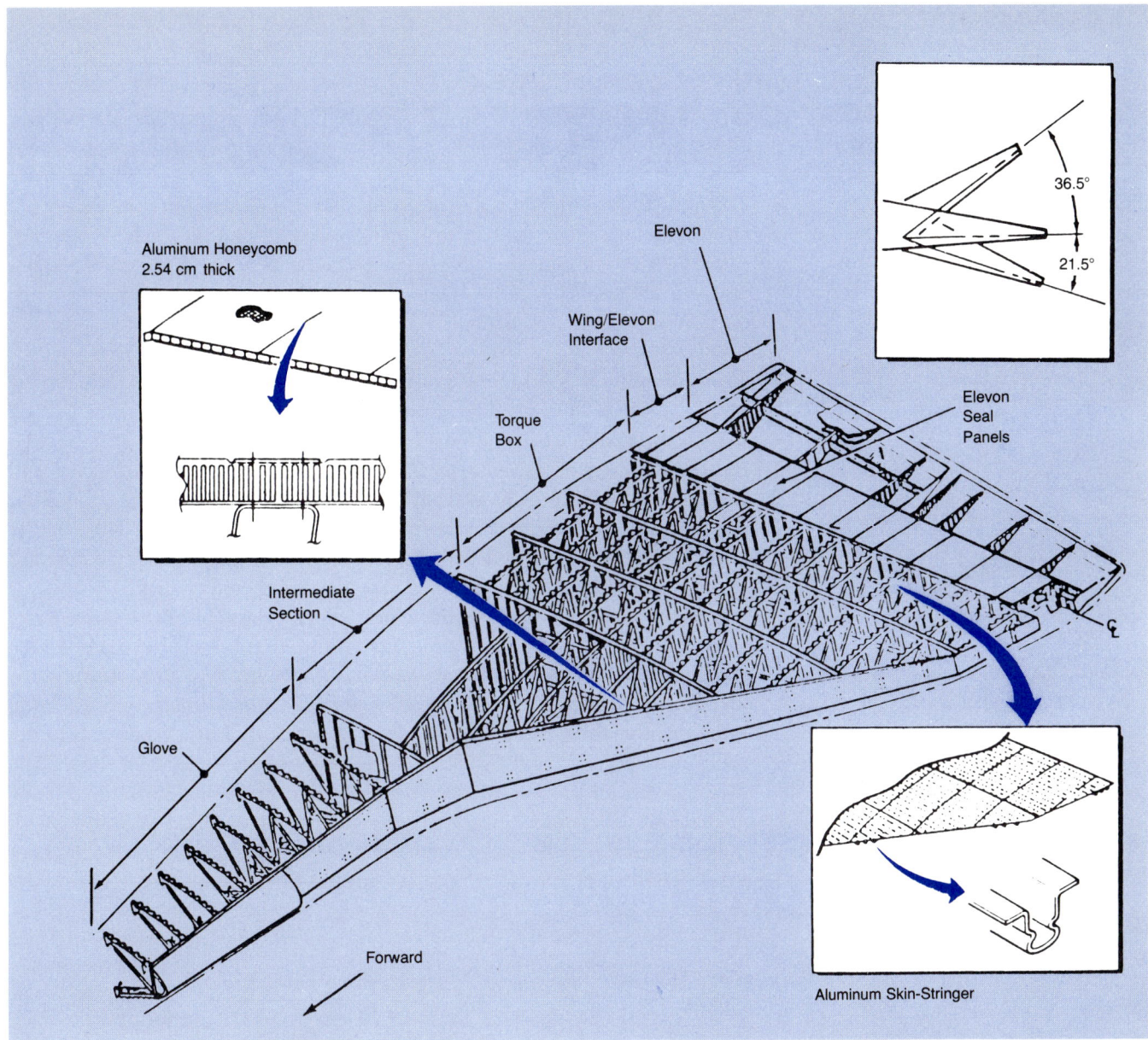

The wing is constructed of conventional aluminum alloy. Its only job is to allow the Shuttle to glide safely back to Earth.

Wings

The Shuttle wings are the lifting surfaces that provide conventional lift and control of the orbiter during gliding descent. The wing sections consist of a glove, an intermediate section which houses the main landing gear, the torque box, the forward spar for mounting the leading edge structure thermal protection system, the wing elevon interface, the elevon interface, the elevon seal panels and the elevons. The wing construction is conventional aluminum alloy with a multirib and spar arrangement. Each wing is 18.3 meters long at the intersection of the fuselage with a maximum thickness of 1.5 meters. The upper and lower skin covers are of aluminum honeycomb structure. The elevons provide flight control during conventional landing.

TO EARTH ORBIT

Space Shuttle Orbiter Systems

During a flight mission, the orbiter must have a complete set of systems to control and maneuver the Shuttle and provide life support. The systems of the orbiter are propulsion, power generation, environmental control and life support, thermal, purge, vent and drain, and avionics.

Propulsion

In addition to the solid rocket boosters and three main engines used during launch, there are two orbital maneuvering engine systems. They are located in pods on each side of the aft fuselage. They provide the final thrust for orbit insertion and are also used for orbit change, orbit transfer, rendezvous and deorbit. The orbital maneuvering system (OMS) engines are designed for one hundred missions and are capable of one thousand starts. The engines are gimbaled by pitch and yaw electromechanical actuators at the forward end of the combustion chamber to provide directional control.

Additional maneuvering thrust is provided by the orbiter reaction control system (RCS). This system is grouped in three modules. One module is in the nose cone and the other two modules are in the two aft fuselage pods. Multiple thrusters are located in each pod to provide redundancy for mission safety. These thrusters control pitch, yaw and roll attitude control during orbit insertion, on-orbit adjustments and the reentry phases of flight. The thruster system uses tetroxide as the oxidizer and monomethyl hydrazine as the fuel. The propellants are sprayed under controlled pressure by an injector into the combustion chamber where they combine to produce hot gases. The gases expand and are accelerated through the nozzle to provide thrust.

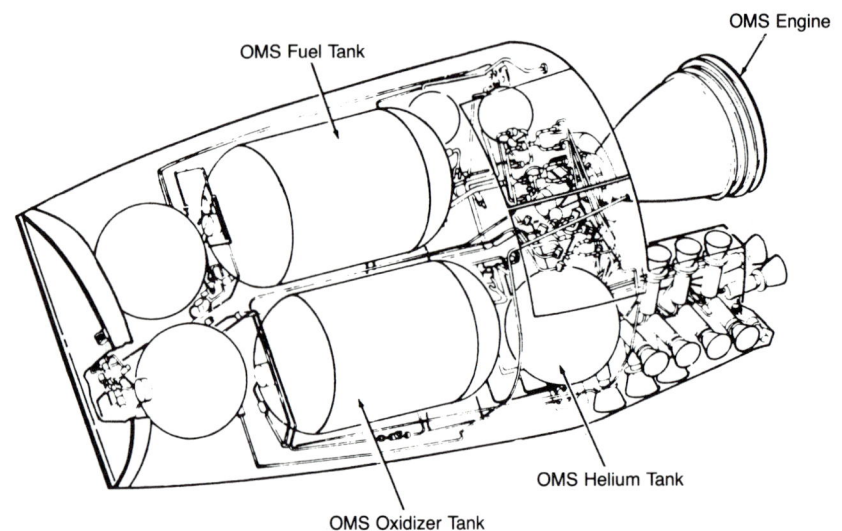

Located in pods on each side of the aft fuselage are the Orbital Maneuvering System engines. They are used for final orbit insertion, and for all changes in orbit, including deorbit.

44

SPACE SHUTTLES

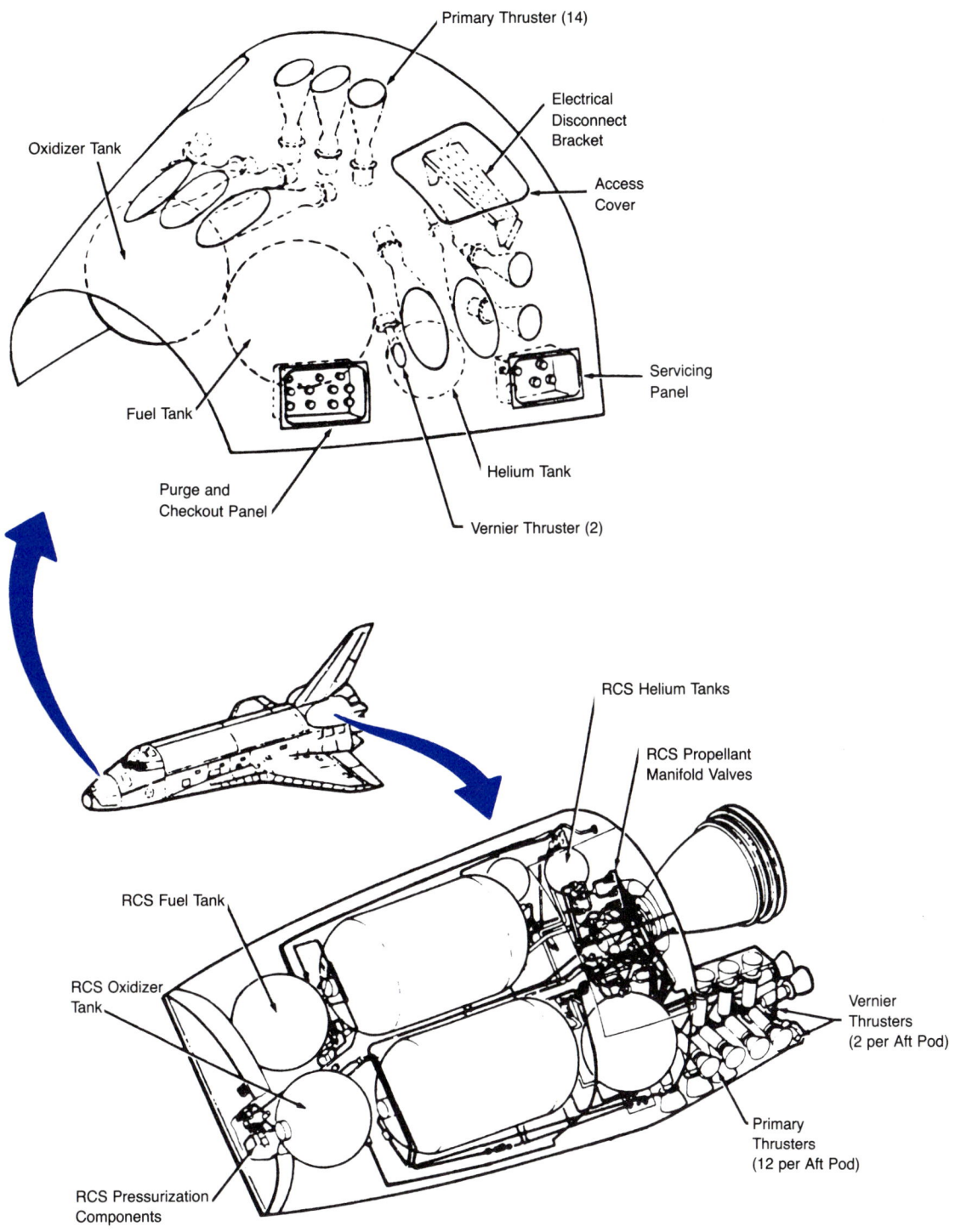

Orbiter maneuverability and orientation are provided by the thrust from the Orbiter Reaction Control system.

TO EARTH ORBIT

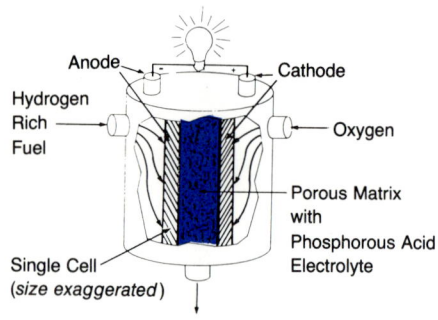

The fuel cells of the electrical power system are located in the mid-fuselage. They provide both electrical power for the equipment and, as a by-product, drinking water for the crew.

Power Generation

The orbiter has two systems to supply power requirements. One system is for electrical power and the other for hydraulic power. The electrical system derives its power from fuel cells which are supplied with cryogenic oxygen and hydrogen reactants. The fuel cell system is composed of three units located in the mid fuselage. Each fuel cell unit is composed of a single stack of cells divided into two parallel-connected substacks of thirty two cells each. The power is produced by the chemical reaction of the hydrogen and oxygen which are supplied to meet the output requirements. The by-product of this power generation is water used by the crew for drinking. Most of the time

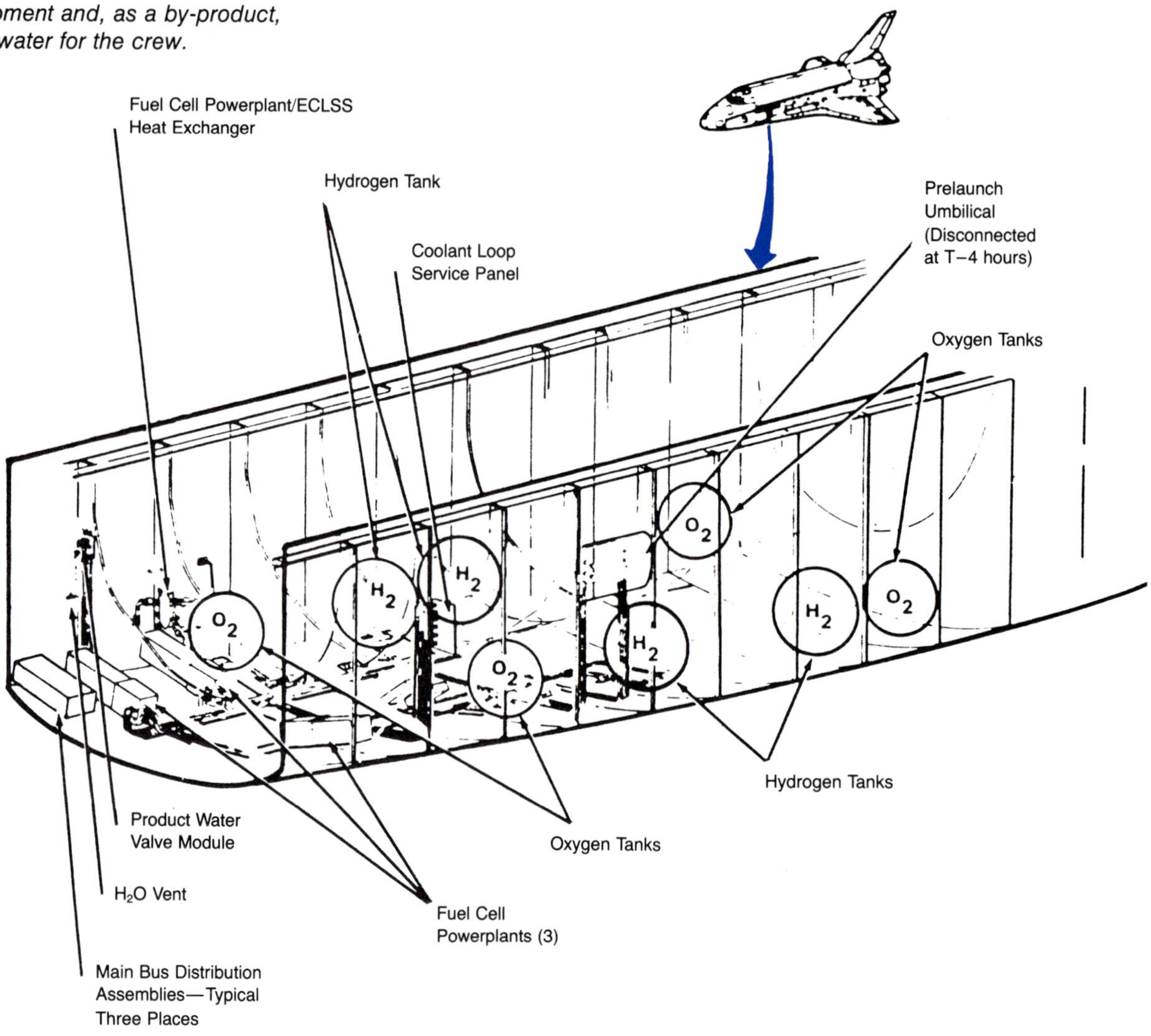

46

SPACE SHUTTLES

only two fuel cell units are in use, while the third stands by until higher energy loads create a need for more power.

The hydraulic power system operates the area surfaces, the main engine thrust vector control and engine valves, the landing gear and other system actuators. The system consists of three independent turbine engines that convert the chemical energy of liquid hydrazine into mechanical power on a shaft which drives the hydraulic pumps. These pumps then provide the power to operate the related systems. The hydraulic power system is started before launch and is used for engine control during launch phases. The system is then shut down during on-orbit operation and is only restarted about five minutes before the deorbit burn. It continues to operate until about five minutes after landing.

The hydraulic system is only used for engine control during launch and after reentry for gliding and landing control.

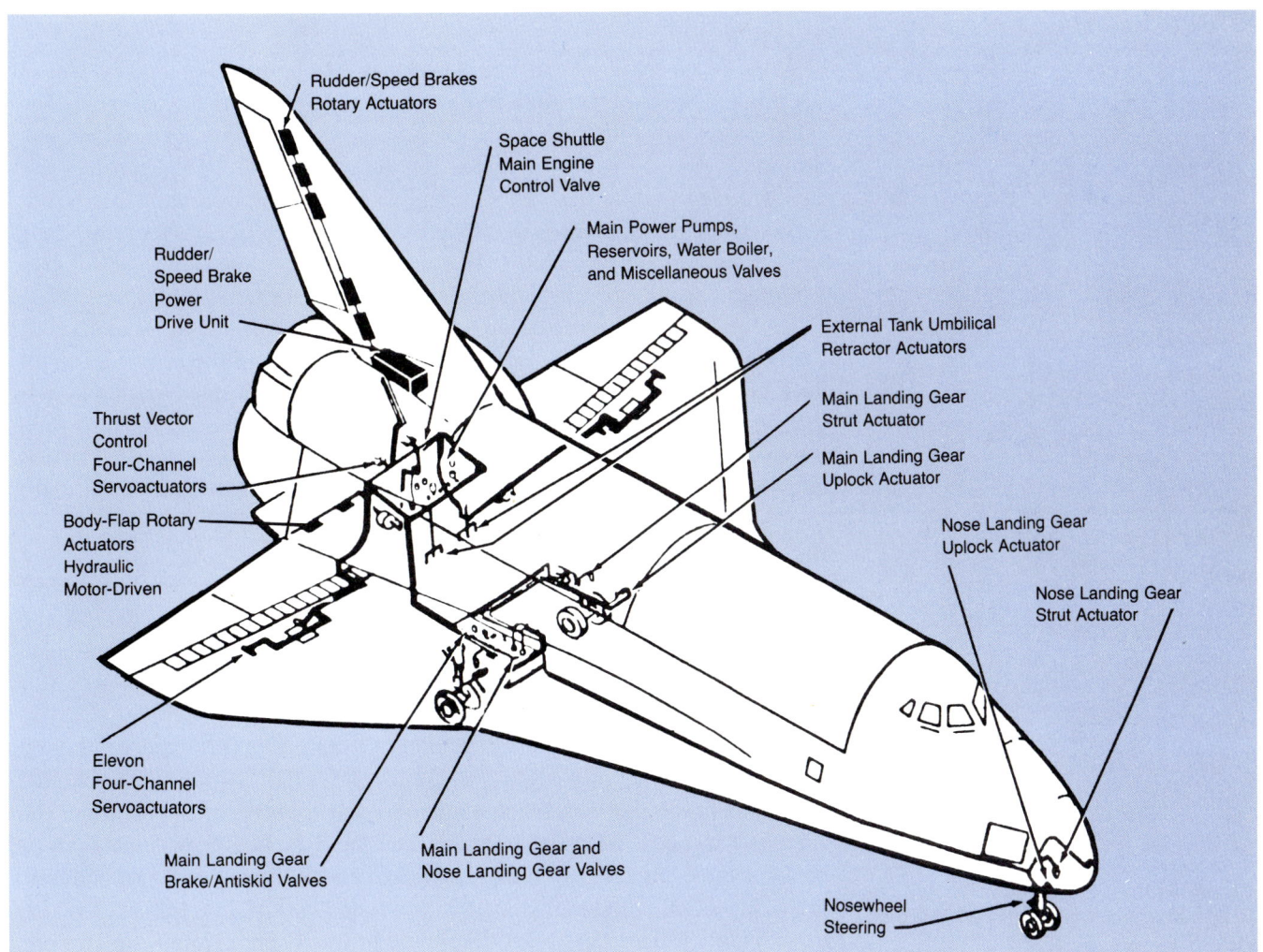

Environmental Control and Life Support

To accomplish as much work as possible in space, the astronauts need to move freely about the interior of the orbiter without the constraints of spacesuits. The environmental control and life support system (ECLSS) enables astronauts to work in shirt sleeves. The system is located in the mid-deck of the orbiter. The pressurization system maintains the cabin pressure at normal sea level conditions on Earth, providing air which is 21 percent oxygen and 79 percent nitrogen.

The oxygen comes from the same cryogenic oxygen tanks that supply the electrical power system. However, the oxygen for breathing passes through restrictors where it is warmed before passing through regulators. The nitrogen comes from four tanks, two of which are redundant. The nitrogen is under pressure so that when it arrives at a valve to mix with the oxygen, which is also under pressure, the gases released for breathing create sea level pressure.

While in space, air is consumed and needs to be revitalized. Two fans in the cabin pass the air through lithium hydroxide canisters to cleanse it. The canisters contain a mixture of activated charcoal, which removes odors, and lithium hydroxide which removes the carbon dioxide. The canisters are changed on a regular basis to maintain clean air. The humidity that builds in the crew compartment is controlled by condensing water vapor out of the air as it moves over cold plates. The air is returned to the cabin, while up to 1.8 kilograms of water per hour is sent to the waste tank.

Another segment of the environmental control system is thermal control. As the air circulates in the cabin, it picks up heat from the crew and flight deck electronics. To remove this heat there are two water circulation systems that work in conjunction with two Freon interchangers. The Freon interchangers in turn pass the heat to the Freon coolant loops. The heat is delivered to radiators which transfer the collected heat into space. This system is necessary to keep Freon gas out of the cabin area for safety reasons, since under certain conditions Freon can be toxic.

The last segment of environmental control is water and waste management. Water for drinking, food preparation and personal hygiene for the crew is provided as a by-product of the fuel cells and fed into storage tanks. If the tanks reach capacity, a relief valve automatically dumps excess water overboard.

The waste collection system is similar to the facilities on today's jetliners. The differences that one might quickly notice are foot restraints, handholds, and a waist restraint which helps maintain a seal between the user and the seat. It has been designed for both male and female crew members. It contains the commode assembly, the urinal assembly, valving, instruments, interconnection plumbing, the mounting framework and restraints. The urinal assembly is designed to handle fluids. In space, high volume air streams

The orbiter waste collection system does the same job as the earthbound toilet. What hazards are encountered in orbit that do not exist on earth?

SPACE SHUTTLES

The Orbiter Environmental and Life Support system provides both the necessities of life and the environment in which to enjoy them. Getting rid of excess heat generated by human activity is one of the functions of the system.

substitute for Earth's gravity in forcing the fluids into collection receptacles. The commode system handles solid wastes in the same manner. Airstreams also assist in the water flush mechanism. The waste matter is chemically treated and stored. After the orbiter returns to Earth, the commode is serviced in a similar fashion to those on airliners.

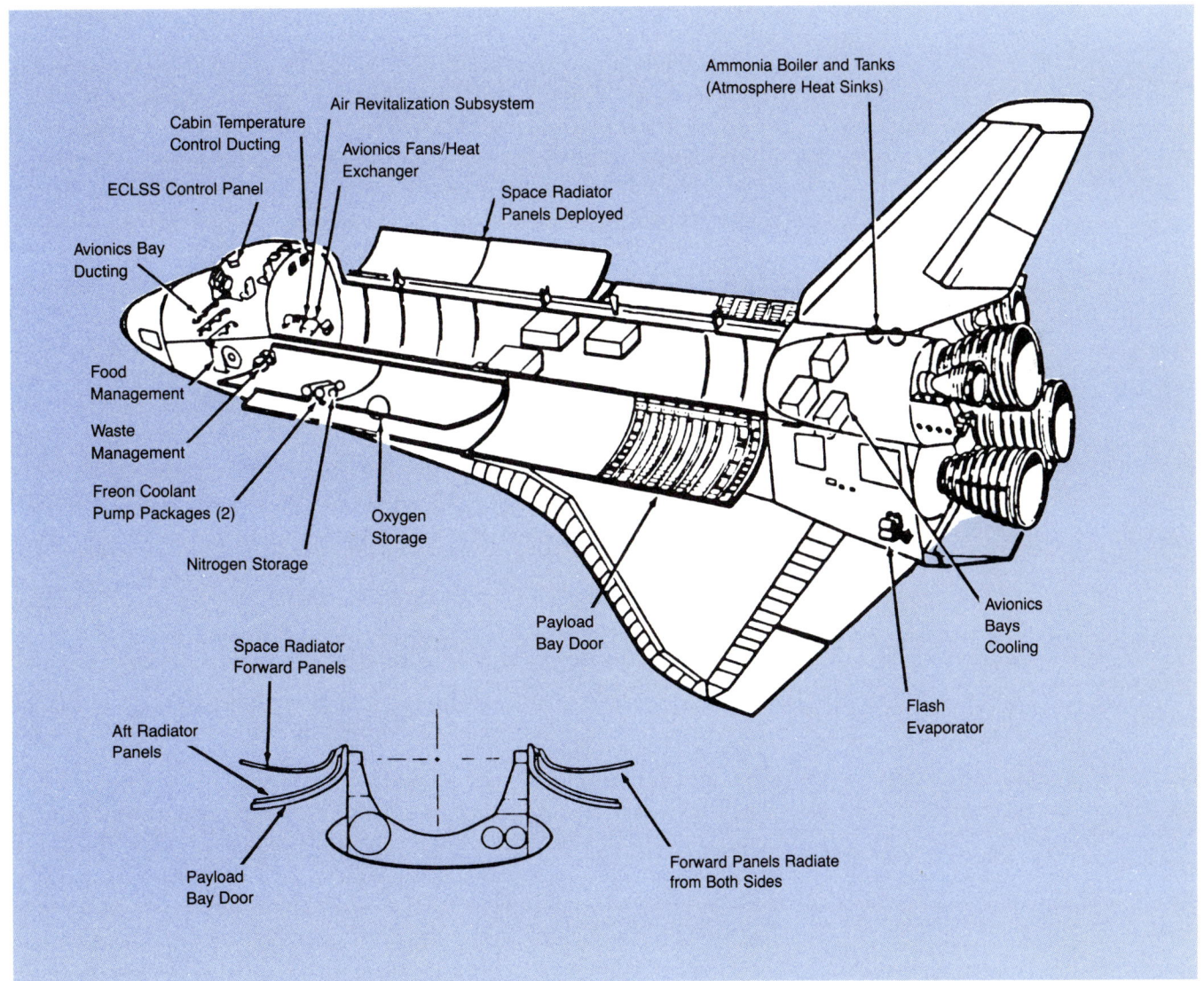

Thermal Protection

The external thermal protection system protects the orbiter from the heat generated by atmospheric reentry. It is a passive system using four materials which are lightweight and stable at high temperatures.

1. Coated reinforced carbon material is used on the nose cap and leading wing edges where the temperatures exceed 1260° Celsius. The carbon composite is made of layers of graphite cloth. The outer layers are chemically converted to silicon carbide to prevent oxidation at the high temperatures.
2. High temperature reusable surface insulation is used for areas that reach a maximum of 704° Celsius. This requires approximately 20,000 tiles primarily on the lower surface of the vehicle. The tiles are made of a low-density, high-purity silica fiber made rigid by ceramic bonding.
3. Low temperature reusable surface insulation is used for areas that do not exceed 649° Celsius. This consists of approximately 7000 tiles applied to the upper wing and fuselage side surfaces of the orbiter. They are the same as the high temperature tiles, except that the coating is designed to reflect most sunlight.
4. A flexible reusable surface insulation is used for areas that do not exceed 371° Celsius. A felt material is coated with a silicone elastomeric film to waterproof it and give it the desired optical properties of low solar absorbance and high solar emittance. The felt is applied to the upper parts of the payload doors, the sides of the fuselage and the upper wing.

The different surface tiles are applied to the aluminum skin of the orbiter with a silicone resin cement.

In addition to the exterior thermal control system there are numerous insulator blankets and thermal coatings. These insulators are used throughout the interior walls of the orbiter to help maintain temperatures at acceptable levels where the external system cannot adequately maintain required temperature levels.

Purge, Vent and Drain

The purge, vent and drain system removes gases and fluids that accumulate in unpressurized areas. During prelaunch, the purge system circulates a conditioned gas through the fuselage payload bay and tail, and orbit maneuvering system pods to remove toxic gases, as well as maintaining proper temperatures and humidity levels. The vent system (18 vents and outlets in the fuselage skin) allows various spacecraft cavities to depressurize during ascent and to repressurize during descent and landing. Electromechanical actuators are used to open and close the vent ports. The drain system removes accumulated water and other fluids from the orbiter. There is also a separate system which controls pressure between the window panes and prevents fogging and frosting of the windows during flight.

SPACE SHUTTLES

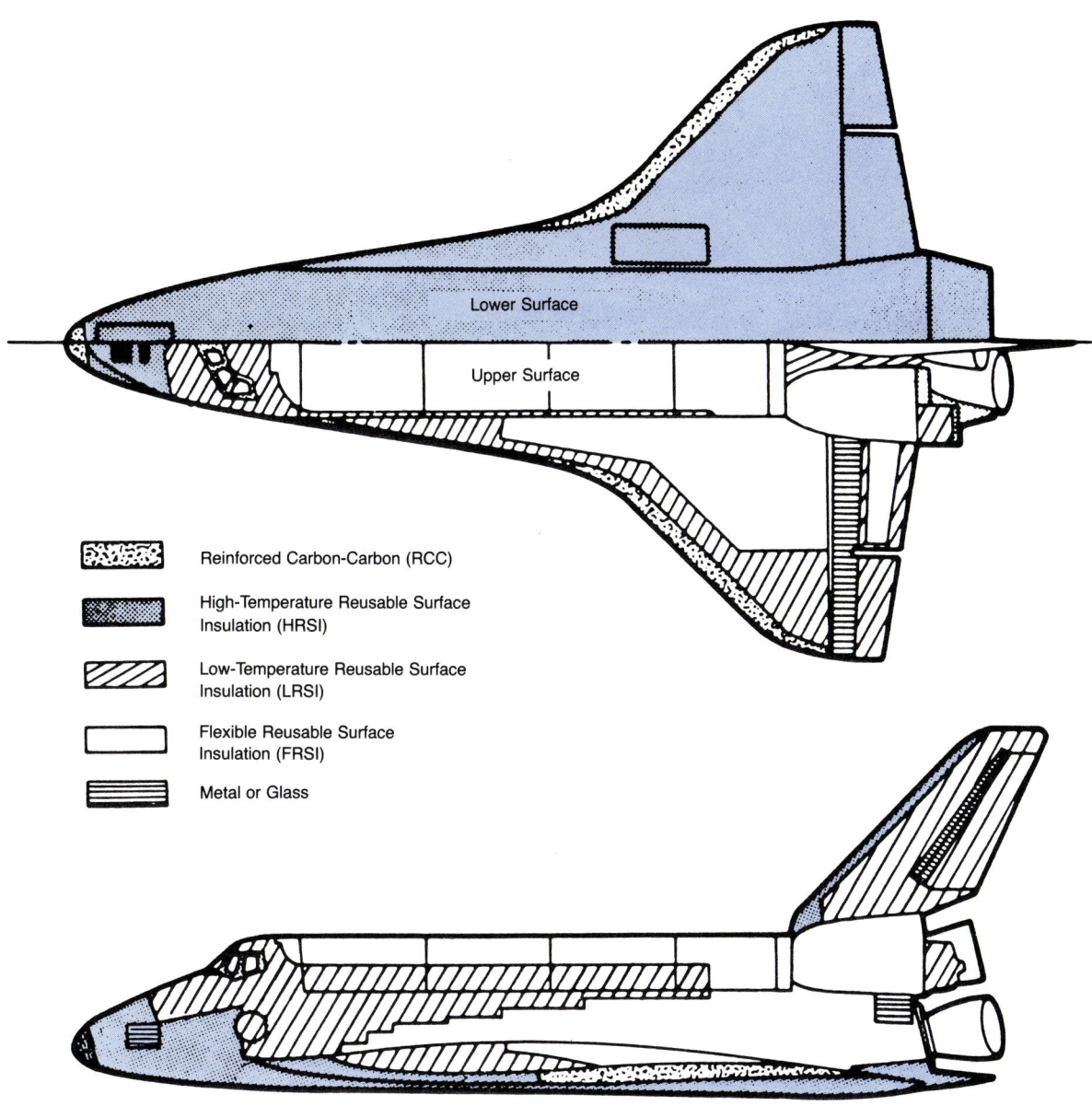

The Orbiter Thermal protection system prevents the Shuttle from becoming a meteor upon reentry.

Avionics

The Shuttle avionics system controls or assists in controlling most of the Space Shuttle systems, including guidance, navigation, control, electrical power, external tank and solid rocket boosters. Avionics automatically control the orbiter status and operational readiness, and also provide the sequencing and control for the external tank and solid rocket boosters. The avionics equipment is installed in three major areas of the orbiter: the flight deck, the forward avionics equipment bays and the aft avionics equipment bays. The system contains many redundant features, all connected to five computers which check themselves against each other. So much information is needed to perform orbiter operations that the programs are stored on tape and only called up as specific flight operations are activated.

Guidance, Navigation and Control

The orbiter is a unique transportation vehicle in that it is a launch vehicle, a space orbiter and an atmospheric glider. Computers use the flight control module program to control the orbiter through all of its phases. The guidance, navigation and control system is composed of four computers and other major components that make up the primary control system. A fifth computer is used as a backup.

During launch, most computer commands are directed to the gimbaled main engines and solid rocket boosters. In orbit, the flight control commands are directed to the reaction control system and the steering engines. During deorbit, the computer directs the orbiter aerodynamic control surfaces, which include the elevons, speedbrake, rudder assembly and body flaps.

Although computers are capable of all this work, the flight commander can select any of three flight modes. They are: automatic — when the computer system flies the vehicle; control stick steering — when the flight crew flies the orbiter with computer augmentation; and direct — when the flight crew flies the orbiter with no augmentation. The flight crew can also select different rates for pitch, roll and yaw, as well as the speed brake and body flap.

In the automatic mode the flight crew monitors the instruments to verify the trajectory. The guidance, navigation and control systems compute the flight equations that command the movement of the spacecraft. In this mode, only the landing gear extension and braking are performed by the crew.

In the control stick mode, the crew flies the spacecraft by operating a small pistol grip stick known as a rotational hand controller. If the orbiter is in aerodynamic flight, rudder pedals are also used. The system interprets the motion on the stick and rudders as commands in pitch, roll and yaw. The larger the hand motion on the stick, the larger the command

SPACE SHUTTLES

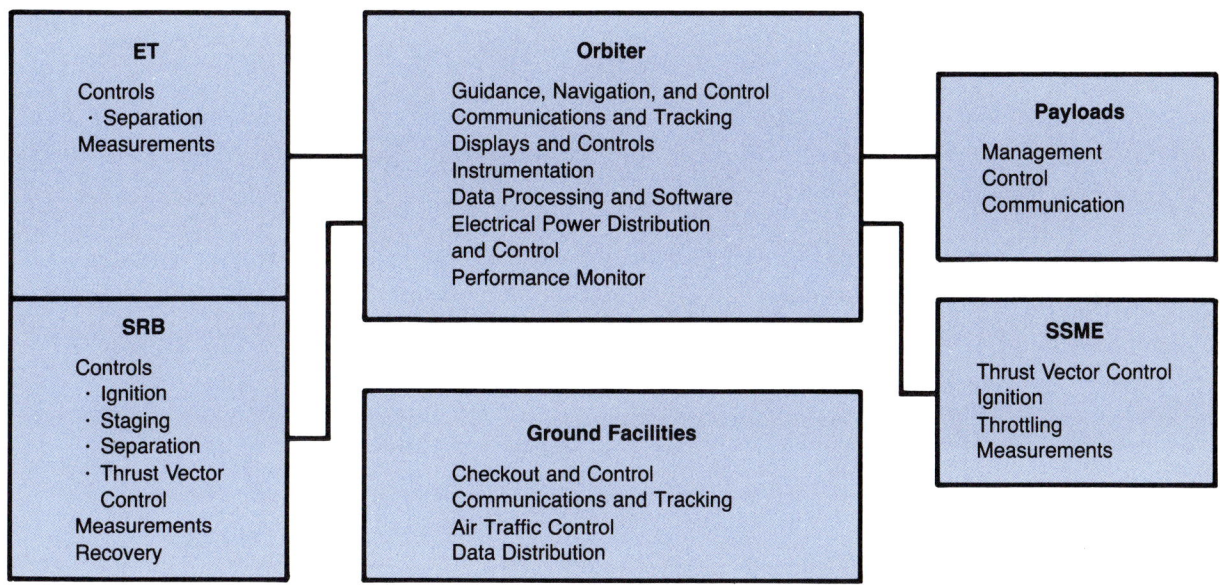

Five separate computers control the Shuttle Avionics System.

Quantity	Display or control
827	Toggle switches
430	Circuit breakers
415	Pushbutton switches
53	Rotary switches
29	Thumbwhell switches
4	Timers
97	Vernier potentiometers
3	Rotational hand controllers
2	Translational hand controllers
1	Crew optical alignment sight
88	Meters (round, tape, straight)
58	Event and mode lights
2	Horizontal situation indicator
2	Attitude direction indicator
4	Cathode-ray tube
[a]3	Caution-and-warning panel (includes fire panel)
[b]1	Computer status board

[a]170 indicator lights.
[b]25 indicator lights.

action. The flight control system compares the hand commands with measurements from the rate gyros and accelerometers that indicate exactly what the vehicle is doing. It then generates control signals to produce the desired movements in each axis.

In the direct mode, the orbiter only responds to inputs from the flight crew, although the commands by the crew are relayed through the computer. The pilot must coordinate all movement to maintain the proper attitude. Mission control and the shuttle pilots decide on the specific mode of flight based on mission requirements.

Displays and Controls

Over 2000 readouts and control devices surround the cockpit area of the orbiter. They are grouped by function and arranged in operational sequence from left to right or top to bottom.

The left panel contains circuit breakers, controls and instrumentation for the environmental and life support system, the communications equipment, heating controls, trim and body flap controls, and the commander's speed brake and thrust controller. The right panel contains additional circuit breakers, controls for fuel cells, power units and the hydraulic system. The pilot's electrical power distribution controls and development flight instruments are also on the right panel. The pilot's speed brake and thrust controller is to the left on the center console.

The overhead rack contains lighting controls, the computer voting panel and all purge controls. (Each computer makes a decision based on the

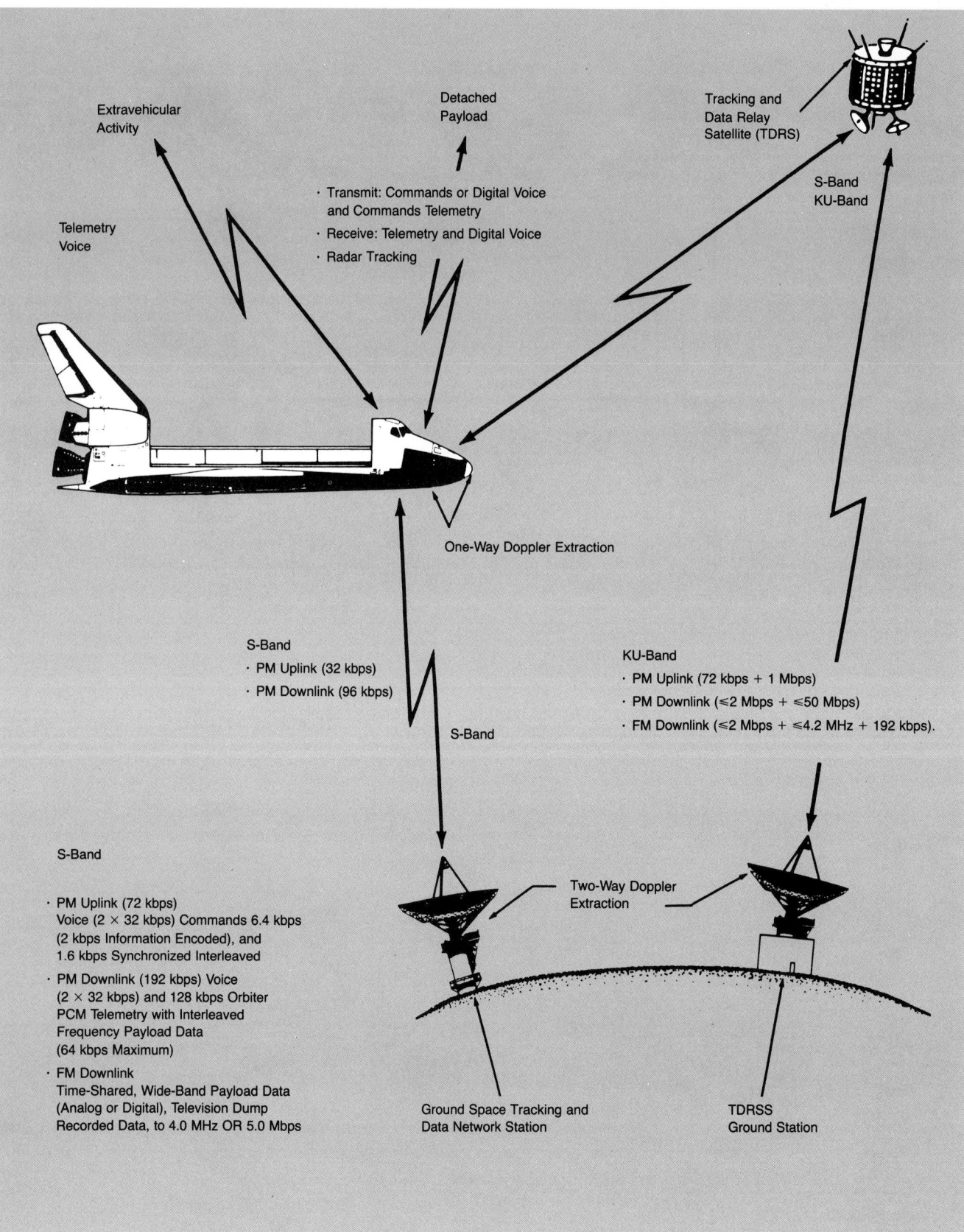

SPACE SHUTTLES

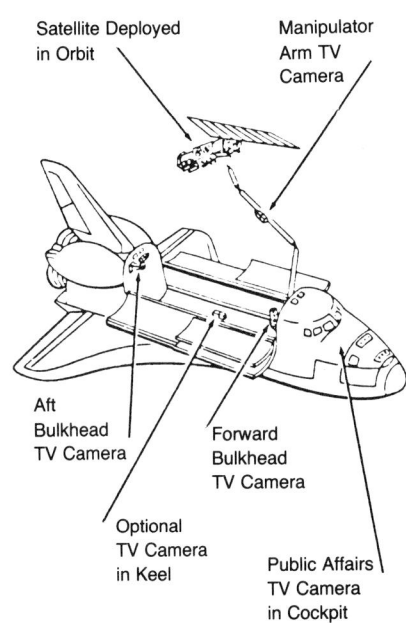

Space Shuttle orbital communication and tracking links are necessary to keep both earth-bound technicians and working astronauts aware of everything happening on the mission.

available information. When the computers disagree as to an action, a computer vote is taken and displayed on this panel.) The center console contains the flight control system channel selection, the air data computer equipment, the communication and navigation control set, the fuel cell circuit breakers, and the pilot's trim and body flap controls. The center forward panels contain the cathode ray tube (CRT) display sets, the caution and warning system, aerosurface position indicator, backup flight control displays, and fire protection system displays and controls.

In addition there is an aft mission specialist station which contains readouts and controls for the payload bay area including lighting, the remote manipulator system, and a television system, as well as unique controls for specific payloads.

Communications and Data

The communication and data systems must cover the wide range of Shuttle activities and payloads. The orbiter system consists of a radio system, a computer system, a special processor for interfacing between payloads and radio system, a television system and a tape recording system.

In conjunction with the Shuttle system, there are support systems on earth. These include the Space Tracking and Data Network (STDN), the Tracking and Data Relay Satellite System (TDRSS), the Mission Control Center and the Payload Operation Control Center.

The orbiter contains a closed circuit television system for on-orbit operations. The cameras are used to record crew operations, hardware inspections and experimentation. The cameras are also used to observe out of the window to view the Earth, payloads, and exterior of the orbiter.

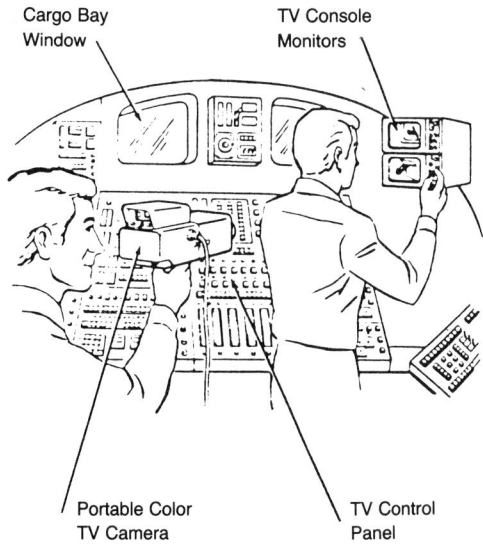

An on-board TV system is used to monitor all mission activities — and to get views of Earth.

55

TO EARTH ORBIT

Mission Operations, Support, Launch and Landing Facilities

The Space Shuttle is a giant step in the evolution of the United States space program. As the first reusable vehicle, it was designed for cost savings. However, reusability was not the only cost saving feature of the program. Much of the existing launch facility at the Kennedy Space Center was adapted to the Shuttle requirements. The program took maximum advantage of existing buildings and structures, and modified them for the Shuttle. The only new facilities that were required were the Shuttle landing facility and the orbiter processing facility.

The Shuttle uses launch pad 39A, the same launch complex used for the Apollo launches with the Saturn V rocket. The vehicle assembly building for the Saturn V rocket has had its internal platform modified so the Shuttle can be assembled in a vertical position atop the mobile launcher platform. The orbiter is connected to the external tank and solid rocket boosters. When the assembly of the Shuttle is complete, the platforms are moved to one side and the doors of the vehicle assembly building are opened. This permits the crawler transporter to move the mobile launcher platform and assembled Shuttle to the launch pad. The Shuttle is connected to the fixed service structure on the launch pad in preparation for launch.

The Apollo launch control center has been adapted for Shuttle requirements. The Shuttle launch sequence requires approximately 45 people, as

The crawler transporter is used to move the mobile launcher platform and the Shuttle from the assembly area to the launch site.

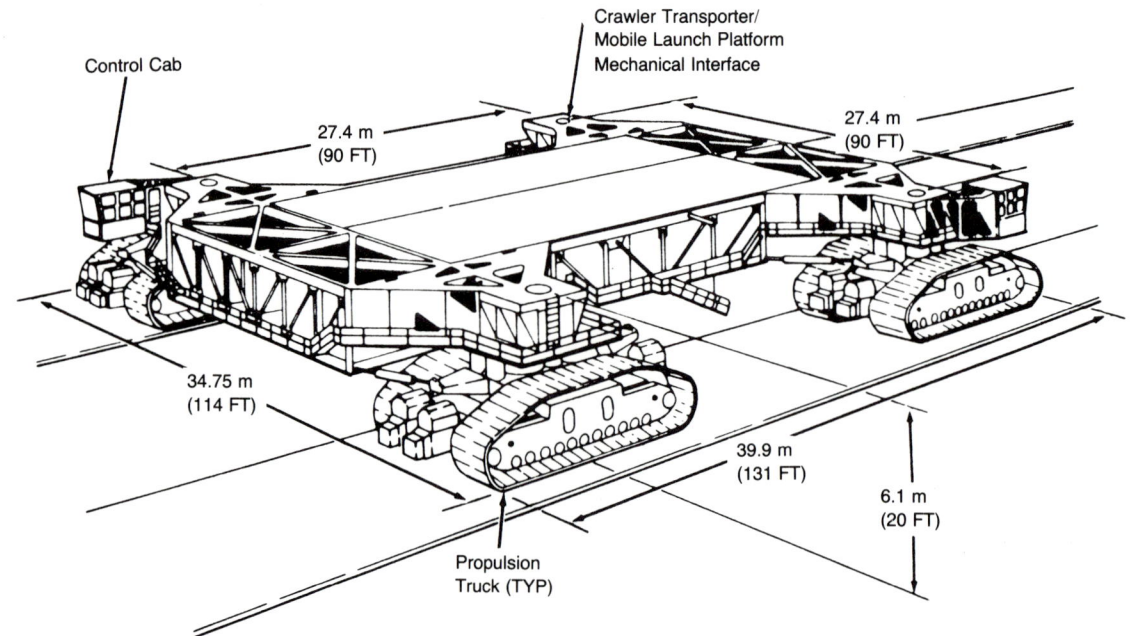

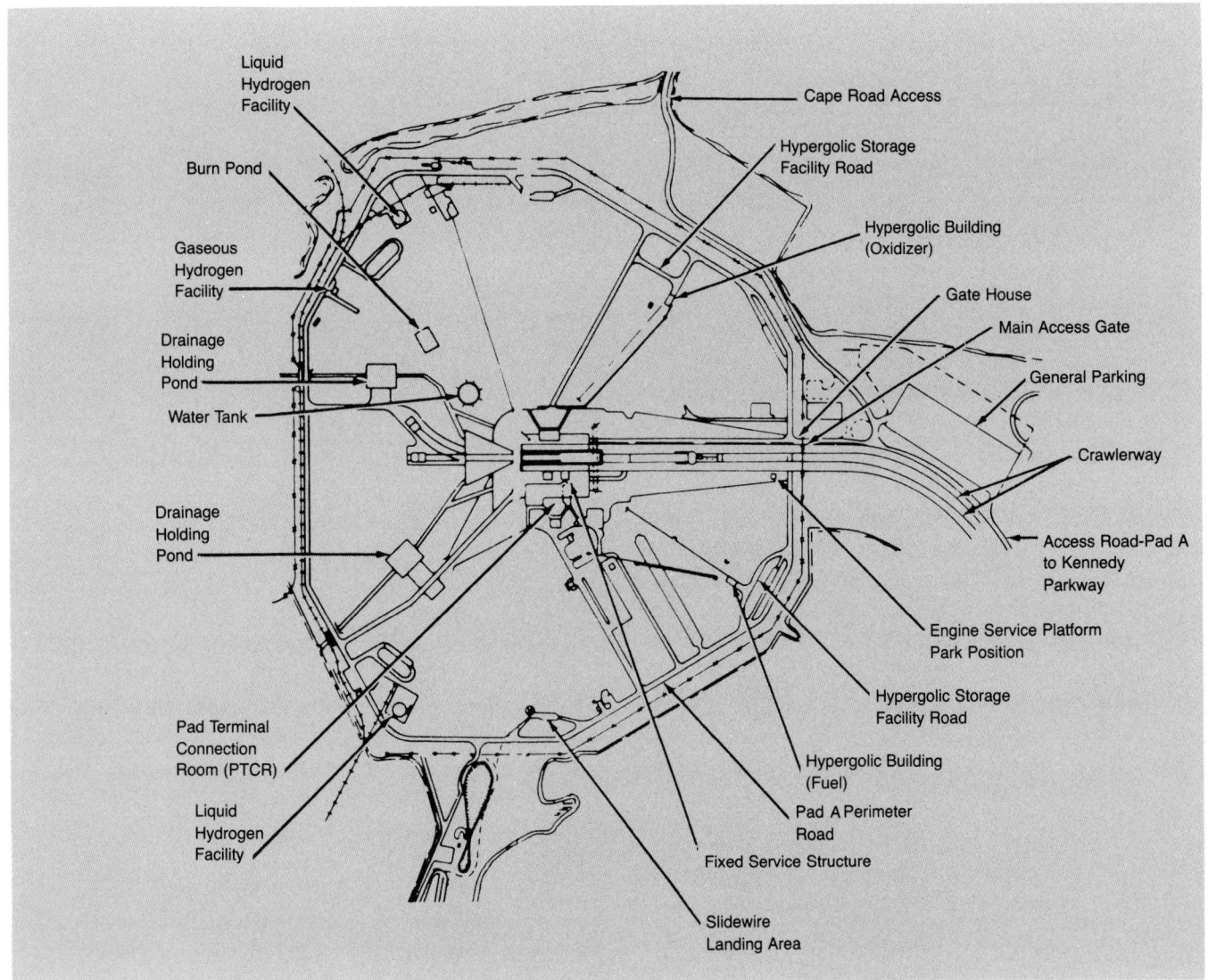

Launch Pad 39-A overhead view.

compared to 450 required for the earlier Apollo launches. When the Shuttle is ready and launch occurs, some new procedures are undertaken. Immediately after the launch, the solid rocket boosters are recovered and returned to the launch complex to be refurbished. After the flight, the orbiter lands on a runway specially constructed for the orbiter. The orbiter uses a sophisticated microwave scanning-beam landing system to help land on the runway in a high speed glide. Since the orbiter has no propulsion system, it must accomplish the landing perfectly the first time. Once the orbiter returns, it is sent to the orbiter processing facility where it is checked and refurbished for the next flight.

TO EARTH ORBIT

Flightcrew Training

When astronauts go into space on the shuttle their tasks must be accomplished correctly the first time. Preparation for any mission will include time in or on several training devices. At the Johnson Space Center (JSC) they have an Orbiter one G trainer which has a full scale flight deck, a mid deck and a mid body complete with payload bay. The flight crew gains experience in training, habitability, extra–vehicular activity, ingress, egress, television operation, waste management, stowage and routine housekeeping and maintenance.

Another device used to train astronauts is the Orbiter neutral bouyancy trainer. This trainer consists of a full scale crew cabin, mid deck, an airlock and payload bay door which are all immersed in a huge tank which provides a zero G environment for training which includes extra vehicular activity.

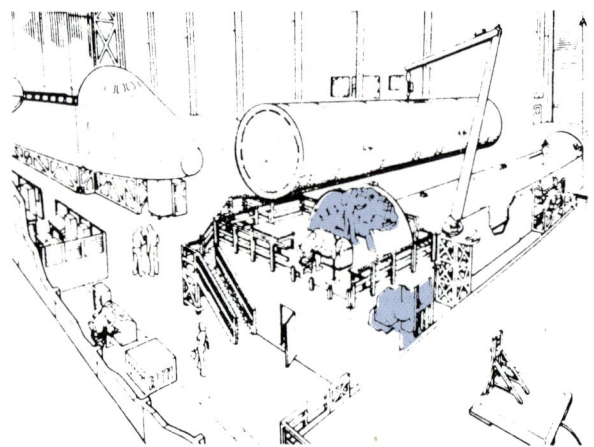

Remote manipulator system task trainer

There is also a Shuttle Mission Simulator (SMS) which consists of forward and aft crew stations. The SMS is computer controlled and uses mathematical models to simulate real flight dynamics. Another device is the Spacelab Simulator (SLS) which consists of a core and an experiment segment interior with computer modeling for training the flight crew and ground crew support members.

One of the more interesting trainers is the Remote Manipulator System task trainer. It consists of mockups of the aft crew station, payload bay and a mechanically operated arm. Here the astronauts can practice using a mechanically operated arm for payload grappling, berthing, payload bay camera operation and manipulator software operation. Helium inflated models of payloads are used to simulate the space environment.

All operations must be mastered in the training facilities so that they are second nature to the astronauts, as on the shuttle flight they will have to do the job right the first time.

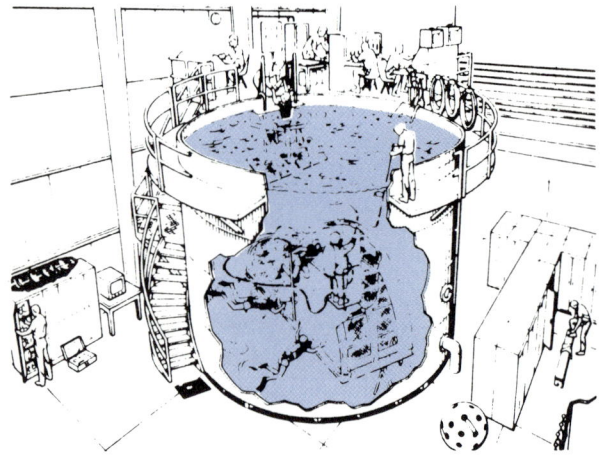

Orbiter neutral bouyancy trainer

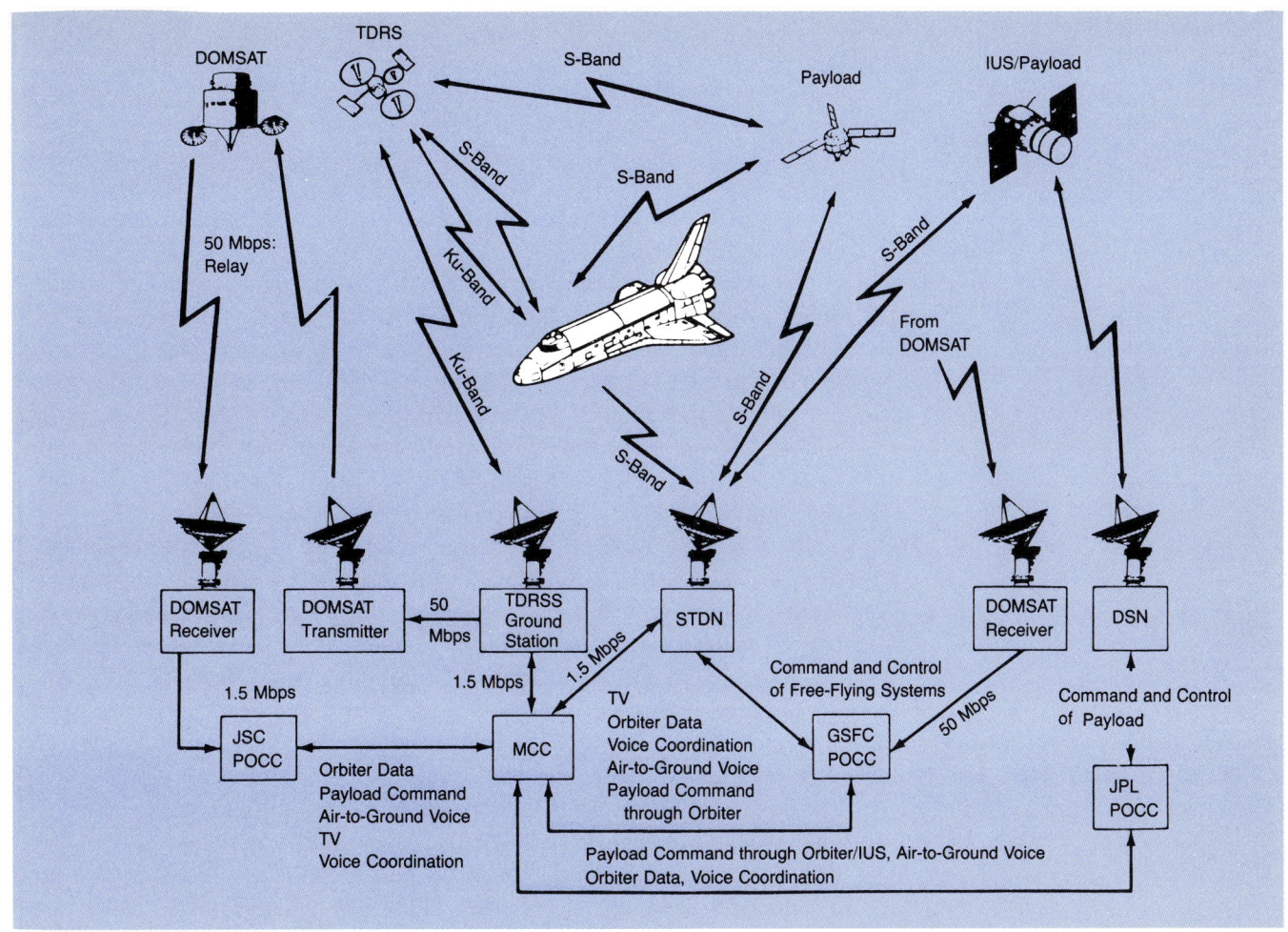

DOMSAT	Domestic Satellite
DSN	Deep Space Network
GSFC	Goddard Space Flight Center
IUS	Inertial Upper Stage
JPL	Jet Propulsion Laboratory
JSC	Johnson Space Center
MCC	Mission Control Center
POCC	Payload Operations Control Center
STDN	Space Tracking and Data Network
TDRS	Tracking and Data Relay Satellite
TDRSS	Tracking and Data Relay Satellite System

The Shuttle communicates with earth in two ways: by direct radio and by satellite relay.

Tracking, Communications, Flight Operations and Mission Control

Communications with the Shuttle orbiter take place constantly from launch to landing. Two ways of communicating with control centers are provided for the orbiter. The first way is with radio links through the TDRSS satellite system. Voice, television and data can be communicated to and from the orbiter by relaying radio signals through these NASA satellites and their single ground station in New Mexico. The radio antennas on the orbiter do not always point toward earth, but instead continuously point at one of the two TDRSS satellites. The second way to communicate is to point the radio antennas at the STDN ground stations located around the Earth.

As in past space programs, the Johnson Space Center houses the Mission Control Center for Space Shuttle missions. The mission control computer complex is divided into three systems. The first is the communication interface system. It gives the control center great flexibility in routing communications, using voice, teletype and video. Computers compress out-going data and route incoming data. It deals with data in both real and delayed time and uses the computer to restore data to the proper time format. (Real time provides information as the event is occurring. Delayed time processes information, stores it in the computer and releases the information

TO EARTH ORBIT

to the shuttle and crew when the shuttle can process the information while in communication range.)

The second mission control system is the Shuttle data processing complex, which processes communication, trajectory data, and telemetry data. This system is essential during mission events such as launch and landing. Trajectory and telemetry is converted to meaningful information that can be used by the flight controller. The third mission control system is the display control system. It transfers the computer-processed data to readout devices including strip chart recorders, scribing plotboard, event lights and a television system. Most data is available on the television system.

The mission control center operations for the Space Shuttle are different from those of previous programs in that operations planning and management are the main tasks. The other functions of flight control and coordination of payload operations are now handled at the Goddard Space Flight Center, the Jet Propulsion Laboratory or the Johnson Space Center depending on mission requirements.

International Shuttle Design

Soviet Union

The Soviet Union has made more progress than any other country except the United States in experimenting with Space Shuttle concepts. In the 1950s, during the development of space shuttle technology, the United States developed reentry vehicles that could maneuver like a glider. This type of vehicle was known as a "lifting body." It is believed that the Soviets have also flown missions with such a vehicle.

Plans call for the Soviet Shuttle to have jet engines so that if it should not be on course for landing, it could make adjustments or fly by and make a second approach. This is an improvement over the American Shuttle, which has only one chance to land. The launch system (Energia) for the Soviet shuttle is also being designed with an all-liquid fuel system as opposed to the combination solid and liquid fuel system used by the United States. Infor-

An early gliding re-entry vehicle from the 1950s shows how far the design has advanced in thirty years.

mation on the Soviet vehicle is limited. However, unmanned tests of the orbiter *Buran* began in 1988, and manned flights are expected in the 1990s.

France

The French are developing a small Shuttle known as Hermes. It is very similar to the United States Shuttle in that it is planned to service space stations and to transport cargo. It will be capable of performing scientific experiments, on-orbit repairs, maintenance and refurbishing satellites. The proposed launch vehicle will be the Ariane 5, which will have a large central body with cryogenic engines and strap-on solid rocket boosters. When in orbit, the Hermes will use two engines mounted in the rear fuselage. The entire system is very similar to that developed by the United States. Hermes is in the concept planning stages and an operational vehicle may appear late in the 1990s.

Japan

The Japanese are also exploring the possibility of developing a Shuttle with the name of HOPE (H-II Orbiting Plane). They are considering different design options. The final design will be chosen to balance payload size against crew size so that the rocket chosen will be capable of generating enough thrust. The missions to be performed will be a major factor in determining the optimal configuration. They hope to undergo tests of vehicles sometime in the mid 1990s.

JAPANESE SHUTTLE OPTIONS

Design Option	Vehicle Weight(Kg)	Lift Capacity(Kg)	Crew Size	Propulsion
1.	10,000	3,000	0	none
2.	10,000	1,000	2	none
3.	20,000	4,000	4	none
4.	27,000	1,000	2	internal
5.	10,000	1,000	2	jet

Germany

The Germans are exploring the concept of the Horus Shuttle. It is a different concept from the American Shuttle in that the Horus vehicle would ride atop a Sanger aerospace plane and be launched from this vehicle. It would look similar to the original American Shuttle riding atop a 747 jetliner. The Horus will carry a crew of two and could service space stations and do reconnaissance work. The scientists involved with this project are carefully monitoring other Shuttle efforts to help improve the Horus concept. The Horus will enter development stages in the mid 1990s and operations may begin early in the twenty-first century.

TO EARTH ORBIT

The Space Shuttle at Work

IMAGINE YOU ARE a mission specialist on a space shuttle mission that is ready to begin. You are strapped in an acceleration seat, ready to be launched from Cape Canaveral. You think about all the preparation and training you have had over the past months. There were classes on the shuttle systems, training for the weightless environment in the watertank, and even courses in first-aid and emergency procedures. Of course, as a mission specialist, most of your time was spent learning how to use the RMS. You are the expert for this mission. Without you, the mission of deploying and retrieving satellites during the next five days could not be accomplished. You are confident, but still nervous and excited.

The countdown continues. Finally, the main engines are started. You feel the whole shuttle sway slightly. Then you hear the thundering roar of the solid rocket boosters. The shuttle accelerates straight up into the air and you are pushed into your seat. You hear the pilots talking in short choppy sentences to ground controllers. After a short time, you feel the shuttle rotate and slowly change direction. You are heading toward the desired orbit. The shuttle jolts when the solid rocket boosters are jettisoned. Later you are jolted again, as the main engines turn off and the external tank is jettisoned. At this point you realize that you are in orbit. Instead of being pushed into your seat, you are floating. Only your seatbelts hold you in your seat.

For the first few orbits, you wait as the pilots check all of the systems on the shuttle. You are in a low-Earth orbit, so it only takes an hour and a half to orbit the Earth. While you wait, you watch a couple sunrises and sunsets over the planet below. After the systems checks, the pilots put the shuttle in automatic control. Then you all break for a meal. As you unstrap yourself from your seat, you have to adjust to weightlessness. At first you feel clumsy and out of control, as you pull and glide through the shuttle to the mid-deck. It gets easier though, and after a few days you move like a pro and enjoy the sensation. However, since you know that muscles and bones lose strength in space, you are glad that this mission will only last for five days.

After your meal, you begin work at the RMS control console. You run many checks to see if it is ready to be used. This activity takes the rest of this first workday in orbit. When you are through working, you join the other astronauts for dinner and then take a break. You read a science fiction book and feel like a character in the story. After the break you spend some time talking to astronauts on the space station by radio. You will be deploying a load of fuel and supplies to them tomorrow, so you must make sure they are ready to receive it. After this, everyone radios home and speaks with their families. Despite the half-second time delays, you are glad that there are such satellite radios to use.

At the end of the day, you all climb into light sleeping bags which are tethered to the walls. It is the first trip in space for you and one other

Artist's conception shows the Space Shuttle ready to deploy an upper stage space vehicle and its payload, a tracking and relay satellite.

astronaut, so you both have difficulty falling asleep while floating. However, you are so tired that after a while you fall asleep anyway.

Eight hours later you all wake up. You eat breakfast and then bathe with premoistened towels. Then it is time to get back to work. First the shuttle is turned and the payload doors are opened. You activate the RMS and practice some manipulations. After lunch, you use the RMS to deploy two small science experiments. After dinner, you ship the supplies to the space station. You use the RMS to lift the orbital maneuvering vehicle (OMV) and its payload out of the cargo bay. After you release it, the OMV glides slowly away. The ground controllers take over its guidance. When it is safely away from the shuttle, the OMV fires its propulsion system. It begins to accelerate to a higher orbit, where it will rendezvous with the space station. This ends your second day in orbit. Sleep comes easier now that you have had practice.

You spend the next day working at a computer console. A communication satellite must be deployed. Two astronauts don space suits and go out into the cargo bay area to prepare the satellite. When it is ready, you activate the release mechanism. The shuttle sways slightly as the spinning satellite is pushed up and out of the cargo bay. You use a radio to run many tests on the satellite which is now far away from the shuttle. When all the tests pass, you

TO EARTH ORBIT

send the radio command for the upper stage booster rocket to fire. It propels the satellite into its correct orbit.

The next day is spent monitoring experiments in the cargo bay. The day after that is the most challenging. You must pick up another OMV which is in orbit nearby. This one has been in space for a year, in service around the space station. You talk to the OMV controllers on the ground by radio as they guide it closer to the space shuttle. When it gets close to the shuttle, you take over control of the OMV and guide it to the RMS. After grabbing it, the RMS slowly pulls the OMV into the cargo bay. The astronauts out in the cargo bay lock it into place so that it can be returned to Earth.

The last day of your mission is spent rechecking shuttle systems as you prepare to return to Earth. You close the payload doors and prepare for landing. Strapped in your seat, you realize that you will soon feel gravity again. It has become easy and comfortable to float around, and you are sorry to see the mission coming to an end.

With direction from ground controllers, the pilot turns the shuttle around and fires its engines. This slows the shuttle down and causes its orbit to decay. Before entering the atmosphere, the pilot turns the shuttle around again so that the nose of the shuttle is facing forward. Soon you are traveling at hypersonic speed in the upper atmosphere. There is a roar and blinding light outside as you are pressed into your seat. Then the pilot steers the shuttle down through some long turns and you are pushed into your seat even harder. After a last turn, you glide into the California desert at Edwards Air Force Base. The touch down is very smooth and your mission is finished. Gravity again has you in its grasp. You feel very heavy, and are rather sad that it is all over. However, you have every reason to be proud. Your training and hard work helped make this a successful mission. You are now one of the few human beings to have flown into space and orbited the Earth. Someday you may look back on this and tell the story to your grandchildren. However, by the time your grandchildren are born, space travel may be commonplace!

Summary

The Space Shuttle is part of the evolutionary growth of the United States space program. It is the backbone of what has become known as the United States Space Transportation System (STS). The program was initiated in 1972 and became operational in the 1980s. The technology for the reusable space vehicle undergoes continual upgrading in the areas of propulsion, guidance, navigation, control, structures and support. The Shuttle provides a low-cost, reusable vehicle which makes space operation routine. Several other countries are now planning for the development of Space Shuttles to accomplish on-orbit missions and service space stations.

SPACE SHUTTLES

Terms

actuators	kilonewtons
aft	longerons
bulkhead	mandrel
cryogenic	redeployed
deorbit	reefing
drogue	redundancy
elastomeric film	Remote Manipulator System
elevon	slosh baffles
external tank	solid rocket boosters
frustrum	Spacelab
gimbaled	stringer panels
honeycomb	thrusters
jettison	vortex

Important Ideas and Events

- Late 1960s — idea for reusable Space Shuttle was conceived.
- 1972 — STS is approved.
- 1979 — First test flights of the STS.
- 1981 — First successful launch, orbital flight, non-powered reentry and landing of the Space Shuttle Columbia.
- 1986 — Explosion during Shuttle launch grounds the Shuttle for over two years.
- 1988 — Shuttle flights resume late in year.

Interesting Things to Do

1. Order films from NASA about the Space Shuttle.
2. Write to NASA for information on future Shuttle plans.
3. Chart the progress of Shuttle programs of other countries.
4. Construct a project demonstrating a technological concept relating to the Shuttle guidance, navigation or control systems.
5. Keep a log on Space Shuttle flights and events with information obtained from newspapers, news programs and news magazines.
6. Sketch the major events in a current Space Shuttle mission from launch to landing.

What technological difficulties must be overcome before spaceports become possible?

Chapter 3   AEROSPACE PLANES

For many years people have imagined traveling in space rockets out of Earth's atmosphere and through space to the moon, planets and stars. Early science fiction stories described these rockets as missiles. However, after the Wright brothers proved that wings can lift vehicles into the air, another possible shape for space rockets emerged. That was the aerospace plane. We use the word "aerospace" because it can propel itself both in an atmosphere and in the vacuum of space. The word "plane" is used because wings are used for flying in the atmosphere.

The first serious proposals for building aerospace planes were made by a man named Sanger in the late 1930s. In the 1980s, the idea of building and using aerospace planes became a more popular topic. They may be used by the military, space agencies, or even airlines. The United States, Germany, and Great Britain have proposed modern versions of aerospace planes. They are unlikely to be flying soon. Some very difficult technological problems must first be solved. The most difficult problem will be designing air-breathing engines that can propel an aerospace plane all the way into orbit. If successful, the aerospace plane will be the most complicated transportation device ever built.

Historical Development

The aerospace plane was first seriously considered as a bomber. During World War II, Hitler planned to attack distant countries, including the United States. His research engineers experimented with different ways to do this. The Nazi German Army developed missiles, such as the infamous V2, which were to be used on long range targets. These missile development efforts continued until the end of the war. A scientist named Eugene Sanger was working as a research engineer for the Nazi German Airforce on an aerospace plane, the "America Bomber," for similar bombing missions.

TO EARTH ORBIT

The America Bomber was to have been 28 meters long with a wingspan of 15 meters. Behind the cockpit, two 18-meter-long tanks would hold fuel and liquid oxygen. Its launch would be boosted by a rocket sled. It then would burn 82,000 kilograms of fuel climbing to an initial altitude of 280 kilometers. Gathering speed as it fell under the pull of gravity, the plane would enter the denser layers of the atmosphere at an altitude of about 40 kilometers and skip back up, similar to a flat stone skipping across water. This skipping would be repeated until the plane reached its target. After dropping a bomb, it would enter a stable gliding descent back to its point of launch. This program was canceled in the middle of the war, and the aerospace plane was never built. After the war, Sanger continued proposing that an aerospace plane be built, but for peaceful missions.

In the 1980s the aerospace plane has again received attention and research money. One reason for this is the high cost of getting satellites into space. European and American space agencies hope that aerospace planes will provide inexpensive transportation to space. Some people estimate that an aerospace plane could deploy satellites at one-fifth the cost of a shuttle mission. The aerospace plane may also be used as an extremely fast airliner and by the military for strategic application.

Technology of Aerospace Planes

The main reason for creating aerospace planes is to have air-breathing space launchers. Other launchers, such as expendable launch vehicles and space shuttles, must lift both fuel and oxidizer. The oxidizer is often liquid oxygen and is needed for combustion of the fuel for propulsion. Aerospace planes would use the oxygen in the air they fly through as an oxidizer, just as most airplanes do. Since they wouldn't have to carry oxidizer, aerospace planes could be smaller than rocket launchers. Also, since they can fly like airplanes, they may someday fly in and out of airports.

The wings and engines of an aerospace plane make it a cross between the Shuttle and an airliner. Like the airliner, the air-breathing engines can only be used in the atmosphere. Shuttle-type rocket thrusters will be needed in the vacuum of space. Like both the shuttle and an airliner, the aerospace plane's wings are also only useful in the atmosphere. Space vehicles can only change the direction of velocity by rotating and then firing thrusters.

The aerospace plane will be designed for reusability and rapid turnaround time. It should be able to land after a mission, and then quickly refuel, receive routine maintenance, and be ready for its next mission. This will be a major improvement over the Space Shuttle. Between missions, it requires weeks to repair the Shuttle and assemble it onto the solid rocket boosters and external fuel tank. Making maintenance routine for an aerospace plane complicates the technological development of the engines

AEROSPACE PLANES

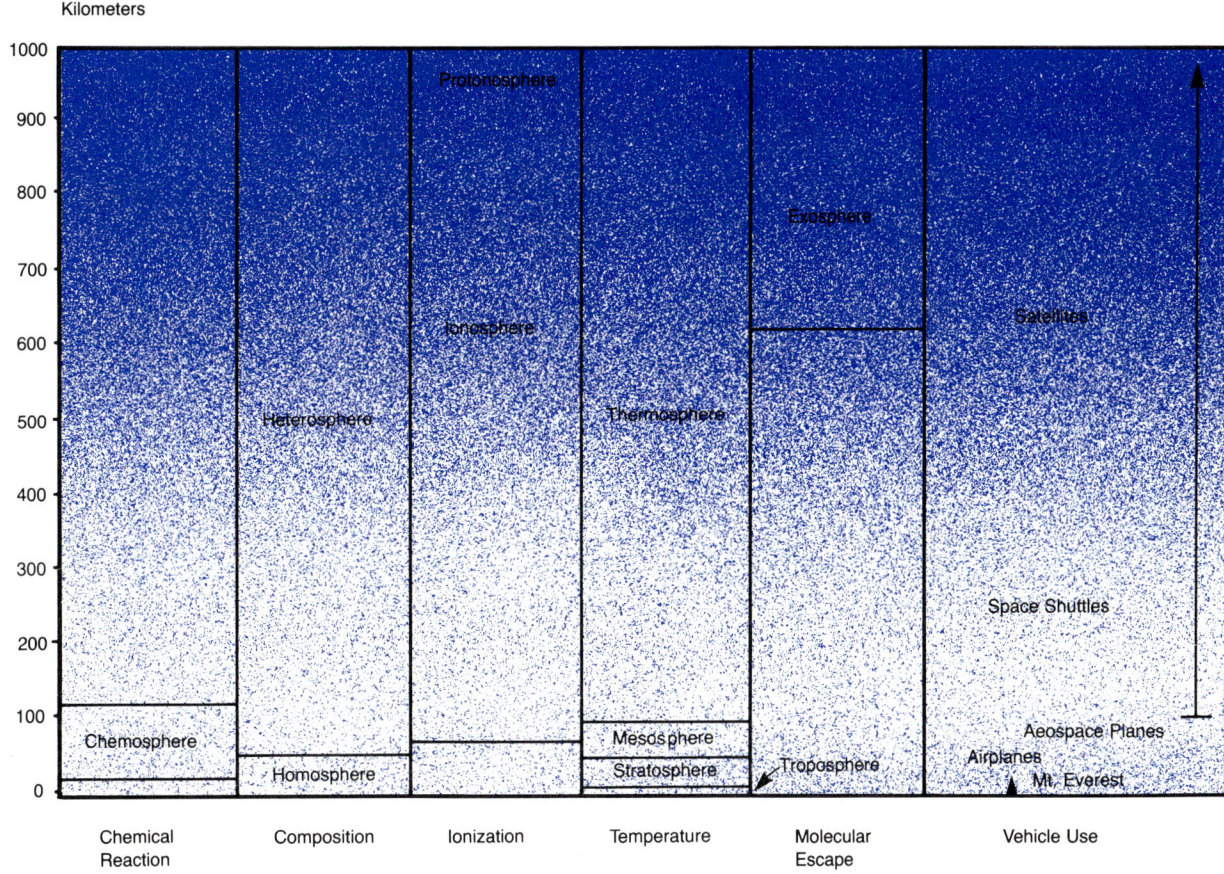

Layers of the Atmosphere

Scientists have different ways of labeling the layers in the atmosphere. Names can represent layers with different temperatures, compositions, chemical properties, or electrical properties. The name can also represent the ability of the molecules to escape the atmosphere.

The boundary between the atmosphere and space is also difficult to establish. Some scientists define the boundary as the exosphere. This is the altitude where light gas molecules can escape the gravity of Earth. Other scientists define the boundary as the region where there is not enough air to provide lift on a plane's wings. This occurs at an altitude of about 160 kilometers.

Aerospace planes can skip in the atmosphere between 160 kilometers and 50 kilometers. Skipping happens when a vehicle flies down into the atmosphere very fast. When the vehicle tries to level out at a constant altitude, it is moving so fast that its wings generate enough lift to push it back up into higher altitudes.

and other parts. While these engines must be designed for new levels of performance, they must also be designed to be sturdy and simple.

Before aerospace planes become possible, some technological problems must be solved. Air-breathing engines such as turbojets, ramjets, and scramjets must be designed to provide propulsion up to hypersonic Mach numbers and orbital velocity.

Hypersonic Mach Number

The Mach number is a parameter named after an Austrian scientist, Ernst Mach (1838-1916). It represents the ratio of the speed of an object to the speed of sound in the surrounding air. The speed of sound in air at sea level is 1200 kilometers per hour. For example, if you are traveling in an airliner at 600 kilometers per hour, you are traveling at one-half the speed of sound, or Mach 0.5. If you are traveling in the supersonic Concorde airliner at twice the speed of sound, you are traveling at Mach 2.

The Latin word sonus, meaning sound, is the root for the word sonic which is used to indicate the speed of sound. A prefix indicates how fast an object moves relative to the speed of sound. Subsonic means below the speed of sound, or less than Mach 1. Transonic means crossing the speed of sound, or crossing through Mach 1. Supersonic means faster than the speed of sound, or greater than Mach 1. Hypersonic means much faster than the speed of sound, and is commonly used to mean greater than Mach 5.

Orbital Velocity

Gravity pulls meteors into the Earth's atmosphere while satellites stay in orbit around the planet. The orbital velocity of an object in orbit above earth is the horizontal speed it must have so that it will be a satellite instead of a meteor. The satellite principle describes the need for an object to maintain a certain speed to stay in the same orbit above earth. If an object in orbit slows down, gravity will pull it down into the atmosphere. To get into a low-Earth orbit, an object must be accelerated to orbital velocity. The concept of velocity includes both speed and direction. The orbital velocity at a 320 kilometer altitude orbit is about 28,000 kilometers per hour in a horizontal direction. Some people use Mach 25 to refer to this speed in terms of speed of sound in the upper atmosphere.

Turbojet

Since World War II, turbojet engines have supplied propulsion for most military and commercial airplanes. These engines take in surrounding air, compress it, mix it with jet fuel, ignite the mixture, and let the resulting hot gases shoot out the back at very high velocities for propulsion. Some of the energy of the hot gases is used to turn turbine blades on a wheel. This wheel is connected by a shaft to the wheel for the compressor blades. Thus

Mach Numbers

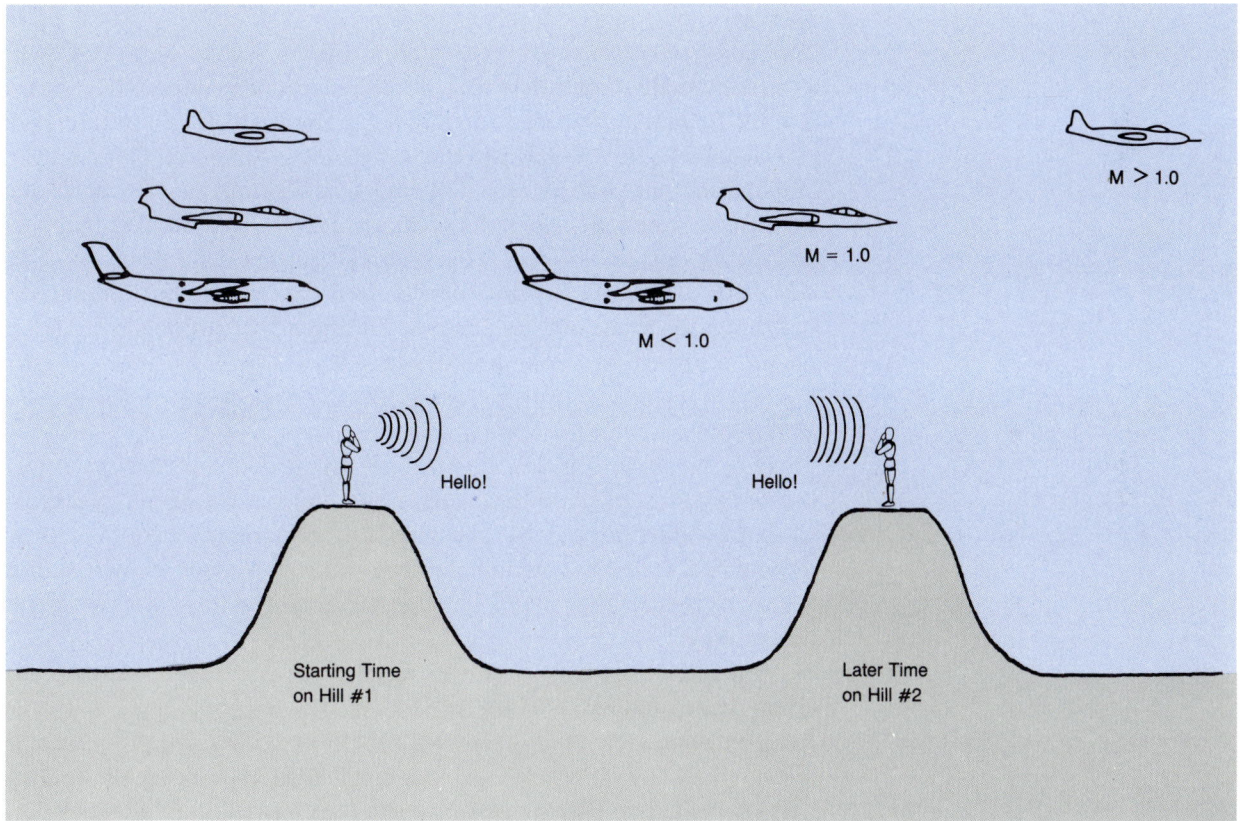

Mach 1.0 is the speed of sound. At Mach numbers less than 1.0, an object travels slower than the speed of sound; at numbers greater than 1.0, an object travels faster than sound.

What does moving faster or slower than the speed of sound mean? If you are on a hill and someone shouts at you from a far away hill, it takes time for the sound to reach you. This is because the shout travels through the air at the speed of sound.

Imagine that three planes are passing over the distant hill just as the person shouts. The plane traveling slower than Mach 1.0 will fly over you after you hear the shout. The plane traveling at exactly Mach 1.0 will fly over you at the same time the shouting is heard. The plane traveling faster than Mach 1.0 will fly over you before sound waves even reach you; you won't hear the shout until after this plane passes.

the energy of the hot combustion gases is used partly to compress the air, but mostly for propulsion. Turbojet engines are used at subsonic and some supersonic speeds. Above Mach 2, the turbine blades get so hot that they melt.

Ramjet

The ramjet engine has no compressor or turbine blades. Thus, it is really just a carefully shaped combustion chamber and exhaust nozzle. To begin operating, the aircraft must already be moving at about Mach 1.5. At this speed, air comes into the engine inlet so quickly that it is "rammed," or compressed and heated enough to be mixed with fuel for combustion. The air is rammed because it must be slowed down enough to sustain combustion with petroleum-derived jet fuel. This is similar to how a burning match fails to sustain combustion when you blow air past it too quickly. After combustion, the hot gases shoot out the back of the engine for propulsion. The ramjet engine begins to overheat around Mach 6.

Scramjet

This engine is similar to the ramjet in that it does not require turbine or compressor blades. A faster burning fuel, such as liquid hydrogen, is used so that combustion can be sustained with supersonic airflow. The scramjet engine has been shown to produce thrust at speeds as high as Mach 7. Scientists predict that it will produce thrust all the way to Mach 25 without overheating.

Other Technologies

Because some jet engine parts are prone to overheating at supersonic and hypersonic Mach numbers, new materials must be developed. Some scientists are confident that structures made from pressed metallic powders will do the job. These metallic powders are formed by a Rapid Solidification Rate (RSR) process. Normally, molten metal is allowed to solidify in crystalline structures when it is cooled or quenched. But with RSR, the molten metal is cooled so quickly that a non-crystalline metal is formed as a powder. When this powder is pressed into shapes, it has superior strength properties, even when very hot.

Many calculations must be made to design an aerospace plane. Propulsion forces, lift, drag and overheating must be accurately predicted. Scientists will use both wind tunnels and computers to make these predictions. Wind tunnels provide useful answers up to about Mach 8. Above Mach 8, scientists often rely on mathematical descriptions, or models, of combustion and hypersonic airflow. These models are very complicated and require so many calculations that supercomputers are often used. Supercomputers are powerful computers that can make many calculations very quickly. Normal

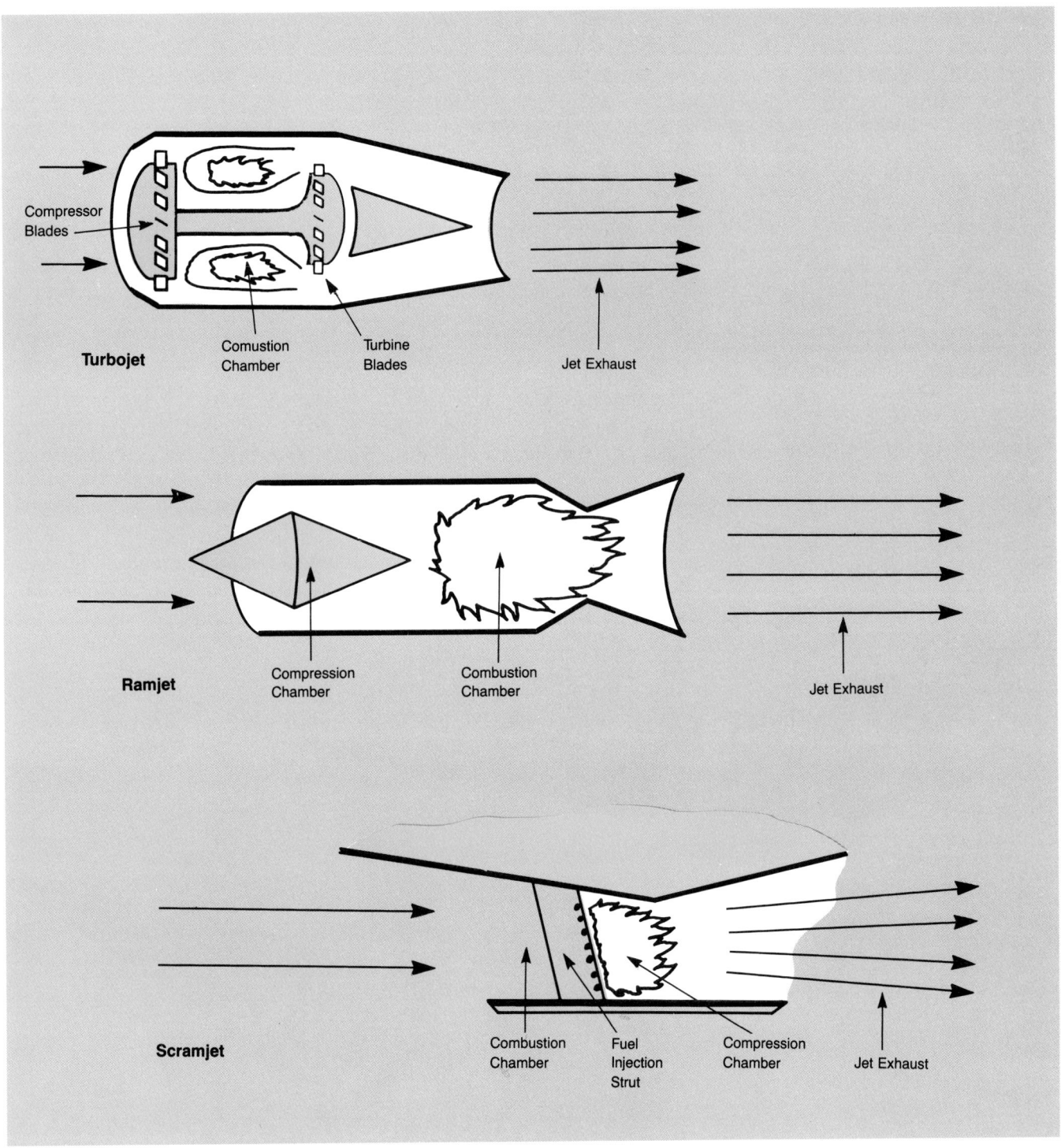

Although the turbojet, the ramjet and the scramjet all operate on the same principle, their performance is vastly different. With no moving parts to overheat, the scramjet is thought to be able to attain speeds of Mach 25. The ramjet, using a petroleum fuel, can reach Mach 6. However, both these engines must already be moving at Mach 1.5 before they can function. The rapidly turning turbine blades of the turbojet limit its top speed to Mach 2; but it can take off under its own power.

TO EARTH ORBIT

computers would take days to calculate what a supercomputer can calculate in minutes.

Computers are also used to help engineers design the shape of the aerospace plane. Using Computer-Aided Design (CAD) programs, a design can be created, changed, and viewed very easily. These designs can then be used as part of the supercomputer calculations.

Aerospace Plane Designs

Germany

The aerospace plane proposed by Germany is called the Sanger II. This design, by a company called MBB, would be a 455,000 kilogram two-stage plane. The first stage would be a hypersonic airplane. It will carry the second stage to its separation speed of Mach 7 at a 35 kilometer altitude. The second stage would be a 82,000 kilogram version of the American Space Shuttle, but with its own fuel. There are plans to have two different versions of this second stage. One would be manned, while the other would be remotely controlled. Payloads of between 3,600 and 13,600 kilograms are planned.

Payloads of 13,600 kg are planned for the German designed Sanger II. A supersonic plane would launch the manned or remotely controlled space plane at Mach 7 in the upper atmosphere.

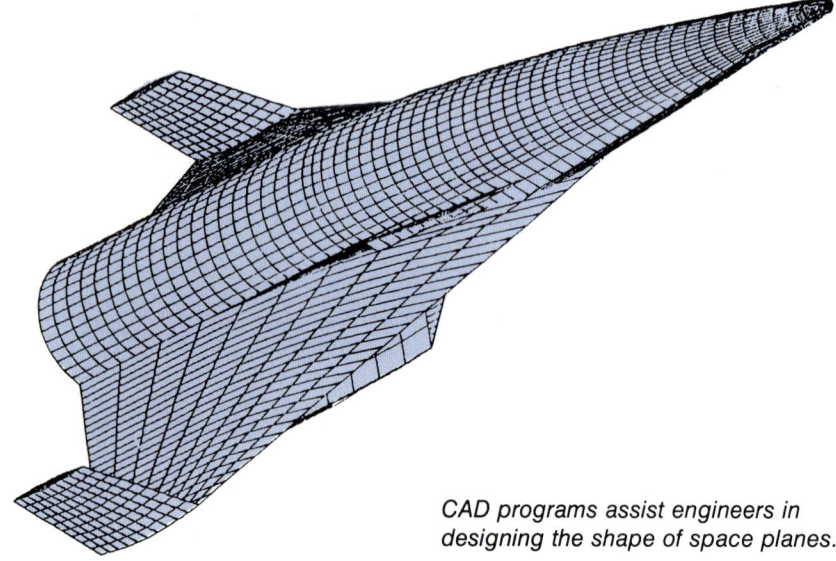

CAD programs assist engineers in designing the shape of space planes.

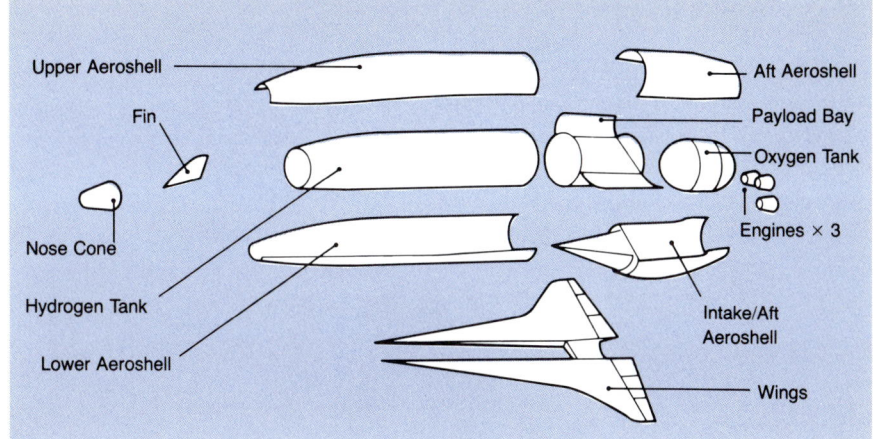

The British designed HOTOL is a single stage vehicle that will deliver a 6400 kg satellite at 1/5th the cost of the U.S. Shuttle. Take-off will be assisted by an accelerating trolley.

Great Britain

The British HOTOL is being designed to provide 6,400 kilogram satellite delivery at one-fifth the cost of the American Space Shuttle. The single stage aerospace plane should weigh 209,000 kilograms at take-off and about 46,000 kilograms when landing. There are plans to assist the take-off of this vehicle by launching it from a laser-guided accelerating trolley.

United States

In October of 1987, the National Aeronautics and Space Administration (NASA) and the Department of Defense gave contracts to three airframe manufacturers and two engine manufacturers to continue developing the National Aerospace Plane (NASP). It is called the X-30 by the Air Force. The capital X indicates that it is an experimental vehicle. Experimental programs only attempt to prove that something is possible. Therefore, a fleet of aerospace planes will only be built if two things happen. First, the X-30 program must be successful, and second, the government must decide that it is worthwhile to fund.

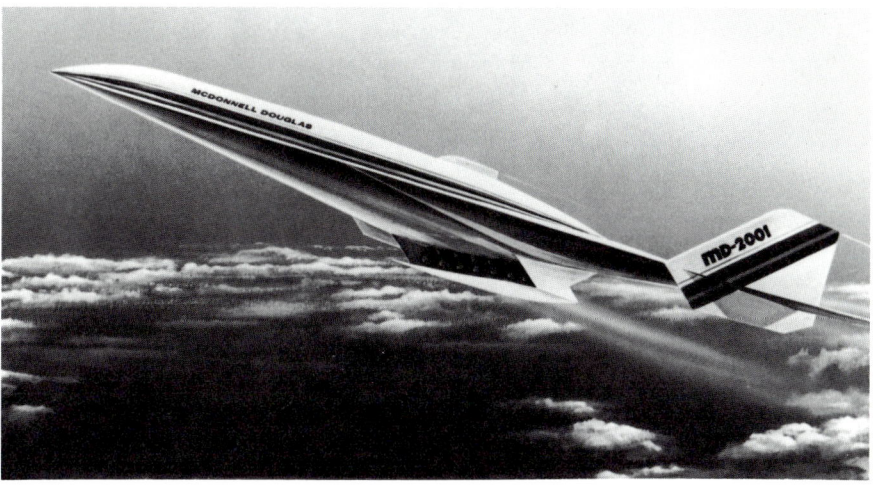

Before the aerospace plane can fly, experimental programs must succeed and governments must decide whether the great expenditures required are worthwhile.

TO EARTH ORBIT

The Orient Express

Jules Verne wrote a story about Phileas Fogg who traveled around the world in eighty days. This concept was considered outrageous for quite some time. But with an aerospace plane, it will be possible to travel around the world in a little over eighty minutes. We have come a long way since Phileas Fogg set out in 1872.

Even though we now talk about distances in terms of minutes instead of days, nicknames for impressive vehicles are often borrowed from the past. For example, the aerospace plane has come to be known as the Orient Express. This title refers to a certain train route from Europe to the Orient. The American press has eagerly adopted this title for the aerospace plane, since it would theoretically be possible to travel from New York to Tokyo in two hours!

Such a plane trip would be very different from one today. There probably would not even be time for a mid-flight meal! Much of the time would be spent accelerating during ascent and decelerating during descent. Therefore you would spend much of the time sitting pressed into your seat. Expense will probably preclude any windows on the aerospace plane for passengers. Any views of the Earth below will appear on television screens. Also, the fiery glow of hypersonic airflow around red-hot wings might be an unsettling sight for passengers. Disadvantages of traveling so quickly would be jet-lag and adapting to new time zones. However, a big advantage is that the world will seem to be a much smaller place.

The Aerospace Plane at Work

IMAGINE YOU ARE an active pilot in the fleet of United States Aerospace Planes. After a routine satellite-deployment mission two days ago, you had been looking forward to some rest. But the emergency alarm sounds, waking you up to the reality that an unplanned mission is in progress. After suiting-up, you attend a flight briefing where the exact nature of the problem is explained. The astronauts on the space station are in trouble. Some space debris has damaged both the descent module and their main cabin. They are slowly losing air, so a new descent module with extra air must be brought to the space station within the next few hours. Since a space shuttle or ELV launch takes weeks to prepare, you are chosen to go instead. As the briefing ends, you realize that all over the planet people are learning from news bulletins that the fate of the space station astronauts is dependent on your rescue mission with the aerospace plane. Nothing must go wrong.

Upon arriving at the hanger, you verify that the aerospace plane has been properly refurbished since the flight two days ago. Meanwhile, the copilot verifies that the payload has been properly installed in the cargo bay. The descent module has passed its readiness tests and is attached to the Orbital

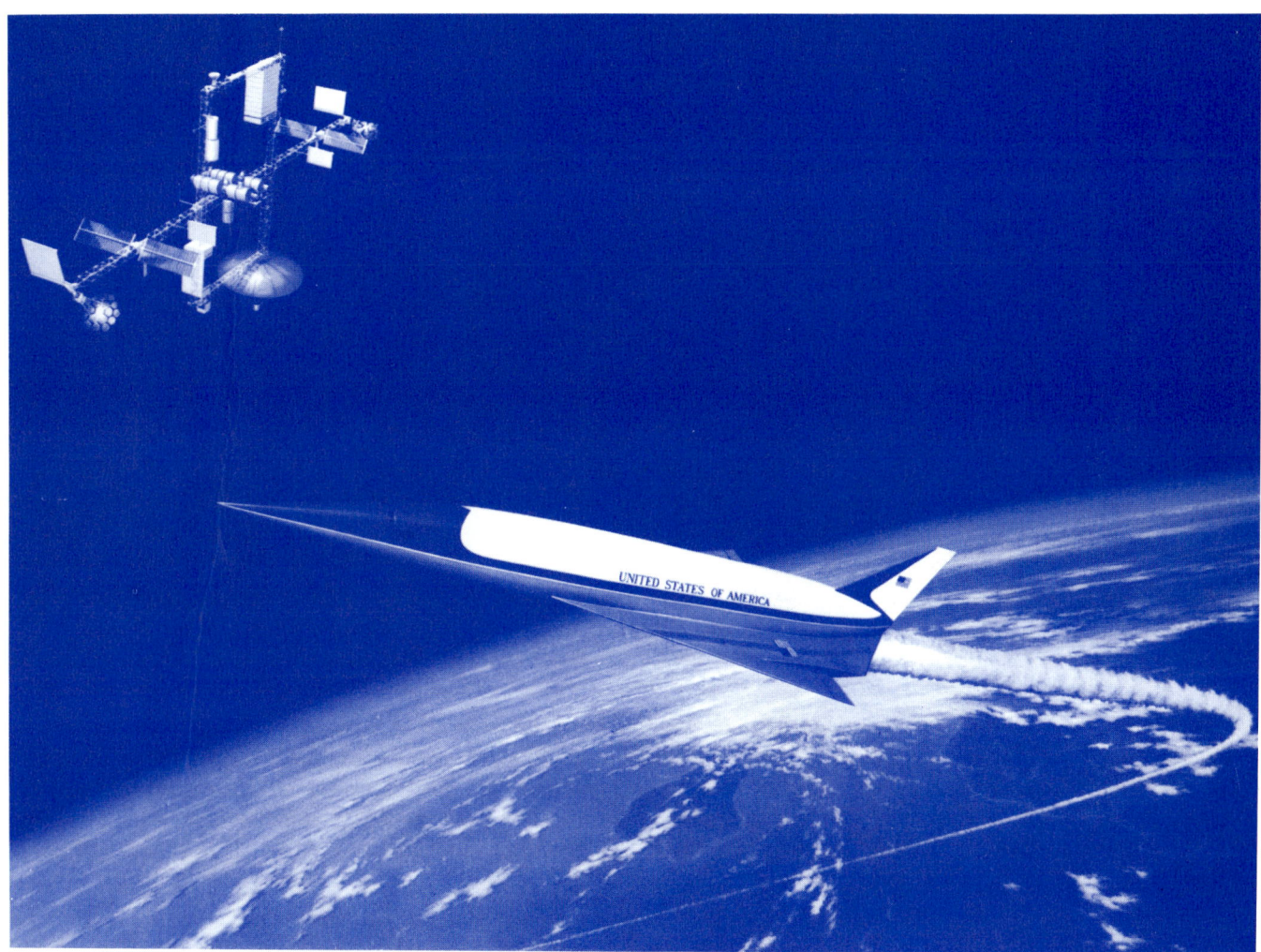

A low orbit intercontinental flight would make the world seem much smaller.

Maneuvering Vehicle (OMV). The OMV will transport the descent module up to the space station after it is released into space from the aerospace plane. With all systems operational, you board the plane and start the turbojet engines. After taxiing out onto the runway, you have to wait in the early morning fog until the correct takeoff time for proper rendezvous with the station. You and the copilot spend this time wisely by checking and rechecking the equipment on the aerospace plane and in the payload bay.

Mission controllers finally give the command to depart. You increase fuel flow to the turbojet engines and roar down the runway for a quick and steep takeoff. Soon you are breaking through the fog and soaring up above the morning sunrise. You are pressed into your seat as you continue to accelerate into the sky. The plane shakes a little as you break through the speed of sound. Soon after, you are jolted as the ramjet engines take over for the turbojets and you continue to accelerate up. Despite wearing radio headphones, the whistling roar of the supersonic airflow begins to be very loud. When the aerospace plane reaches the proper speed, fuel is supplied to the scramjet engines and you are jolted again. After more time, the hypersonic

TO EARTH ORBIT

airflow around the plane creates so much heating and blinding light that you must cover the windows in order to see your instruments.

When orbital velocity is reached, you shut down the scramjet engines and use rocket engines for final path corrections. After a time there is no longer any noise or blinding light. You have reached the vacuum of space. However, there is little time to enjoy the quiet blackness of space above or the delicate clouds, oceans, and continents below. The payload must be deployed.

When mission controllers radio you to prepare the payload for deployment, your copilot verifies that the payload doors have been swung open. Final tests of the OMV and descent module are run before deployment. Then, after your copilot commands the release mechanism to nudge the OMV and descent module from the payload bay, the payload becomes a satellite. It continues to orbit the earth until it is commanded to move on. Some last-minute radio communication with the OMV verifies that it is ready to go. You inform mission controllers, who now take over control of the OMV by way of a radio communication satellite.

After closing the payload doors, your main job is finished and the return trip begins. Some additional rocket firing brings you down and into position for atmospheric reentry. The fiery glow and noise return as you steer the plane, just as you did on your previous job as pilot for the space shuttle. There is no need to turn on the scramjet or ramjet engines since slowing down is the goal now, not speeding up. After some banking maneuvers that press you into your seat, you see that you have arrived back at your base. The turbojets are started after you drop below the speed of sound and you land the aerospace plane just like a traditional airplane.

After touchdown and coming to a stop, you breath a sigh of relief. After flying around the planet, the day is again just beginning as the sun rises over the cold desert runway. Your mission is done, but the mission of the OMV and the space station astronauts is just beginning. You and the rest of the world wish them a successful rendezvous and a safe trip home.

Summary

The aerospace plane is not a new idea. It has, however, taken on new significance. Its potential commercial and military usefulness has renewed interest in its development. The aerospace plane will takeoff like an airplane and soar into space. After delivering satellites into orbit, it will return as the shuttle does, except that it will be able to land like a plane instead of a glider.

Engine technology must be developed to propel the plane to orbital velocity in the upper atmosphere. The aerospace plane must have both air-breathing engines and space-rocket thrusters. These engines will be housed in a structure that will have room for the pilots, cargo, and fuel. When these technological problems are solved, the aerospace plane may be built.

An aerospace plane could be used by the military for bombing, satellite delivery, or reconnaissance. Commercial use of the vehicle for satellite deployment is also considered likely. It is the hypersonic transport, or Orient Express, that stirs the imagination the most. Some people even predict that the aerospace plane will do to the airlines what the airlines did to the shipping business. Only time and technological development will tell.

Terms

CAD	ramjet
HOTOL	RSR metals
hypersonic	Sanger II
Mach number	scramjet
NASP	supercomputers
orbital velocity	turbojet

Important People, Ideas, and Events

- During World War II, a German scientist, Eugene Sanger, made the first serious proposals for an aerospace plane.
- In the 1970s, movie makers popularized the concept of an aerospace plane that propels itself equally well in air and in space. A good example is Luke Skywalker's X-wing, T-65 fighter in *Star Wars*.
- In 1986, the United States committed money to solving technological problems so that an aerospace plane could become reality. Other countries, including Germany and Great Britain, have also proposed their own development programs.

Interesting Things to Do

1. Build models of single-stage and two-stage aerospace planes.
2. Determine what direction an orbiting aerospace plane must fire retrorockets to descend into the atmosphere.
3. Request information from NASA about the NASP.
4. Decide which way is best to fly around the earth, with the direction of rotation, or against it.
5. List the differences between the Space Shuttle and an aerospace plane.

PART TWO

WITHIN EARTH ORBIT

Orbiting 300 miles above the earth, the Hubble Space Telescope (HST) will "see" to the observable edge of the universe, 14 billion light-years away. The Space Shuttle along with the Orbital Maneuvering Vehicle and Manned Maneuvering Unit (both described in this section) will be essential in positioning and maintaining the HST. Once in orbit, the 94-inch Cassegrain reflector is scheduled to operate for 15 years.

Satellites and space stations in Earth orbit are transportation devices themselves. They circle the planet at high speed. However, satellites launched to Earth orbit may later need corrections to their orbit. They also may need repair. Thus there is a need for other vehicles which help satellites to change orbits and be accessed for repair. Space stations also make missions within Earth orbit necessary. Space station structures can be assembled and changed with the help of mobile humans. Space stations may also need to have their orbits adjusted. These are only a few examples of the reasons why space transportation technology is needed within Earth orbit.

Missions within Earth orbit frequently require moving orbiting objects close together. Doing this can be dangerous, especially if humans are aboard. Precise and reliable control of such maneuvers is essential. Thus, whereas launch vehicles had to supply great amounts of energy, vehicles which are used within Earth orbit must supply greatly controlled energy.

The development of transportation for zero-gravity and vacuum conditions required technological advances. Thrusters and control systems had to be invented for stabilizing the orbits of space stations, transporting humans in space suits and moving satellites with a space tug. The technology of these vehicles is introduced in the following chapters. Because these vehicles are very complex, they will also be explained in terms of the parts, or subsystems, which together make up the whole vehicle, or system. Here, then, are some technological systems which are used to transport people and products within Earth orbit: space stations, manned maneuvering unit, and orbital maneuvering vehicle.

The OMV is shown using the module change-out service kit.

Chapter 4 ORBITAL MANEUVERING VEHICLE

In the past, the only way to accomplish tasks in space was to launch either expendable rockets or a Space Shuttle into orbit. Expendable rockets can only be used once to launch satellites. The Space Shuttle is more versatile. It gives astronauts tools such as the Manned Maneuvering Unit and Remote Manipulator System. With these tools, they can launch, retrieve, and repair satellites in space. However, astronauts in the Shuttle can not perform certain types of missions.

The Shuttle was designed to stay in space for short missions only. It was not built to go higher than approximately 300 kilometers or make large changes in altitude during a mission. Although shuttle astronauts proved that satellites with small booster rockets could be manually refueled in space, it was considered dangerous. To accomplish tasks which were lengthy, distant, or dangerous, NASA proposed adding a remote-controlled, unmanned tugboat in space to the National Space Transportation System. This space tug is known as the Orbital Maneuvering Vehicle (OMV).

Mission Requirements

The OMV will be carried into space by the shuttle. It may travel to the Space Station, remain based in orbit, or return with the shuttle when its tasks are completed. The OMV must be able to survive at least forty shuttle launches and landings during its ten year life. It is required to perform twelve types of low-Earth orbit missions, called reference missions, from its base in either the shuttle or the Space Station. These include satellite launch, retrieval, reboost, deboost, and viewing. The reference missions are summarized in the following paragraphs.

WITHIN EARTH ORBIT

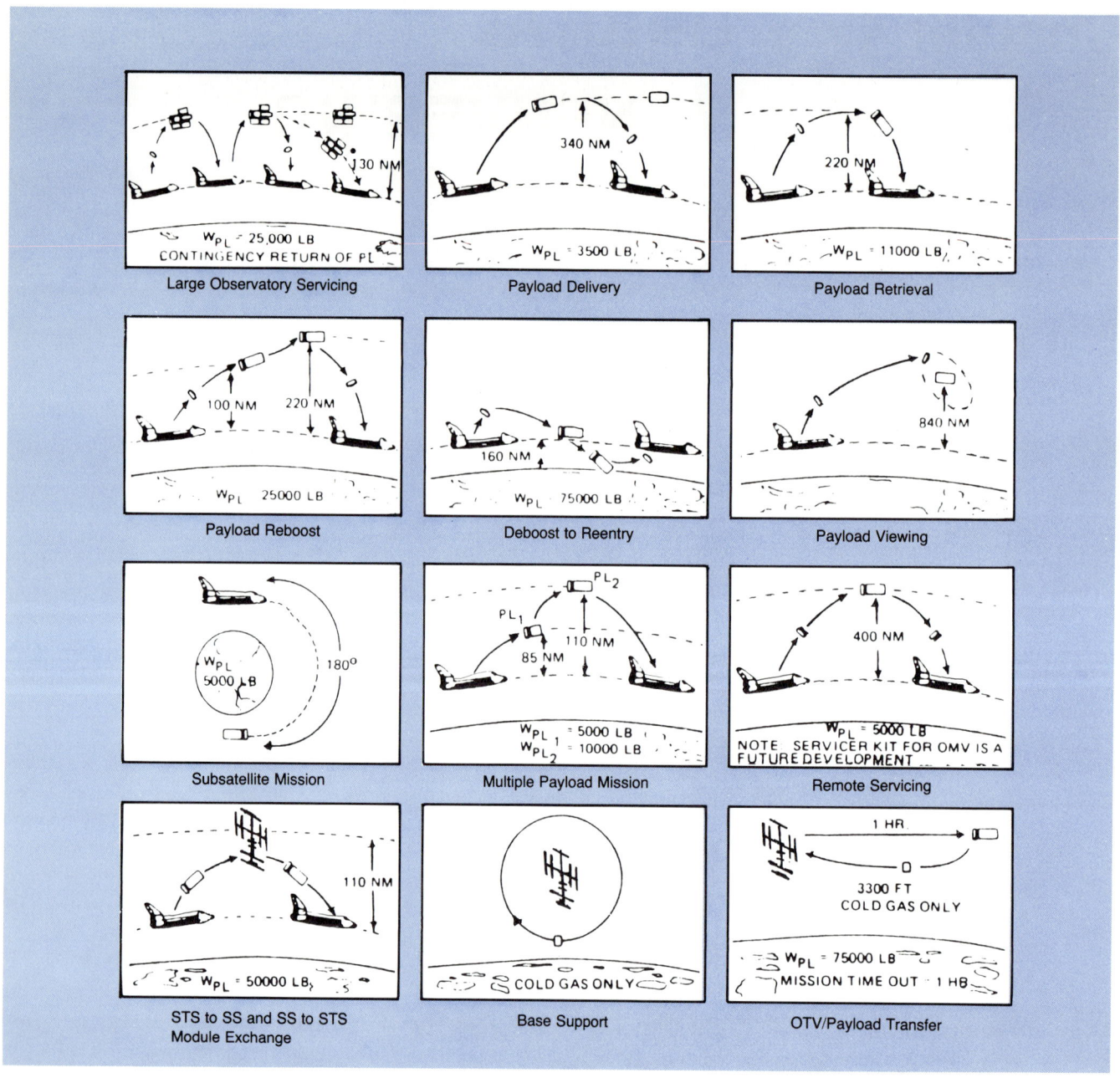

NASA requirements for the OMV are stated in terms of reference missions, which include a variety of space transportation duties.

ORBITAL MANEUVERING VEHICLE

The OMV will take large observatories to an orbiting base for servicing. Because of its very accurate control of acceleration, the OMV will be able to move observatories without damaging their delicate instruments.

Large Observatory Servicing
The new observatories in space, which include the Gamma Ray Observatory and Hubble Space Telescope, are designed for on-orbit servicing. The OMV will be able to move the observatories between the base and the observatory's original orbit for servicing at the base. Acceleration during transport of an observatory must be very small to avoid damage to the observatory.

Payload Delivery
An OMV payload is any object that the OMV transports. Most payloads are satellites. Satellites such as those that gather weather pictures and scientific data need to be delivered to altitudes above that of the base. A typical mission would be to deliver a 1600 kilogram satellite from the shuttle orbit at 300 kilometers to an altitude of 925 kilometers. Larger satellites also can be moved, but not as high, while smaller satellites can be delivered to higher altitudes.

WITHIN EARTH ORBIT

To retrieve a satellite, the OMV must first latch onto it.

Payload Retrieval

This mission serves the opposite function of the payload delivery mission. The OMV will take the payload from its original orbit to either the Shuttle to be returned to Earth, or to the space station for examination. A 5000 kilogram satellite originally at 700 kilometer altitude would be a typical payload.

Payload Reboost

Any object which is currently in orbit around the Earth, including satellites and observatories, can be lifted into a higher orbit by the OMV. An 11,300 kilogram satellite could be lifted from a 480 kilometer orbit to a 700 kilometer orbit. This may be required after a satellite loses speed and drops into a lower orbit.

Deboost to Re-entry

Low-Earth orbit is littered with boosters, satellites, and pieces of satellites, which have become a menace to space flight. The deboost mission will help solve that problem by using the OMV to slow an object down until it cannot maintain an orbit and falls safely into an ocean. An object of up to 34,000 kilogram mass can be deboosted from a 300 kilometer orbit.

Payload Viewing

In order to inspect a satellite at a higher orbit than the shuttle, the OMV must be able to travel up to an altitude of 1850 kilometers, circle around the satellite, and then return. Television cameras will provide long range and close up views for up to four hours.

Subsatellite Mission

The OMV can be used as a space platform for a variety of short-term subsatellite experiments. A subsatellite is a payload which is not able to operate completely by itself. The OMV will provide propulsion, electrical power, and radio communication to any experiment which is attached to it. These experiments can be carried away from the base to anywhere at the same altitude, up to 180° around the Earth, for up to seven days.

Multiple Payload Mission

This mission is a combination of the payload delivery and payload retrieval missions. The OMV will accomplish both without refueling. For example, the OMV might take a 2300 kilogram satellite from the base up to a 450 kilometer altitude, and then continue up to 500 kilometers. There it would dock with a 4500 kilogram satellite and return it to the base. As in the delivery and retrieval missions, there are trade-offs involved with how distant and how massive the satellites can be.

Remote Servicing

This mission requires the OMV to bring fuel and other refurbishing materials to satellites in orbits as high as 1040 kilometers. It will perform service while the satellite is in its orbit. Special servicing kits of up to 2250 kilograms will be developed for each mission.

Module Exchange between Shuttle and Space Station

The OMV will transport space station modules up from the Shuttle's orbit at 300 kilometers, to the space station's orbit at 500 kilometers. Used or troubled modules will be transported back down to the Shuttle by the OMV.

Base Support

The OMV will perform a variety of tasks when it is assigned to work near the space station. Transportation, exterior visual inspection, communication, and homing beacon are possible tasks that it will perform.

WITHIN EARTH ORBIT

Payload Transfer

This mission is a special case of the base support mission. The OMV will transport the Orbital Transfer Vehicle (OTV) and the OTV payload one kilometer away from the Space Station and return alone. This mission will take one hour using cold-gas thrusters. The combined mass of the OTV and its payload can be up to 34,000 kilograms. The OTV will then transfer satellites up to geosynchronous orbit.

Mission Kits

Since new satellites and new missions in space are always being planned by NASA, the OMV must have the capability to be easily modified to support these activities. To do this, mission kits are used. These kits, when attached to the OMV, allow it to recover space debris, travel with an astronaut, or service the Space Telescope and other satellites in their orbits.

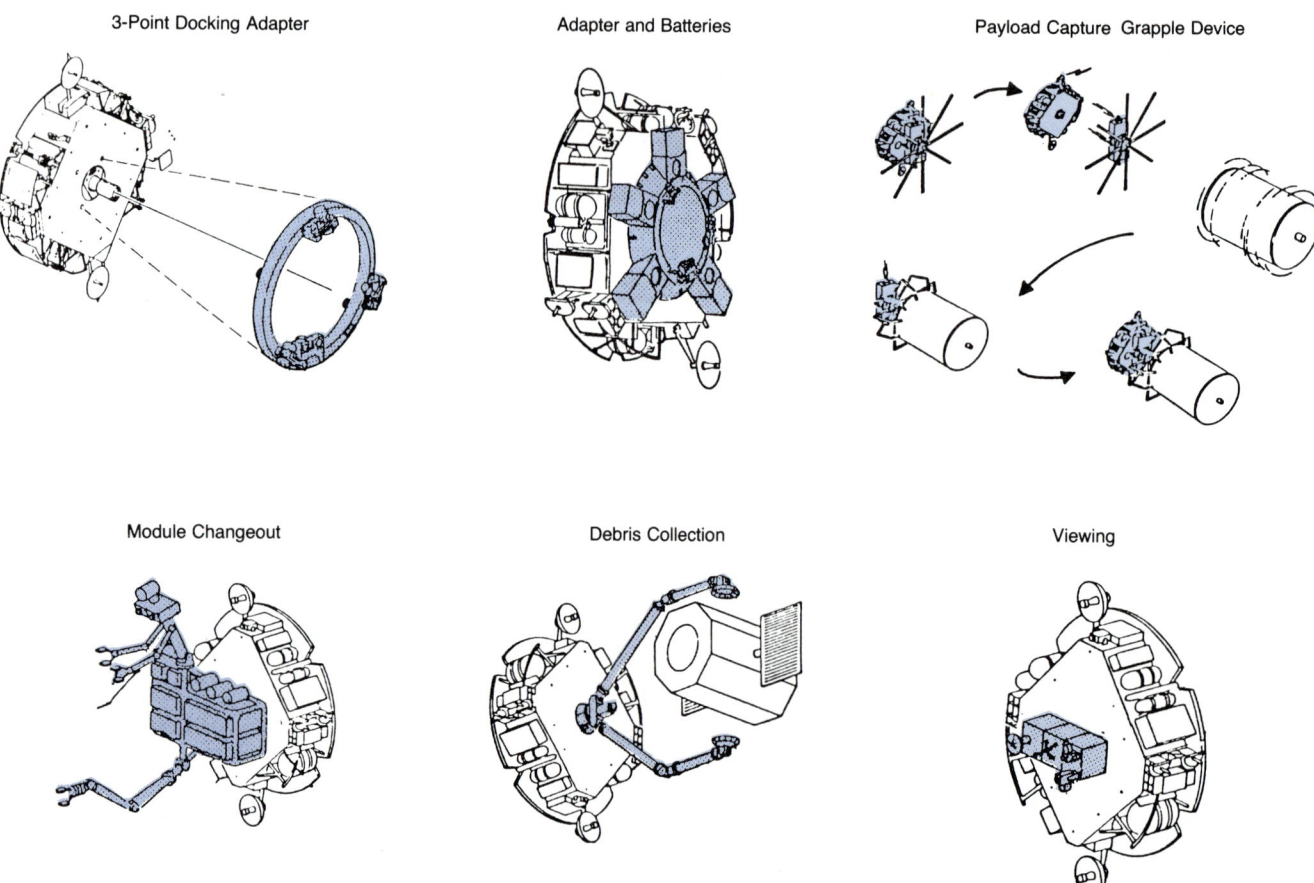

Many adapters or mission kits make the OMV a versatile tool.

ORBITAL MANEUVERING VEHICLE

OMV Description

The OMV is approximately 4.5 meters in diameter and 1.5 meters thick. When fully fueled, its mass is over 8000 kilograms. It is small in comparison to the shuttle. This feature allows it to perform many missions which the shuttle is not able to perform using today's technology.

The OMV will be based in space. A consequence of this is that it must be possible to refuel and repair the OMV while it is in space. To make this easy and inexpensive, the physical design of the OMV is modular. It consists of a central platform, nine types of Orbital Replacement Units (ORUs), and the Propulsion Module. Each type of ORU can be easily removed and replaced, and those of the same type are completely interchangeable. Each ORU is attached to the platform using the same type of connector, which can be loosened and fastened manually or with the Remote Manipulator System on the Shuttle. The Propulsion Module can also be replaced in the same way. This allows the OMV to receive a full tank of fuel without the danger of transferring fuels from one tank to another.

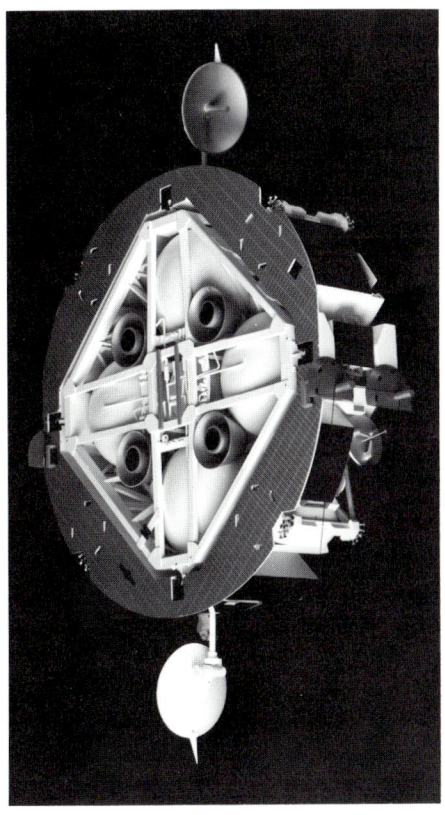

A rear view of the Orbital Maneuvering Vehicle shows the thrusters will allow it to maneuver in space. This unmanned space "tug-boat" is capable of performing lengthy, distant and/or dangerous missions. It can remain idle in orbit between missions.

At 4.5 meters in diameter and 1.5 meters thick, the OMV is nestled in the Shuttle's cargo bay.

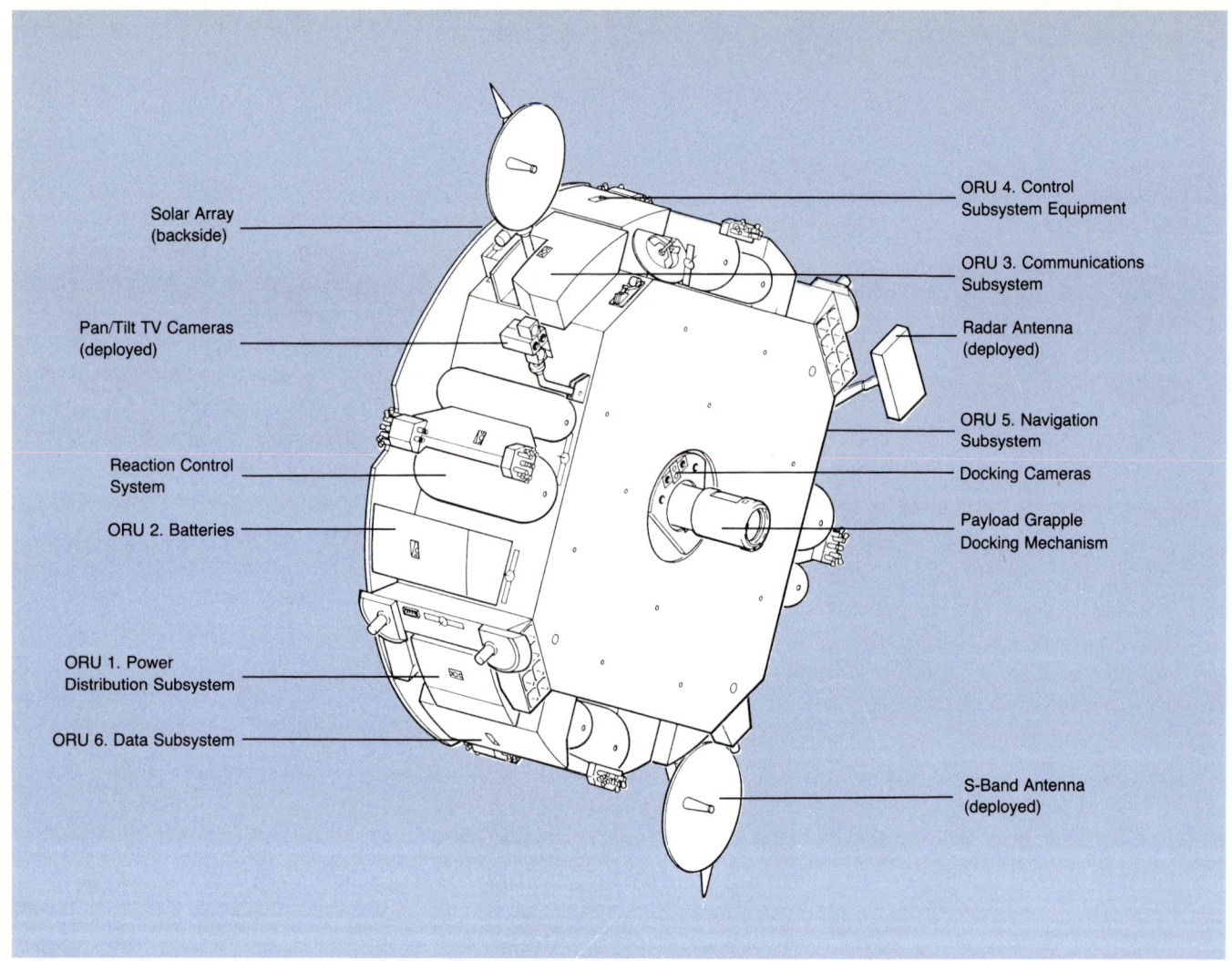

Because of its modular design, components of the OMV can be easily removed and repaired, refurbished or replaced.

In engineering terminology, the OMV is referred to as a system. While the physical design of the OMV is modular, the conceptual design of the OMV system is organized by function. In order to design and build a space vehicle as complicated as the OMV, the system is broken down into more easily understood parts, called subsystems. Each subsystem performs a specific function. This organization helps the designers identify which things they are responsible for, and insures that all of the OMV's capabilities are planned for. It also helps NASA keep track of how much the vehicle should cost.

The complete OMV system includes the vehicle, tracking equipment, and a control station on the ground. A person at the control station, called the pilot, is responsible for the remote-control operation of the vehicle. Each part of the system must work together in order to accomplish OMV missions. The vehicle subsystems, which are described below, must also do their part to insure that the OMV mission is successful.

Materials Selection

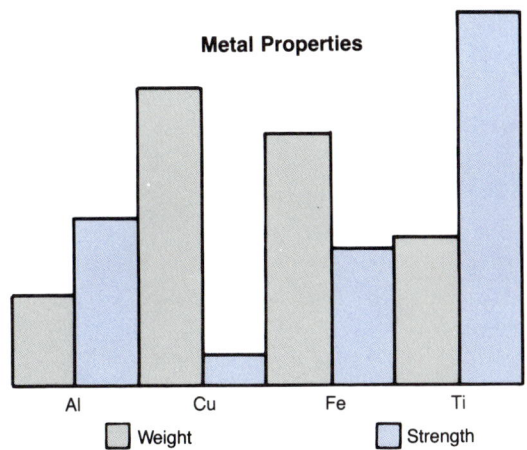

When designing the structure of a spacecraft, there must be a tradeoff between weight, strength, and cost. Each part must be strong enough to provide structural integrity, yet neither too heavy nor too expensive. The OMV is made from aluminum and titanium. Aluminum is used for most of the structure. Titanium is used when great strength is needed. It is used sparingly, however, since it is very expensive.

Comparing the properties of these metals with other familiar metals reveals why they are chosen for spacecraft structures. Iron has about the same strength as aluminum but is seldom used because it is much heavier. Copper is not often used in spacecraft structures since it is not very strong and it weighs much more than aluminum.

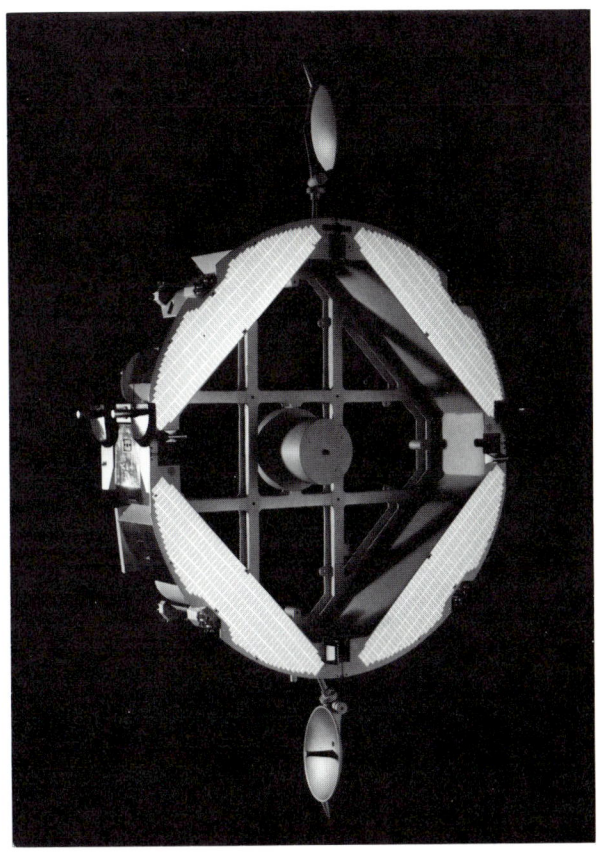

The vehicle platform structure must support and stabilize the ORUs which are attached to it. It must also withstand the Shuttle launches and landings.

Structure and Mechanism

Structures form the body of the OMV. All components and equipment are mounted to these structures. The modular structure of the OMV consists of three major assemblies: 1) a vehicle platform structure, 2) a Propulsion Module structure, and 3) ORU structures.

The vehicle platform structure is made of machined aluminum pieces which are bolted together. It is designed to be strong enough to support the Propulsion Module, ORUs, and satellites through 40 launches and landings. The supports which connect the OMV to the Shuttle, called trunnions, are made from titanium, which is a stronger metal than aluminum. This is necessary since some missions include bumpy Shuttle launches and land-

WITHIN EARTH ORBIT

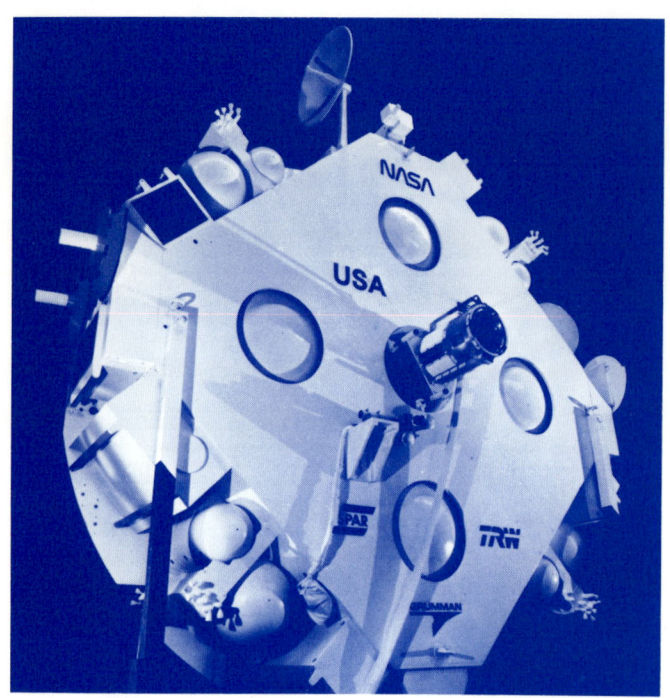

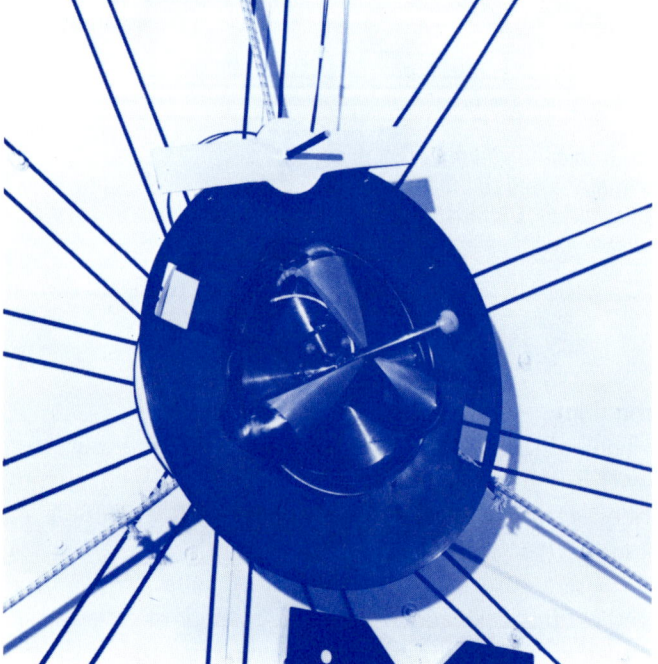

The OMV grapple is shown along with its mating piece and a simulated docking.

ORBITAL MANEUVERING VEHICLE

ings. At the center of the vehicle platform structure is the grapple docking mechanism. This is a vital component of the OMV. The grapple is used to latch onto any object which the OMV needs to dock with or move. To insure that missions are successful, it must never fail.

The Propulsion Module structure is a large framed box which holds the main propulsion fuel tanks and thrusters. It is also made of bolted, machined aluminum pieces with titanium trunnions. Since the Propulsion Module is removable, it is connected to the vehicle platform structure by latch mechanisms. Astronauts will be able to unlatch this structure in space and replace the entire Propulsion Module.

The ORU structures are small frames of aluminum. They attach to the outside of the vehicle platform structure with a bolt that can be fastened and unfastened by the Shuttle Remote Manipulator System. There are two types of these frames. Box-shaped frames house electronic equipment. Star-shaped frames are used to support small fuel tanks and thrusters.

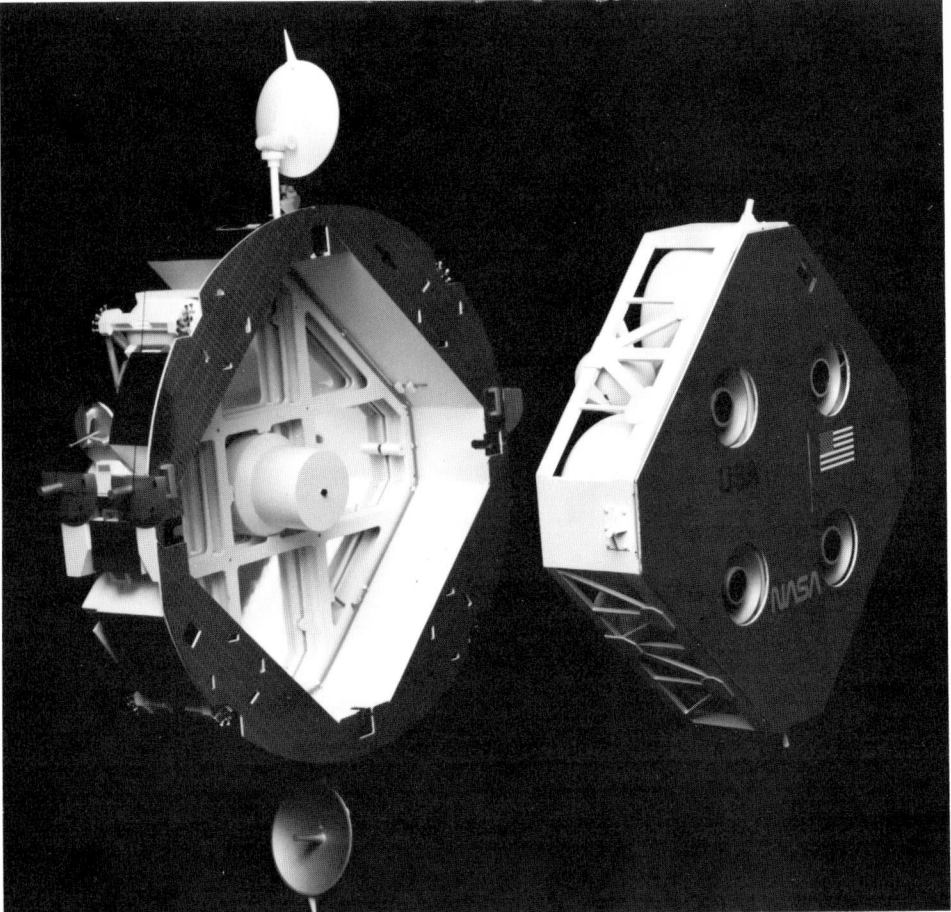

The Propulsion Module fits into the vehicle platform.

Propulsion

Propelling the OMV through space with an attached payload requires a versatile propulsion subsystem. A powerful engine is required to move large payloads. Very precise control is required for docking maneuvers. Special fuels are required to avoid contaminating the payloads. As in the case of all other subsystems, the propulsion subsystem must be very reliable. No single failure should result in the loss of a mission, therefore, every part has a backup on the OMV. If a part such as a tank, valve, manifold, or thruster breaks or clogs, a second component is there to take over its job.

The propulsion subsystem consists of the Propulsion Module and the Reaction Control System. The Propulsion Module includes the main engines and is used for moving large satellites between orbits. Smaller engines make up the Reaction Control System. These are situated in four of the ORUs and help propel, steer, and rotate the OMV. The OMV can be used with or without the Propulsion Module. Without the Propulsion Module it is a short range vehicle which operates using the Reaction Control System only.

The Propulsion Module has separate tanks for fuel and oxidizer. The fuel and oxidizer, when combined, mix and burn similar to gasoline and air in an internal combustion engine. It also has four thrusters which can each deliver from 58 to 580 Newtons, which is equivalent to lifting 6 to 60 kilograms each. While this seems small compared to 34,000 kilogram payloads, it is similar to a tugboat moving a very large ship in a harbor. It just takes time to do the job.

Each Reaction Control System ORU has tanks, valves, and thrusters for two different systems which each use a different fuel. Nitrogen is an inert gas. The nitrogen thrusters are sometimes referred to as cold-gas thrusters. They are included on the OMV because nitrogen will not contaminate payloads or other nearby vehicles. The nitrogen thrusters provide 22 Newtons of thrust. Hydrazine is used by the second system since it is more efficient

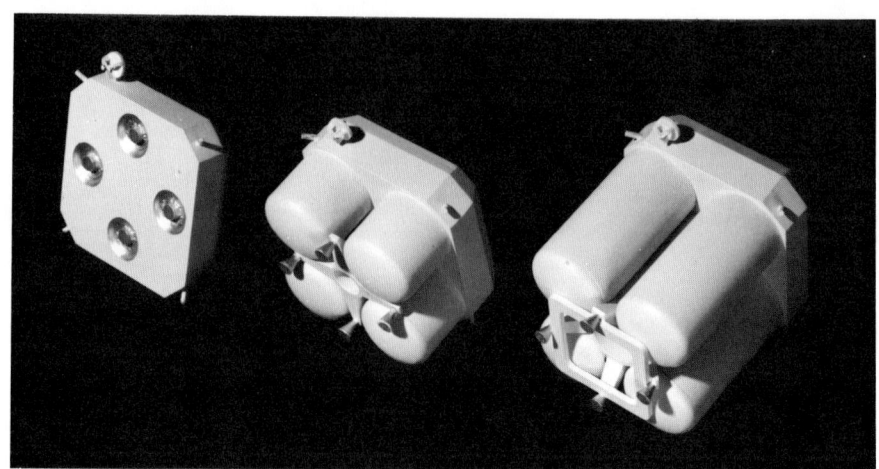

A mock-up of the Propulsion Modules is shown along with proposed modules which could expand the range of the OMV.

ORBITAL MANEUVERING VEHICLE

Radio Communication

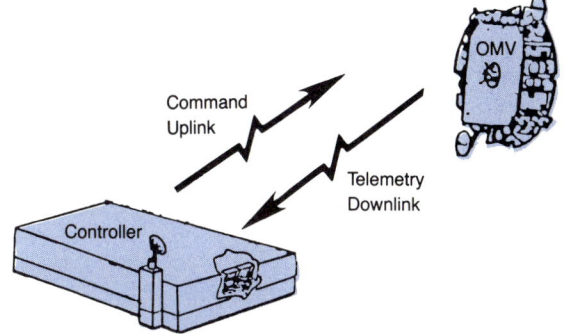

Radios are used to communicate with spacecraft. Data messages and control messages must be exchanged between the controller and the spacecraft. Most space vehicles are designed to be controlled by people on Earth. The OMV, however, can be controlled both by people in space and on Earth.

When controllers want the OMV to perform an action, they use a computer to create the proper messages, called commands. These commands are sent to a radio transmitter which creates a radio message. This radio message is then aimed at the spacecraft by an antenna. The radio waves travel into space and are picked up by the antenna and receiver on the OMV. A computer on the OMV then decodes the message. This is referred to as the command uplink.

When controllers need information about what is happening on the OMV, they use the telemetry downlink. To downlink data, the OMV computer creates messages which go through the OMV radio transmitter and antenna. The radio waves then travel to Earth and are picked up by the antenna and receiver at the control center. The messages are processed by a computer and presented to the controllers.

when payload contamination is not a factor. The hydrazine thrusters provide 53 Newtons of thrust. In each of the ORUs, thrusters for both fuels point in all directions. With careful control of these thrusters, the OMV can be made to move in any direction or spin around any axis.

Communication and Data Management

The communication and data management subsystem has three primary responsibilities: collecting data from OMV sensors, relaying information between the OMV and the control center, and distributing commands to the appropriate subsystems in the OMV. Each of these functions must be performed simultaneously when the OMV is operated in remote-control. Redundant computers direct these activities.

Two types of information are collected by the computers. The first is status data, which is used to verify that all subsystems are working correctly. For example, battery voltage, computer temperature and fuel tank pressure are some of the conditions that the computer monitors. The second type of information that the computer collects is sensor data, such as measurements of movement from accelerometers or fuel flow to a thruster. Both types of information are brought to the computer on a pair of wires called a data bus.

WITHIN EARTH ORBIT

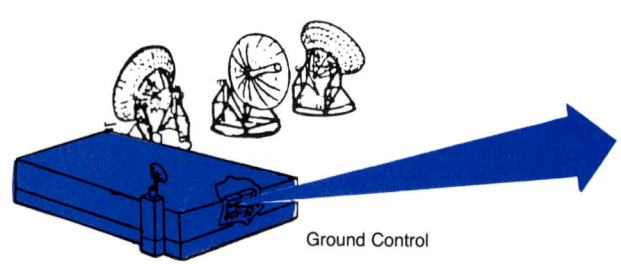

Radio communication is essential to remote controlled operation of the OMV. Any break could be disastrous to a mission.

The information which the computers have collected must be relayed to the control center. The computer also controls this relay, which is a complex operation. Antennas transmit and receive the radio signals. They must always point to either a NASA relay satellite (TDRS), the Shuttle, the Space Station or a NASA ground station. The antennas, radio receivers, and transmitters are located at opposite ends of the OMV in redundant ORUs. This arrangement always makes it possible for the computer to point an antenna correctly, even when the OMV is docking with a spinning satellite.

Pictures from three TV cameras are also relayed to the control center. Two of the cameras are located at the center of the OMV, near the grapple docking mechanism, and one is at the end of a boom that rotates from one edge of the OMV. Images from two of the cameras can be transmitted at the same time. Lights are attached near each of the cameras. These lights are used to illuminate targets up to 60 meters away, so that the pilot can control docking. They are especially useful when the OMV is in the Earth's shadow.

The information sent up from the control center is a set of commands to control various parts of the OMV. All command messages first go to the computer. After verifying that the commands are authentic, the computer sends the messages all over the OMV on the data bus. All ORUs receive the information on the data bus. However, each ORU reacts only to information meant specifically for itself. For example, a Reaction Control System ORU will obey those commands which tell it to fire reverse thrusters for exactly one second.

Guidance, Navigation, and Control

The equipment and computer programs of the guidance, navigation and control subsystem allow the OMV to move through space either automati-

ORBITAL MANEUVERING VEHICLE

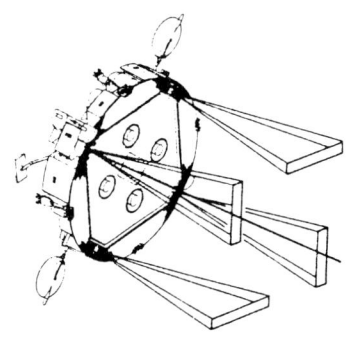

Sun sensor fields of view are oriented along OMV axis.

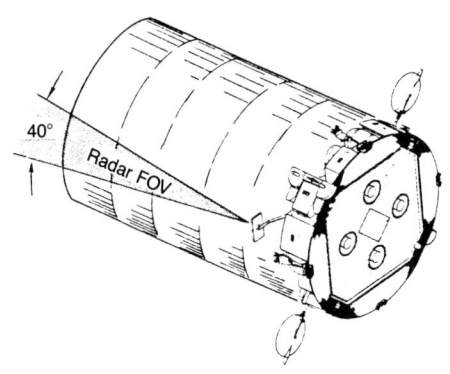

Deployed radar can see around 15-foot payload.

cally or by remote-control. In automatic, the OMV independently transfers payloads between orbits, rendezvous with other vehicles, or maintains an orbital storage mode. In remote-control, it performs any maneuvers that the pilot directs. In order to perform the automatic and remote-control functions, the subsystem measures and calculates the OMV's position, speed and direction. Signals from the Global Positioning System satellites are also used to determine this information. At the same time, the OMV always points the antennas to keep radio contact with NASA.

The orbit transfer mode is used to direct the OMV to a specific point in space. Accelerometers and a navigation radio are used to measure the OMV's position in space. Computers calculate how it must point and fire its thrusters to reach a particular destination. Other devices are used to help navigate and guide the OMV by sensing where the sun and Earth are. The sun sensor, located next to solar arrays, is also necessary when the OMV is stored in orbit. It verifies that the solar cells are always facing the sun while the OMV is kept spinning in space.

The rendezvous mode is used to direct the OMV to a point close to another object. It is an important mode since it controls how the OMV approaches a satellite, the Shuttle, or the Space Station. Yet it is also a difficult mode to implement. A radar, which is mounted on a boom, is deployed and pointed toward the destination. This radar can measure distances from 30 meters up to eight kilometers. Thrusters are carefully fired based on the information from the radar. This allows the OMV to accurately and safely move up to other space vehicles.

Docking and maneuvers which can not be preprogrammed are performed in remote-control. Radio contact is an important element in this mode, because information and TV pictures from the OMV must be relayed to the pilot. Precise calculations of position and velocity are needed so that the pilot can decide how to perform the maneuver. The pilot radios maneuvering commands to the OMV. Radio antennas on the OMV must be carefully pointed in this mode so that communications are constantly maintained.

Some of the equipment and computer programs of this subsystem are shared with other subsystems. For example, the computer that calculates positions and thruster firing also controls the communication and data management subsystem. Sensors are also shared between ORUs. The radar boom is attached to one ORU, while the gyros, accelerometer and navigation radio are within another ORU. Earth sensors, sun sensors and radio antenna gimbal drives are also placed on other ORUs.

Electrical

Electric power for operating the OMV comes from batteries. Electric power is needed during every mission for computers, radios, heaters, solenoids, and motors. One kilowatt of power may also be fed to payloads for up to five continuous hours. Solar cells are used to recharge batteries, and are important for supplying power during the orbital storage mode, during which the OMV is left unused in orbit for up to nine months.

The OMV has a redundant power system, containing two of each component so that if any single piece fails, electricity is still available. Two ORUs contain batteries and switches. Two other ORUs contain the electronics which control the power distribution to the payload, the batteries, and the rest of the OMV. Two sets of wires, which carry power to all of the other ORUs, run throughout the OMV.

Thermal Control

All components of the OMV have a range of temperatures in which they perform properly. Just as a house must be cooled in summer and heated in winter, the OMV must be cooled when in the sun and heated when in the earth's shadow. The thermal control subsystem uses many methods to keep temperatures within reasonable limits. Insulation protects many parts of the OMV against both heat and cold. Thermostats measure temperature and tell the computer whether things are getting too hot or too cold. Components which are likely to get hot are designed with special cooling tubes to keep them cool. Wire heaters are used to increase temperature, which is often necessary when the OMV is shadowed.

Insulation is used to keep the OMV cool when the sun is shining on it. Thin blankets, called heat shields, are attached to much of the outside of the vehicle. These shields also keep the OMV warm when it is not in the sun by keeping the heat in the vehicle. Temperature control is especially important for the fuel tanks, valves, and thrusters because they are more easily damaged by extreme temperature. Up to twenty layers of insulating heat shields are applied to the ORUs containing fuel tanks and thrusters.

Cooling on the OMV is done passively. This means that there are no moving parts such as fans blowing air or pumps pumping fluids. Some cooling is done by conduction, which is how heat moves through a solid material. To keep electronics cool, some ORUs have metal plates to soak up the heat. These plates conduct heat away to other plates which face out into space. Passive cooling of these outer plates is done with radiant heat control. Heat moves through space from warm objects to the cooler surroundings. This is how the plate that is exposed to space stays cool as it radiates heat away. Since space is very cold, some heat is radiated away, even if the plate is only at room temperature.

Most heating on the OMV is done by conduction. Many components have wires wrapped around them. When electric current is passed through such wires, heat is generated and conducted to the components which are in contact with the wires.

As you control the OMV, a TV camera sees for you. Your hands guide OMV movements. You deftly perform intricate maneuvers from afar. You recover a damaged satellite and return it to an orbiting repair facility.

The OMV at Work

IMAGINE YOU HAVE BEEN invited by NASA to witness the OMV at work. This does not require riding on the Shuttle, since much of the remote-control work is done at the OMV mission control center. At the control center, there are people called pilots who sometimes control the OMV. As you wait for the Shuttle to launch from Kennedy Space Center, the OMV pilot explains how a television screen shows pictures from the vehicle. Switches and throttles are used for controlling the OMV. This is all made possible by the radio links with the OMV. However, the pilot is only needed for the critical times when the OMV is near another object. At other times, on-board computers control and guide the OMV.

After the Shuttle launches and enters its proper orbit, the OMV's work begins. The OMV is released from the Shuttle while the Shuttle is at its normal 300 kilometer altitude. It travels automatically to a troubled weather satellite at 700 kilometer altitude. When it nears its destination, the pilot takes over and carefully steers the OMV close to the satellite. As you watch, still-frame pictures flash on the TV screen. Numbers also appear on the screen from the OMV radar. This helps the pilot know the distance to the satellite. Carefully controlling OMV thrusters, the pilot docks with the satellite by commanding the OMV's grapple to grasp the satellite. The pilot then lets the OMV guide itself and the satellite back near the Shuttle, where it receives additional pilot guidance.

Once the satellite is safely in the Shuttle, the next mission starts. One of the ORU batteries is running low, so a Shuttle mission specialist uses the Remote Manipulator System to replace the ORU. Then the much larger Propulsion Module is replaced. Finally, a mission kit is attached to the front of the OMV. Repaired and refueled, you watch as the OMV again leaves the Shuttle.

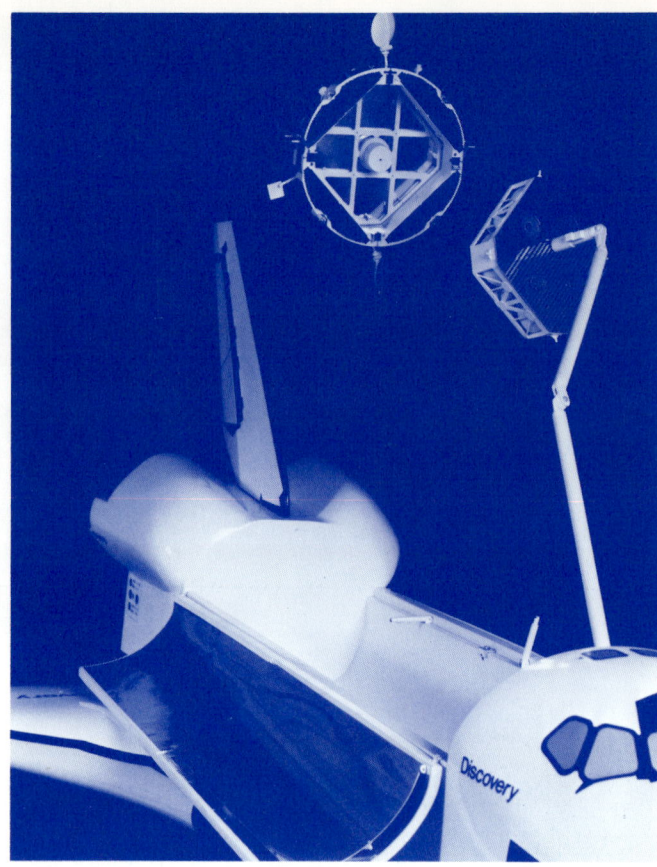

With the cargo bay door open, the OMV is ready to be released.

Installing a Propulsion Module is accomplished using the Remote Manipulation System.

The next piloted session begins when the OMV has gotten close to an old, dead satellite. This space debris is in an orbit which will be dangerous for future launches and must be deboosted. You watch again as the pilot steers the OMV to one end of the satellite. After latching on to it, the view doesn't change. The OMV takes over and slows it down so that it will fall out of its orbit, and then lets go. You see that the satellite slowly moves away with the blue ocean below. The view doesn't last long. The OMV quickly turns around and speeds up so that it doesn't also drop to Earth.

After it returns to the Shuttle, you and the OMV pilot watch as the Shuttle mission specialist now controls the OMV. In the shuttle bay, the mission kit is removed as well as the spent Propulsion Module. Also, Reaction Control System components are replaced. The OMV doesn't need a fully loaded and powerful Propulsion Module for its next assignment at the Space Station. The cold-gas thrusters will be enough to propel the OMV around the Space Station doing odd jobs. The OMV will remain based in space, performing a Space Station support mission.

The OMV controls itself until it is near the Space Station. Now astronauts in the Station guide it in for docking as you watch the final maneuvers. For the time being, the pilot at the mission control center is finished. There will, however, be many more remote-control missions for our pilot on the ground. During its lifetime, the OMV will be keeping pilots busy on the ground, in the Shuttle, and in the Space Station.

ORBITAL MANEUVERING VEHICLE

Summary

The OMV is a space-based transportation system. It is expected to perform many different missions. It can move payloads that are very large or small, using a grapple mechanism to hold them. It can be launched from the Shuttle and returned to it. Most of the time it will be stored in orbit by itself or near the Space Station.

Astronauts can repair and refuel the OMV while in space. This feature made it necessary for the OMV to have a modular design, with easily replaced parts. Every mission in space is expensive, therefore the OMV has a very redundant design. When a part fails in space, a back-up is usually there to allow the mission to be successfully completed.

Terms

conduction	modular design	redundant design
data bus	orbital replacement	reference mission
deboost	unit (ORU)	remote-control
gimbal	payload	subsystems
grapple	radiation	trunnion
low-earth orbit	reboost	

Important People, Ideas, and Events

- The idea of a reusable space-based tugboat originated at NASA as part of a National Space Transportation System.
- Many components of the OMV design have been proven to work on other satellites. Despite this fact, many of these components are redundant so that a failure in space does not ruin a mission.
- The OMV should operate throughout the 1990s. Future versions of the vehicle may include new capabilities, such as being based at the much higher geosynchronous altitude.

Interesting Things to Do

1. Build a model of the OMV.
2. Determine what direction the OMV must fire to deboost a satellite.
3. Imagine the earth is the size of a basketball and determine how far off this basketball the OMV would be if it were in a 300 kilometer orbit.
4. With an earth globe, investigate how an antenna can always be pointed at a relay satellite that sits above the equator at geosynchronous altitude.
5. Request information from NASA on the OMV.
6. Investigate the difference between the OMV and a rocket upper stage.
7. Sketch alternative designs for the OMV.
8. Sketch designs for the control station.
9. Sketch a mission kit that could allow the OMV to mine asteroids.

The MMU has been tested on Shuttle missions. It will be an important transportation device for astronauts working at the Space Station.

Chapter 5 MANNED MANEUVERING UNIT

Extra-vehicular activity (EVA) has become a routine part of an astronaut's work. EVA increases mission flexibility and allows a greater chance for success in planned or emergency situations. However, working in weightlessness during EVA requires some very different considerations than working on Earth. For example, all tools must be attached to the worker or they will drift away. The worker also must be able to maintain position while working. This can be accomplished using tether restraints. When it becomes necessary to move to a different location, the worker can easily travel along by pushing off and landing on any stable object. However, when it is necessary to travel in free space, some sort of propulsion and stabilizing system is necessary. The Manned Maneuvering Unit (MMU) was designed to fill that need.

The MMU allows Shuttle astronauts to operate beyond the confines of the payload bay, to fly to any part of the Shuttle or to nearby payloads and structures. This independent mobility can be used to support activities such as transfer of cargo and personnel, inspection and monitoring of orbital operations, and construction and assembly of large space structures.

Historical Development

The need for independent powered flight during EVA was realized early in the American quest for space. Experiments with personal propulsion systems began in the Gemini program and continued during the Skylab missions.

Gemini

The first powered flight outside a spacecraft taken by a single person occurred on the Gemini 4 mission in June, 1965. During the four day mission, astronaut Edward White spent 21 minutes outside the spacecraft,

WITHIN EARTH ORBIT

using a small, hand-held rocket-gun for propulsion. It was powered by compressed gas. Since this was the first American experiment of this type, White remained tethered to the spacecraft during the entire experiment.

The next step was to develop a maneuvering unit which consisted of a structure with thrusters and controllers attached. The first maneuvering unit was sent up on Gemini 9 in June, 1966. The mission plan called for astronaut Eugene Cernan to fly the maneuvering unit. However, one arm of the device refused to deploy. After several exhausting attempts to move the arm, Cernan was ordered inside and the experiment was scrubbed.

On the Gemini 10 mission, the Gemini spacecraft had to rendezvous with an unmanned Agena spacecraft. Astronaut Michael Collins used the hand-held maneuvering gun to travel to the Agena Spacecraft to retrieve an experiment package. A tube from the Gemini spacecraft supplied compressed nitrogen to the gun.

Skylab

The predecessor to today's MMU was developed in the early 1970s. It was successfully flown by five astronauts inside the Skylab space station in 1973 and 1974. They demonstrated the maneuverability and precise controllability of this type of personal maneuvering system. They were able to accurately maintain a separation of a few centimeters while moving along walls. Fourteen hours of flying time were accumulated during eleven tests during the second and third Skylab missions.

MMU Description

Today's MMU is one piece of a system necessary to support independent, powered EVA. The other components are the Extra-vehicular Mobility Unit (EMU) Spacesuit, the Primary Life Support System (PLSS), and the Flight Support Station (FSS). They are used in conjunction with the Shuttle airlock to accomplish EVA.

Manned Maneuvering Unit

The MMU is a self-contained backpack designed for zero-gravity use. The frame is made of aluminum, and houses a 16.8 volt silver-zinc battery, a control electronics assembly, two hand-held controllers, nitrogen fuel tanks, and 24 thrusters. It is 127 centimeters high, 85 centimeters wide, and 68 centimeters deep with arms folded in, or 122 centimeters deep with hand controllers extended. Its mass is approximately 136 kilograms when filled with nitrogen propellant. The MMU is small enough to fit through the Shuttle airlock and side hatch. It is designed to support a six-hour EVA without battery recharge. However, it may be necessary to recharge the propellant tanks during the six hours, depending on how much the thrusters are used.

A MMU prototype was tested inside the Skylab Space Station.

Designed for zero gravity mobility, the MMU is self-contained and provides six degrees of freedom of movement. With built-in failsafe devices, it allows crewmembers untethered activities outside the spacecraft.

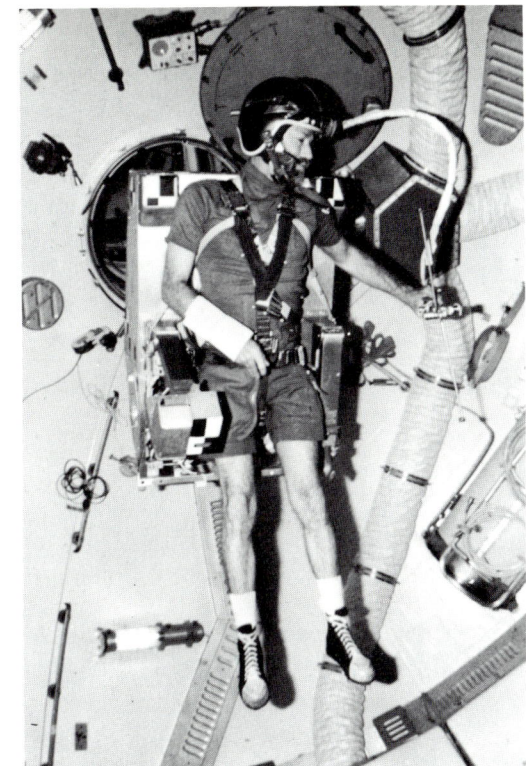

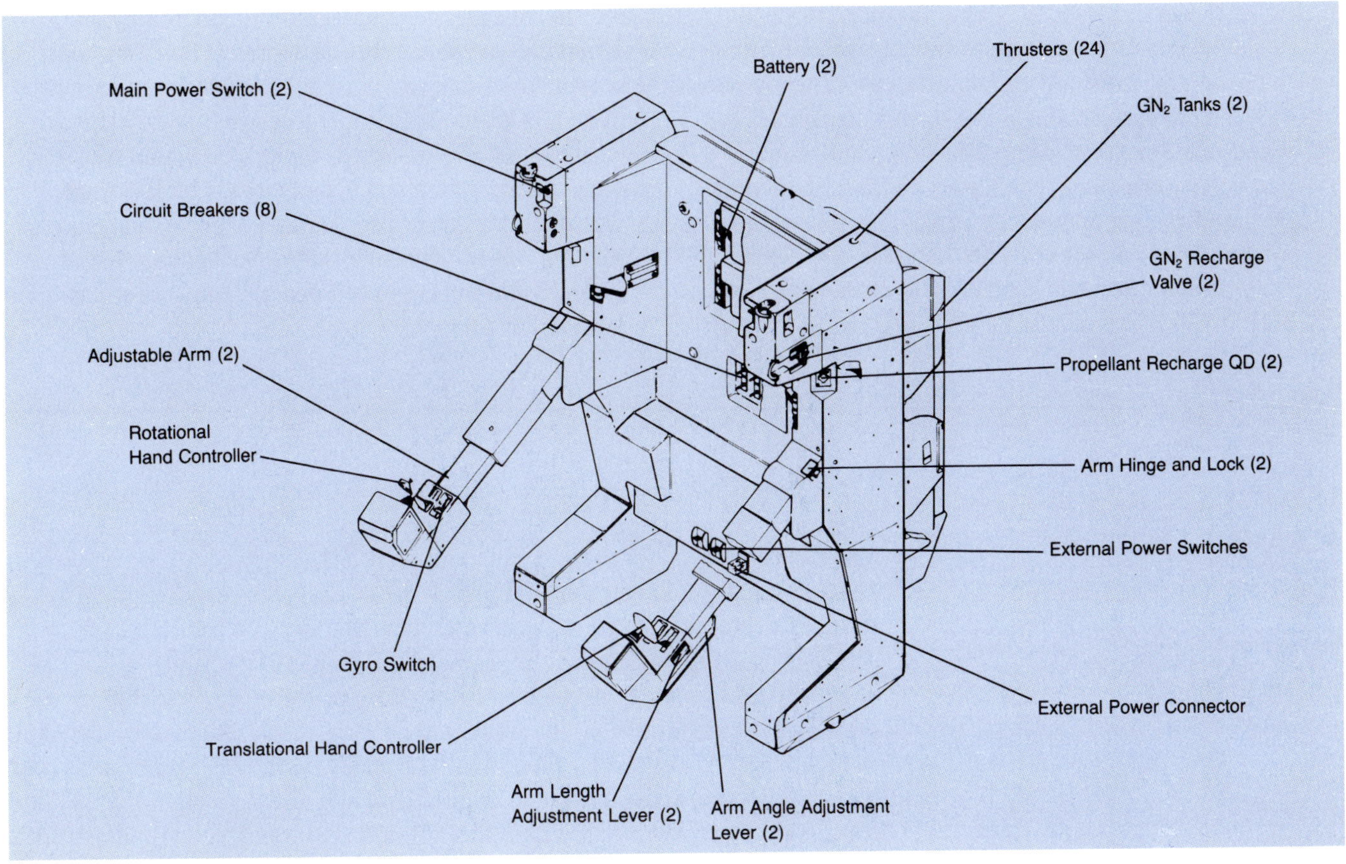

- Main Power Switch (2)
- Circuit Breakers (8)
- Adjustable Arm (2)
- Rotational Hand Controller
- Gyro Switch
- Translational Hand Controller
- Arm Length Adjustment Lever (2)
- Arm Angle Adjustment Lever (2)
- Battery (2)
- Thrusters (24)
- GN_2 Tanks (2)
- GN_2 Recharge Valve (2)
- Propellant Recharge QD (2)
- Arm Hinge and Lock (2)
- External Power Switches
- External Power Connector

105

Degrees of Freedom

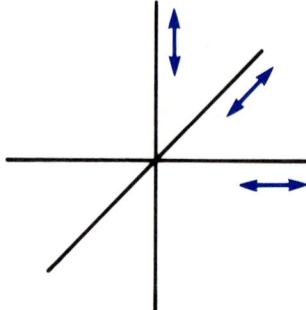

Translational Axes

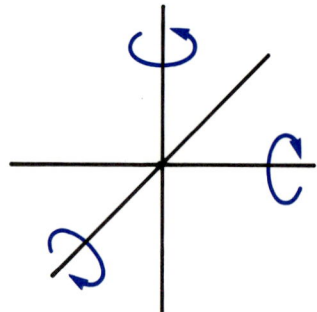

Rotational Axes

All motion is made up of a combination of two types of movement, translation and rotation. Translation is straight line movement and rotation is spinning movement. Both types of movements can take place on three axes. To translate, you can move up or down, forward or backward, and to the right or left. This represents three degrees of freedom. Rotating around these three axes provides three more degrees of freedom. These motions are called pitch, roll, and yaw. Pitch is like doing a somersault. Roll is like doing a cartwheel, and yaw is like a skater spinning. Together, translational and rotational movements provide six degrees of freedom. In the MMU, astronauts use thrusters to propel themselves. They can translate and rotate in any direction; they have six degrees of freedom of movement.

Is it always possible to have six degrees of freedom of movement? To answer this question, imagine that you are floating down a river on an inner tube. If you paddle downstream, you are creating forward translation. If you paddle towards a shore, you are creating sideways translation. A floating inner tube cannot be paddled so that it flies straight up. Therefore, you only have two translational degrees of freedom of motion. For rotation, you have only one degree of freedom. You can paddle so that the inner tube rotates either way around a vertical line. This is the yaw axis. If you tipped your inner tube to the left or right, you would rotate around the roll axis. If you tipped forward or backward, it would be the pitch axis. However, either way you would fall out of your inner tube! Consequently, you only have three degrees of freedom, two degrees for translation and one for rotation.

The propulsion system consists of two fuel tanks which are 76 centimeters long and 25 centimeters in diameter. The tanks are made of aluminum with a kevlar filament overwrap. They each hold 5.9 kilograms of nitrogen at a pressure of 20.69 Megapascals. Each of the 24 thrusters produce 7.56 newtons of thrust. Astronauts have the freedom to move, or translate, forward, and backward, up and down, or sideways, and can rotate in pitch, roll, and yaw. This is known as six degree of freedom movement. Translations and rotations are accomplished by moving hand controllers which are located at the ends of the control arms. The left hand controller commands the thrusters to cause the MMU to translate, while the right hand controller commands the thrusters to cause the MMU to rotate. A control electronics

Spacesuits

Astronauts involved in EVA must be protected from the environment of space. In addition to protecting against vacuum, radiation, heat, and cold, spacesuits must also protect against tiny pieces of debris traveling through space, called micrometeors. First generation spacesuits are made from multiple layers of compressed fabric. They enabled humans to walk on the moon and work in space. However, these suits are difficult to manufacture. They are also very stiff, which restricts astronauts' mobility.

A new type of spacesuit, made of metal, is being developed to overcome these deficiencies. The suit must be designed so that it is easy to seal, yet easy to move around in. The metal that it is made from must also meet stringent requirements. It must be good at radiating heat so that the astronaut stays cool. It must not corrode or react with atomic oxygen that is found in low-Earth orbit, where EVAs typically occur. It must also protect the astronauts from micrometeors, just as fabric spacesuits have done in the past. NASA has shown that astronauts can move around more easily in these new spacesuits, and is continuing to develop them.

assembly converts the hand controller movements into commands to operate the appropriate thrusters for achieving the desired maneuver. In addition to manual control, an automatic attitude hold function is available. It is used to maintain a constant attitude during flight by using the thrusters to automatically stop any rotations which are sensed by gyroscopes within the MMU.

The MMU design is fully redundant and fail-safe. This means that every part has a built-in spare which automatically replaces a failed component. No single failure could prevent an EVA crewmember from returning to the Shuttle. Therefore the MMU can be used safely without tethers or other attachments to the Shuttle.

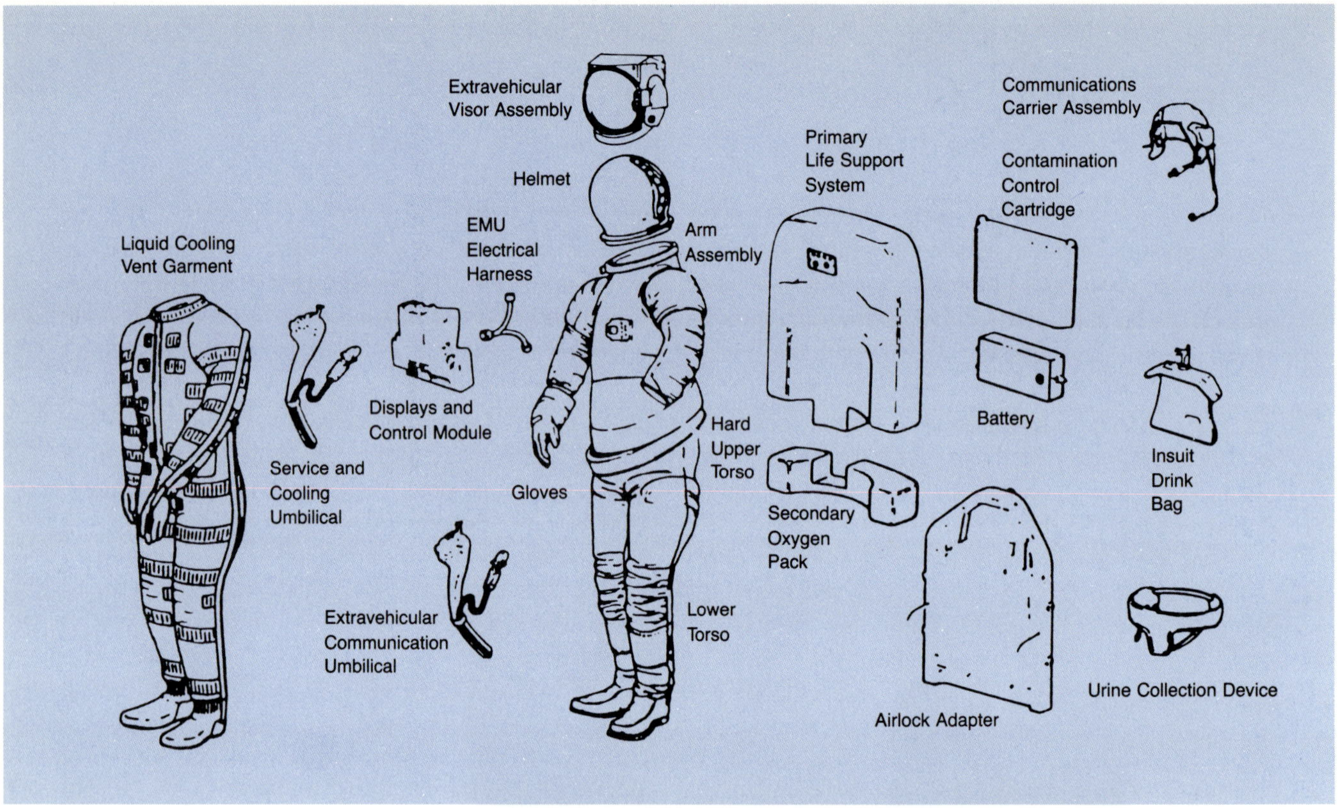

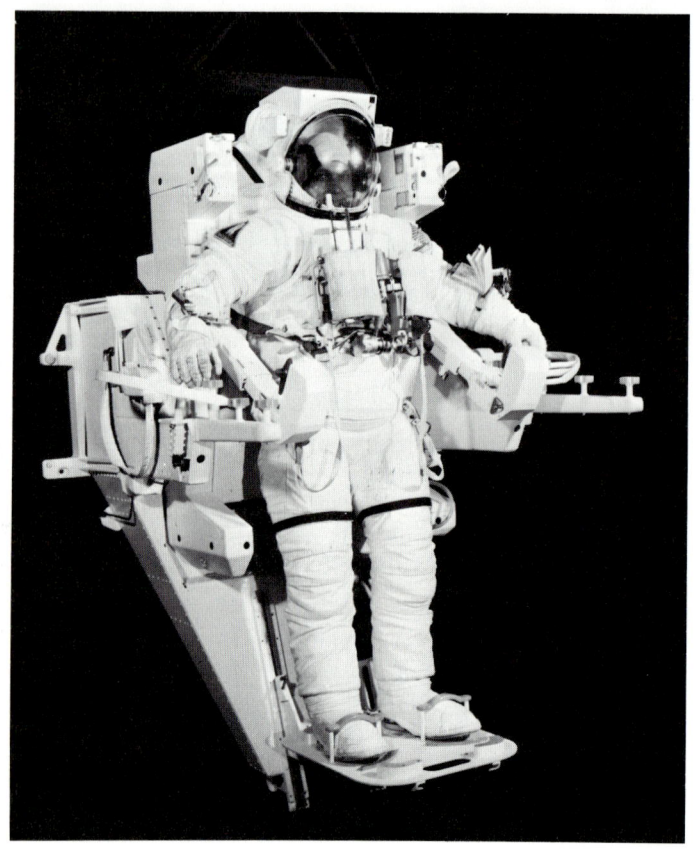

All components of the EMU spacesuit and of the PLSS are designed and made to keep the space worker alive, comfortable and productive. What difficulties must the crewmember overcome and what limits must be recognized for an EVA to be accomplished?

The MMU, still in the FSS, has been donned and is ready for EVA. The FSS recharges the MMU's propulsion system and provides replacement battery packs. The MMU is always ready for the next mission.

MANNED MANEUVERING UNIT

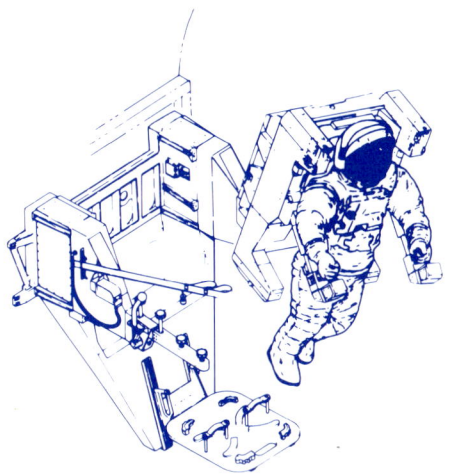

To use the MMU, the crewmember must don the backpack and release it from the FSS.

Extra-vehicular Mobility Unit Spacesuit and Primary Life Support System

The EMU spacesuit and the PLSS provide environmental protection, life support, mobility, and communications for the EVA crewmember. Spacesuits are available for all sized people except for those who are extremely large or small. They have flexible joints for movement of the shoulder, elbow, wrist, fingers, waist, hip, knee and ankle. Breathing oxygen and suit pressure is maintained at 2816 kilograms per square meter. Thermal, optical and micrometeoriod protection are also provided. Voice radios allow communication between the Shuttle and two EVA crewmembers.

Flight Support Station

The FSS is mounted on the port side of the forward end of the Shuttle payload bay. The MMU is stored in the FSS when it is not in use. It is also the place where the EVA crewmember puts on and takes off the MMU, called donning and doffing. This station provides the capability for propulsion system recharging and battery replacement. The FSS and MMU are heated when not in use. The Shuttle provides both electricity for heating and nitrogen for recharging the MMU fuel tanks. Temperature sensors in the FSS and MMU are constantly monitored by the Shuttle caution and warning system.

Airlock

The airlock is used by Shuttle crewmembers for transitioning between the shirtsleeve environment of the cabin and the vacuum environment in space. It is a modular, cylindrical structure with two "D" shaped pressure sealing hatches. Mating hatches are located in the Shuttle bulkhead or at the side of the payload tunnel adapter when the European Space Agency (ESA) Spacelab is flown in the bay. The airlock can be installed inside or outside the cabin, depending on mission requirements. The normal location is inside the mid-deck compartment to allow maximum use of the payload bay.

The airlock provides for stowage, donning, and doffing of the EMU spacesuit. A portable oxygen system allows the crewmember to prebreathe oxygen for denitrogenization when transferring from the cabin air environment to the lower pressure EVA environment. This prevents a painful and dangerous condition known as "the bends", which occurs when nitrogen bubbles form in the body as a person is exposed to a rapid lowering of pressure. The airlock also contains a battery charger for charging the EMU and MMU batteries, and facilities for replenishing the EMU water supply.

Soviet MMU Design

An MMU has been developed for the Soviet Union to support EVA around their Mir space station. It is similar to the American MMU. The space suits that are worn while using it have an interesting feature. The arms and legs can be removed and replaced. This allows the Soviets to tailor the arm and leg lengths of the suits to fit the individual crewmembers.

The MMU at Work

IMAGINE YOU HAVE BEEN chosen to service a satellite using the MMU. The training for the mission is rigorous. In addition to the standard astronaut training, you must learn to work during EVA and learn to control the MMU. After studying all of the written lessons, you fly to Houston, Texas, where NASA has a weightless environment training facility. It is a large water tank which contains full-size mock-ups of the Shuttle payload bay and the MMU. You don your EMU spacesuit with its PLSS and enter the water. Instructors, who are trained divers, assist you in learning to move yourself around in the bay. You push off and land on the objects inside the bay, just as you will do in space.

First you practice the tasks that you will perform with your EVA partner. NASA guidelines call for a two person EVA whenever possible. After you have practiced these tasks many times, you learn how to latch yourself to the MMU and release it from the FSS. Then you begin to try the controllers. As you push the right controller forward, you begin to tumble head over heels. Next you try the left controller and translate forward. Gradually you learn to move yourself where you want to go.

When you have become proficient at controlling the MMU, the mission training begins. You must practice all tasks which you are expected to perform on your mission, and other tasks which might become necessary if there is an equipment failure. You repeat the tasks many times until your instructors finally say that you are ready. You then leave for the Shuttle launch complex at Cape Canaveral, Florida.

The first step in your mission is to get into orbit. The Shuttle launch is very noisy. The engines roar while you feel very heavy as your weight is three times normal. The pilot takes the Shuttle into orbit and brings it close to the satellite which you will repair. It is then your turn to do your job.

First you and your partner enter the airlock to don your EMU spacesuit and PLSS. You doublecheck each other's suits and seals to make sure all is well. Then you both begin to breathe pure oxygen. You continue this for several minutes to make sure that you don't get the bends when you go outside. When this is complete, you depressurize the airlock and enter the payload bay. As you pull yourself over to the FSS, you steal a few glances at the Earth. It is a beautiful sight, but you know that you should perform your

MANNED MANEUVERING UNIT

To simulate the weightlessness of space, astronauts train underwater. NASA operates this weightless environment training facility which includes a full-size mock-up of the Shuttle payload bay.

WITHIN EARTH ORBIT

In space, a crewmember prepares to don the MMU. The MMU is heated while it is stored in the FSS.

mission first and enjoy the sights later. You then don the MMU backpack and release yourself from the FSS. You push away from the station and use the controls to fire the thrusters. As you begin flying away from the bay, your partner wishes you luck over the radio in the spacesuit.

As you clear the bay, you begin to realize that it is sensational to be able to soar wherever you want to go. You feel very powerful, but very small compared to all of space around you. After a little more sightseeing you begin to head to the satellite that needs repair. You activate the autopilot system that will maintain your attitude, thereby freeing your right hand. You use the hand controls to fire thrusters and match your motions to the satellite. You can fly right up to the satellite since the MMU's fuel is nitrogen, which can not contaminate it. Then you begin the repairs that you practiced for so long in the simulator. You encounter a small problem with a valve, and must perform one of the extra tasks which you practiced "just in case" something like this should happen.

After completing the repairs you return to the Shuttle. Since you have only used four hours of the standard six hour EVA, you have time to perform you secondary mission of inspecting the Shuttle. When this is done you return to the payload bay. At the FSS you doff the MMU. You then help your partner complete the remaining EVA tasks and return to the airlock. As the airlock begins to fill, you wish you could stay out a little longer. However, you know that you will be back outside in 16 hours when your partner will perform her mission with the MMU. When the airlock is filled, you both doff your spacesuits and reenter the cabin. The rest of the crew is pleased that the mission was successful. You all then get some rest so that you will be able to perform tomorrow's mission.

Summary

The MMU is a fail-safe personal transportation unit that gives astronauts the freedom of untethered movement in space. It has been used on several shuttle missions. The system is made up of the MMU, the EMU spacesuit, the PLSS, the FSS, and the airlock. Using the MMU, many types of activity are possible in open space, including repair, construction, and rescue. It also allows an EVA crewmember to travel between space structures. In the future there may be a second MMU and FSS on starboard side of the Shuttle payload bay for certain missions. The MMU may also be based at the Space Station to support its operations. The Soviet Union has developed a similar MMU which is used to support EVA around their Mir space station.

Terms

attitude	roll
controller	rotation
deploy	six degree of freedom
doffing	starboard
donning	tether
fail-safe	thruster
pitch	translation
port	yaw

Important People, Ideas, and Events

- The development of personal powered spaceflight began in the 1960s with the Gemini program.
- The MMU is a refinement of an earlier unit which was tested by astronauts in Skylab.
- Six degree of freedom movement is accomplished using translational and rotational controllers.
- Astronaut Bruce M. McCandless becomes the world's first free-flying human satellite during the first flight of the MMU on February 7, 1984.

Interesting Things to Do

1. Demonstrate how the MMU thrusters work by attaching a balloon to wheels and allowing it to deflate. Show how the direction of air released controls the direction of motion.
2. Make a model which demonstrates six degree of freedom motion.
3. Write to NASA to obtain more information about the MMU.

Living and working at the Space Station will require coordination between many complex systems.

Chapter 6   SPACE STATIONS

Tasks in space, including photoreconnaisance and radio communications, can be accomplished by satellites. Yet humans are necessary in space to accomplish tasks related to manufacturing, experimentation and research. There is also the need to learn how humans survive in the weightlessness of space over prolonged periods. If people can remain healthy during long journeys in space, colonizing other planets and building cities in space may be in our future. But first we must learn our limits.

Salyut, Mir and eventually the United States Space Station will initiate permanent residence in space. As Space Stations are launched into orbit, they do not have crews on board. After the stations are in orbit, they are monitored to determine if all systems are operational. When the status of the stations is deemed safe and functional, crews are sent in other spacecraft which dock with the Station.

Soviet Space Stations— First Generation

The Soviet Union has been committed to a manned space program. In 1971, they were the first to have a Space Station, called Salyut, in low-Earth orbit. A Space Station with people on board cannot exist alone; other vehicles must bring replacement crews and supplies. This requirement has led to the ongoing development of space transportation systems.

There have been seven laboratories or Space Stations in the Salyut series. The first five, known as the first generation, had only one docking port. The sixth and seventh had two docking ports and are known as the second generation.

Salyut 1 through 5
The original Salyut Station had three components: one docking and airlock compartment, a laboratory with living quarters, and the control, instrument

WITHIN EARTH ORBIT

The Soviet Union has had orbiting space stations since 1971. With a need to replace crews and replenish supplies, these space stations, like Salyut 4 pictured here, provided the impetus for the continuing development of the space transportation and habitation systems.

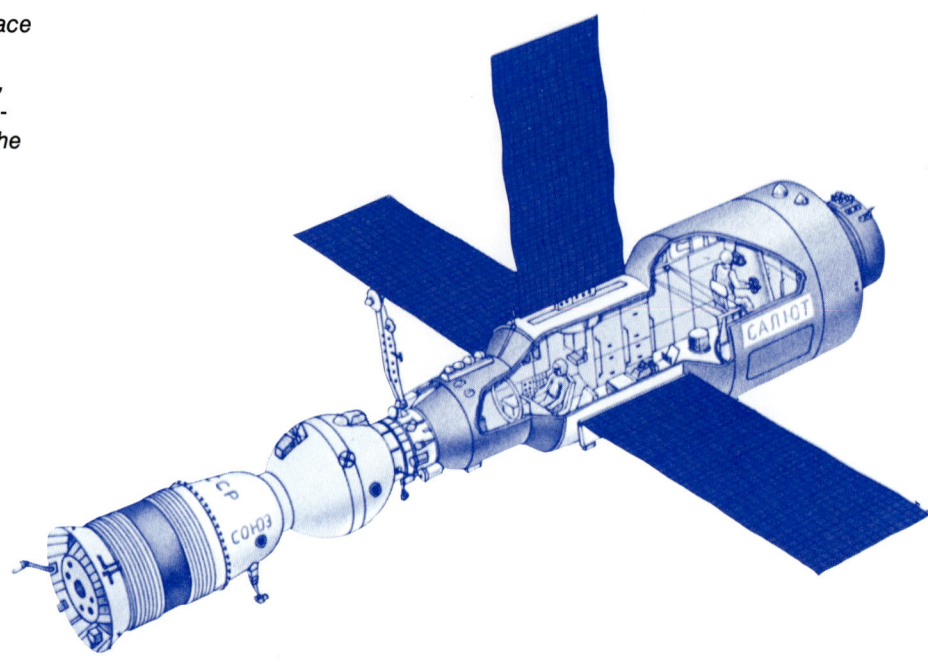

and propulsion module. Salyut was 13 meters long with a maximum diameter of 4.2 meters. Salyut was dependent on other spacecraft for delivery of supplies and replacement crews. The Soyuz manned spacecraft fulfilled this purpose.

Salyut Systems

Life Support
There are a number of systems which enable cosmonauts to live and function aboard Salyut. The life support system controls the atmosphere inside the Station. The composition of the gases for breathing, as well as the regeneration of oxygen and collection of carbon dioxide, are one part of the life support system. The system also collects excess moisture for humidity control and regulates the water regeneration system and the sanitary systems for washing and waste removal. The temperature inside Salyut and any powered delivery vehicle docked with it is regulated by a temperature and control system to protect the scientific and operational equipment. There is also a medical monitoring system to return biomedical data about the cosmonauts to Earth. This is not only for immediate medical feedback, but also to quantify the long term effects of living in space.

SPACE STATIONS

Propulsion, Guidance and Control

The propulsion system includes the low thrust and high thrust maneuvering engines. These are used to keep Salyut in the desired low-Earth orbit. The guidance system can operate in an automatic mode or manual mode to maintain the orientation of Salyut. There is an on-board equipment control system which controls the power supply system, radio links with ground control and deployment sequences for events occurring outside the Station. There is also a separate docking and internal transfer system which handles automatic docking, including the mechanical, electrical, and hydraulic docking functions. This system can be controlled by the crew, controlled by radio from Earth or used in an automatic mode.

Power Supply

The power supply system supplies power to the Station and any craft which is docked with it. The system also keeps the solar panels in the proper orientation to the Sun to keep the batteries charged.

Communications

The communication system has three components. The command and television system radios commands up to Salyut and television pictures down from Salyut. The telephone system communicates telephone signals between ground control, Salyut and the Soyuz vehicle. The telemetry system sends experiment data and other signals from Salyut to the ground control center.

Soviet Space Stations— Second Generation

Salyut 6

Salyut 6 was the first Soviet Space Station to have two docking ports. The forward docking port was used for Soyuz which brought visiting or replacement crews to the Station. The aft docking port could be used for the Progress resupply vehicle or another Soyuz. Progress could only use the aft port because that was where the fuel resupply lines were located. Salyut 6 was similar in size to the first generation stations. When docked with a Soyuz, the Station was approximately 23 meters long.

When cosmonauts arrived in the Soyuz craft and docked with Salyut, they entered through a transfer compartment of about eight cubic meters. This is where the pressure suits and airlock control panels were located. The next work compartment had the Station control panels. In this same area was a table for working and eating plus the storage areas for food and water. Beyond the table was the area for scientific equipment. There was also a shower and two air locks which were used to dispose of garbage. The floor of the Station had cameras and infrared sensors which helped to determine the vertical position of the Station for the navigation system. There was a toilet facility near the hatch which led to the intermediate chamber. This

WITHIN EARTH ORBIT

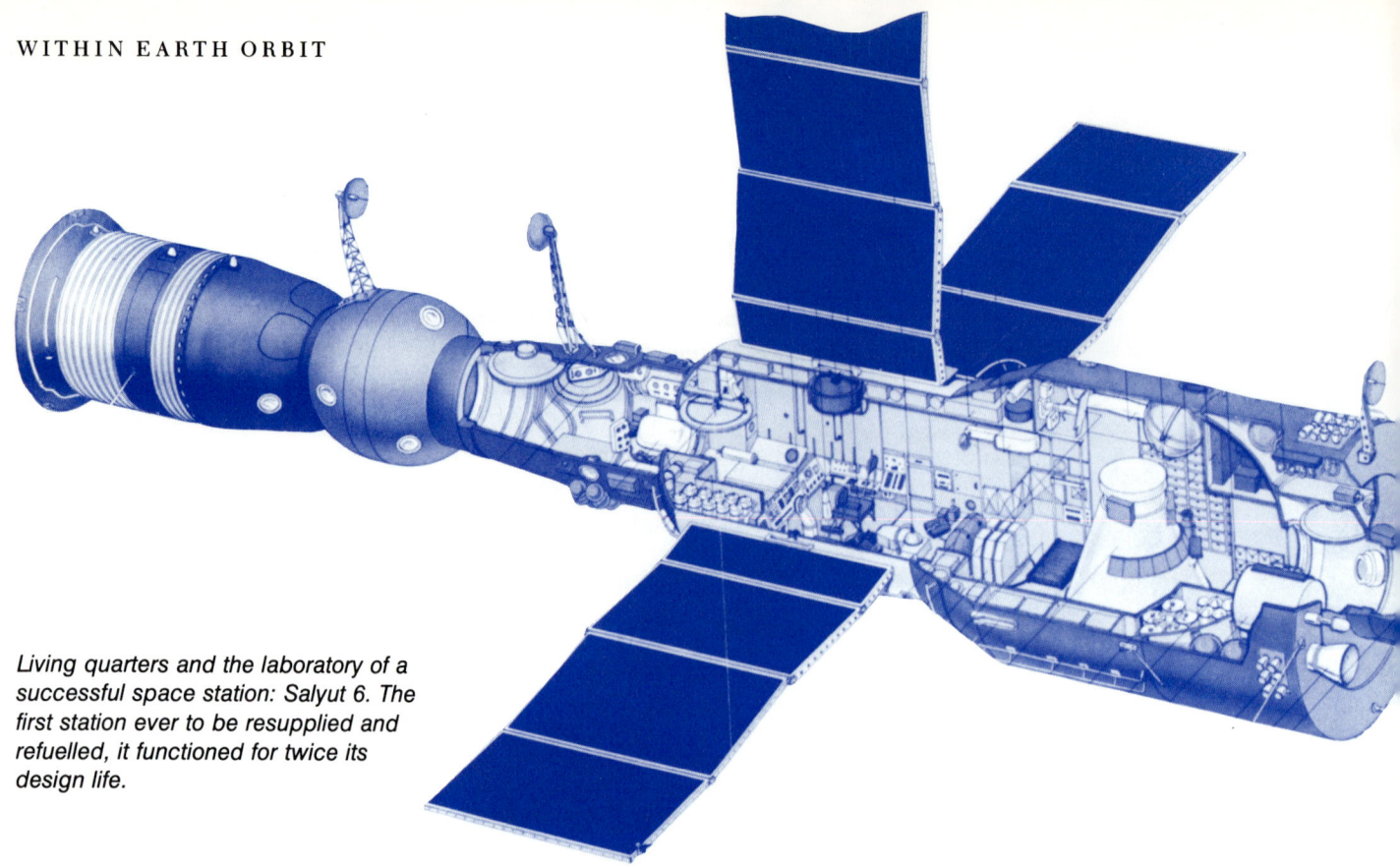

Living quarters and the laboratory of a successful space station: Salyut 6. The first station ever to be resupplied and refuelled, it functioned for twice its design life.

chamber included the aft docking hatch. There were also 20 windows for visual and photographic observation of Earth.

In 1978 Salyut 6 had the distinction of being the first Station to ever be resupplied and refueled. This made it possible to expand the operational lifetime of the Station to 18 months, twice the designed time. The crews were able to do research in the fields of materials processing, Earth observations and astrophysical and biomedical observations.

Salyut 7

Salyut 7 had almost the same configuration as Salyut 6. Improvements were made in the amount and type of scientific equipment it contained and some changes were made for crew comfort. Salyut 7 hosted 10 crews of 2-3 people each, including a number of crew members from other nations. During this time, a variety of experiments and related space activities were conducted.

At a time when the Station was unoccupied, it experienced an electronic systems failure. This led to another historic event. A Soyuz crew of two was sent to Salyut 7, in 1985, to effect repairs. The Station was in a deep freeze condition but repairs were completed and the Station reactivated. A second Soyuz with a crew of three was sent to the Station and all five inhabited the Station for a week. Then one member of the initial two man crew and one from the three man crew returned to Earth, thus effecting the first crew transfer. At a later date, the other three cosmonauts returned to Earth.

SPACE STATIONS

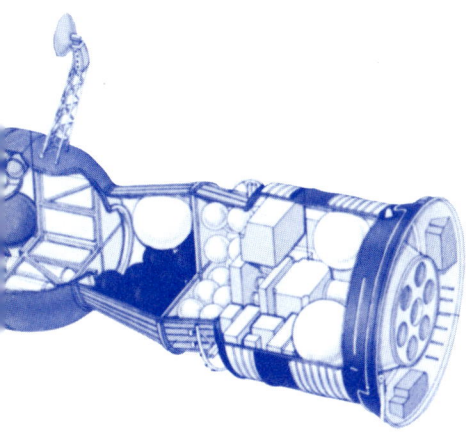

Cutaway view of a Soyuz spacecraft.

Progress Vehicle

Maintaining a Station in space requires that additional supplies be brought to the Station. The Soviets have developed an unmanned cargo ship which is a modified version of the Soyuz spacecraft. It has been stripped of all the life support systems and does not contain a heat shield or parachute system for reentry. It is not intended to survive reentry into the Earth's atmosphere. The Progress vehicle can carry 2300 kilograms of equipment, fuel, water, gas, experiments and replacement parts for Salyut. It operates as a controlled robot, and does its own braking and accelerating to correct its course as it approaches and docks with the Station. Docking is accomplished by fourteen engines which each provide ten kilograms of thrust and eight precision orientation engines which each produce one kilogram of thrust.

Another major function of the Progress is the refueling of the Station, enabling longer onboard missions. As the Progress docks with the Salyut Station, the main pipelines from Progress to Salyut are automatically coupled. The propellant is transferred first, followed by the oxidizer. Another use of the Progress vehicle has been to boost the Space Station into a higher orbit. The Progress engines are fired and the Station is raised to the desired orbit. After the Progress vehicle has completed its mission, it is often filled with waste from the Station and then undocked. As Progress pulls away from

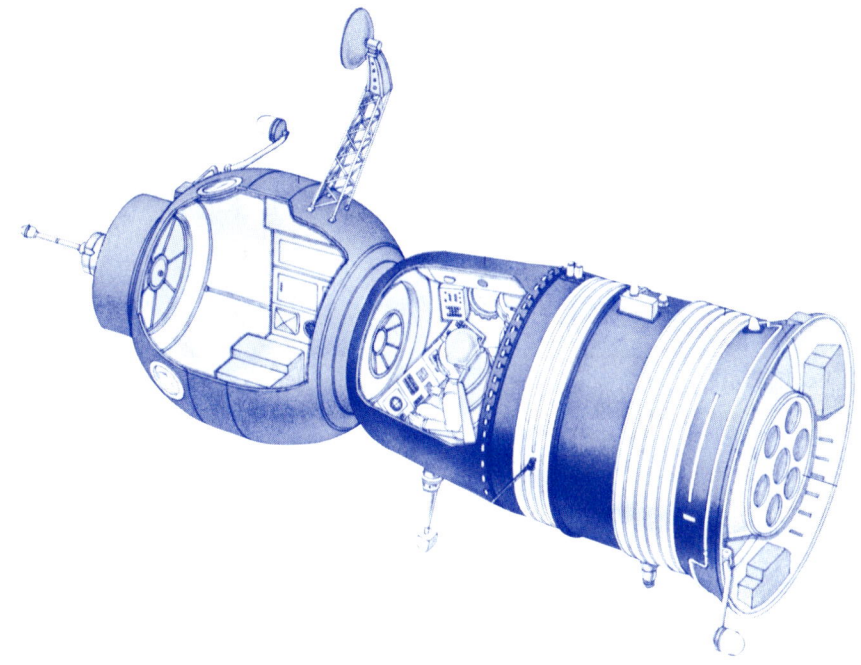

WITHIN EARTH ORBIT

the Salyut Station, its engines are fired for one last time, initiating the deorbit burn. Since the Progress is not to be recovered, it is sent on a trajectory through the dense part of the Earth's atmosphere, where it literally burns up over the Pacific Ocean.

Soviet Space Stations - Third Generation

Mir

The most recent Soviet Space Station is known as Mir, or "peace." It was named as a reaction to the United States Strategic Defense Initiative. Mir is the next developmental step in Soviet Space Stations being built on the technology of the Salyut Station. The most noticeable difference between Mir and Salyut is that there are six docking ports instead of two. One docking port is located at the aft end of the Station and the other five are on a docking pod at the forward end of the Station. The second major improvement is that Mir relies more on computers to perform many routine operations. The Mir Station has two larger solar panels instead of three as were used in the earlier Salyut series. These panels rotate to point toward the Sun at all times regardless of the alignment of Mir.

Mir is designed as a core to which a number of scientific modules can be attached. The core is 13.5 meters long and 4 meters in diameter. The Mir Station can grow as these scientific modules are attached to the core, which functions as living space and a command center. Cosmonauts can go to the different attached modules to conduct the scientific experiments and research work. It is also possible to detach a module and leave it in free-flight near the Station when it is not needed. This frees a docking port for additional modules as research directions change.

The first module, named Kvant, was docked with the Mir Station in April of 1987 and used for astrophysical research. Kvant modules are 5.8 meters long and 4 meters in diameter. Other modules will be outfitted for materials processing, remote sensing and food growing. The Mir Station became a complex of four units in 1987: the Mir core Station, the Progress Freighter, an improved Soyuz TM2 space vehicle and the Kvant module. This was the first time a research complex of four spacecraft had been achieved through successive dockings. As newly arriving craft dock with Mir, they dock at the axial or end docking port. Once docked they can be moved to a side docking port using a manipulator arm.

Mir Systems

The Mir systems are similar to those used on Salyut. Mir has a propulsion system which contains the main orbital maneuvering engines, propellant, air tanks and other equipment. The engines are powered by hypergolic nitrogen tetroxide and hydrazine. The engines are used to maneuver the Station and, in addition, the Progress vehicle can be used to boost the Station into a higher orbit.

SPACE STATIONS

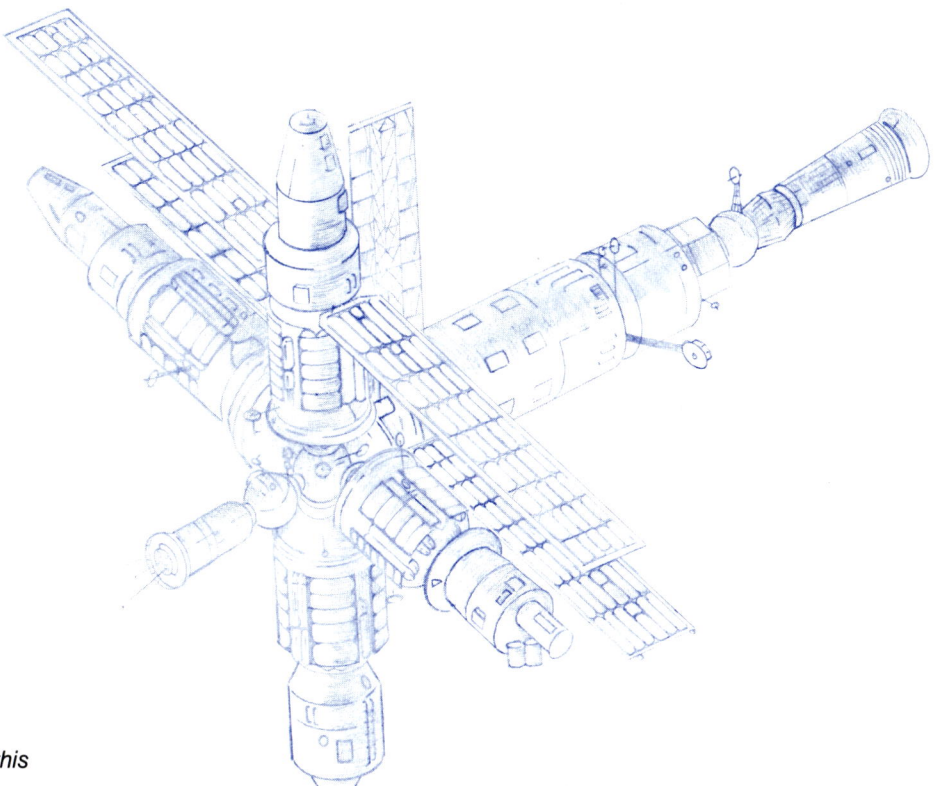

An artist's conception of a future MIR configuration. The modular design of this station allows for future expansion.

The temperature of the Station is maintained between 18° Celsius and 28° Celsius. Humidity is also controlled. Lithium hydroxide filters clean the recirculated compressed air.

The communication system uses a radio complex which provides continuous voice and data communication for the crew and ground control. The Soviets use a global network of tracking ships to provide live coverage during part of each orbit.

Living In Mir

As new crews are sent to Mir, they will arrive in the updated Soyuz TM2 spacecraft. It has a new avionics system, called Kurs, which provides for automatic docking. The Soyuz vehicle does all the maneuvering necessary to dock with the Mir Station. Essential supplies are delivered by the Progress ferry or tanker. Eight computers operate all the systems and control the flight path, attitude control, orbital maneuvers and docking of visiting craft. The zero gravity complex has a table and chairs for eating and working as well as exercise equipment. There is a hand and face washing facility, but no shower. Wet wipes are used for other necessary washing. There are books,

WITHIN EARTH ORBIT

videos, television links with families and sound tapes which play the familiar sounds of Earth: birds singing, wind blowing, sea waves breaking and other familiar sounds. The Mir complex also has a ceiling and floor to help provide an Earth-like orientation.

The Soviet plan for work in space is done on a daily task basis. Future plans call for a crew size of up to six cosmonauts when an additional living module is added. One of the more unique work events occurred when a crew which had spent 51 days in Mir entered their Soyuz spacecraft and taxied over to the Salyut 7 Space Station where they spent 50 days closing it down. They then taxied back to Mir and remained another 19 days before returning to Earth. This was the first crew to transfer between two space facilities.

Salyut 7 was then placed in a higher orbit. It is not expected that the Salyut 7 will be occupied again. It will be monitored to see how its systems decay over time in space. It is expected that the Mir complex will be completed in the early 1990s and that crews will eventually stay on board for two years to test human ability to remain in space for this length of time. It will take two years to fly to Mars and back. The future of Soviet Space Stations appears to be taking shape with the development of the Soviet Energia heavy lift vehicle. If this booster is successful, it will have the capability of lifting a new Space Station which could be as large as the entire Mir complex.

United States Space Stations First Generation

Skylab

The Skylab Space Station was the first American effort to have a long term manned space facility where astronauts could live and work. It was built from a Saturn IV B rocket stage and launched on a Saturn V rocket used in the Apollo program. Because of the weight of the Station and the orbit to be achieved, the Saturn rocket used five F-1 engines for the first stage and five J-2 engines for the second stage to place Skylab in orbit. The launch of the Station took place on May 14, 1973. Unfortunately, problems during the launch resulted in the meteoroid shield being torn away and one solar wing being ripped off. The Station was virtually without power when the other solar wing was jammed and never deployed.

The Skylab Space Station was to be occupied by three crews using the Apollo command module launched by a Saturn I B rocket. The first crew, launched on May 25, 1973, was sent to assess the damage to the Station and make repairs. They were able to erect a sunshield over the workshop where the meteoroid shield had been torn off. During extra-vehicular activity they freed the solar wing and let it fully deploy to produce needed electrical power. This first mission lasted 28 days.

The second mission to Skylab was launched on July 28, 1973. Efforts on this mission were directed toward experimentation and manufacturing in space. This mission lasted 59 days. The third mission to Skylab was launched

America's pioneer space station, Skylab, was used for less than a year.

on November 16, 1973. It was to last 56 days but was extended to 84 days because of the exceptional successes which were achieved.

Skylab was America's pioneer Space Station. It was only used for less than a year, but Skylab remained in orbit for a little over six years before drifting down into the denser parts of the Earth's atmosphere. Heat and friction caused Skylab to break apart and fall to Earth.

There had been hopes that the Space Shuttle would be ready for launch prior to the Skylab reentry. The Shuttle would have been used to boost the facility into a higher orbit. However, prolonging Skylab's useful life through a Shuttle mission was not to be. Skylab's lack of a propulsion system left it helpless as its orbit decayed.

United States Space Station - Second Generation

The United States developed many programs that led to the entry and exploration of space. The largest endeavor, Project Apollo, was initiated by President John F. Kennedy in his 1959 decree: "I believe that this nation should commit itself to achieving the goal, before this decade is out, of landing a man on the moon and returning him safely to Earth." Since the successful lunar program, other programs such as Apollo-Soyuz, Skylab and the Space Shuttle have been the building blocks toward the next major undertaking in space. In 1984, President Ronald Reagan made a bold commitment for the nation. He set the national goal of developing a permanently manned Space Station within a decade.

WITHIN EARTH ORBIT

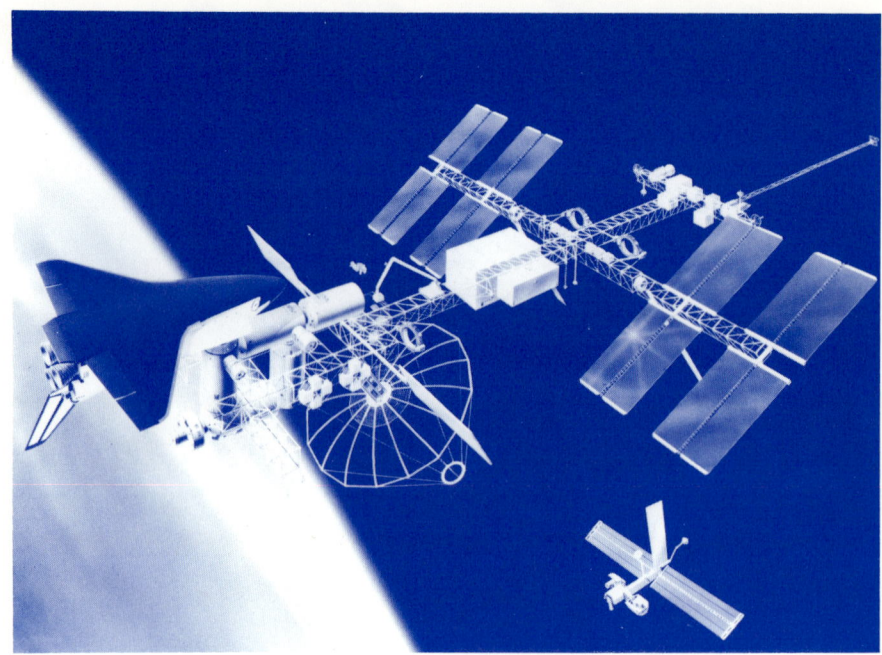

Although initially judged to be the best design for a space station, the power tower was rejected. Its tendency to oscillate would cause problems for scientists and their delicate instruments.

Space Station Initial Planning

In every major undertaking of this magnitude, many designs and sequences of operation are explored. For the Apollo lunar program, three major plans were conceived to accomplish the task (see DeOld, 1986, p. 420). Of the three plans proposed, the one judged to be the best became the Apollo program. A number of major plans were also considered for the Space Station. Several initial design concepts were considered. The configuration which was at first judged to be the best design was called the power tower. However, further engineering studies indicated that this single truss of 130 meters, with habitation modules at one end, would tend to oscillate or vibrate. This would cause problems for scientists who needed to direct sensitive instruments at distant objects with great precision. The power tower also lacked sufficient area for attaching payloads and storing payloads or other materials when not in use. Much of the scientific experimentation and commercial work planned needs low gravity conditions which exist in space. This would not be achieved in the near zero gravity configuration of the power tower.

The most recent engineering studies have led to the dual keel design which is rectangular and provides a stiffer frame. The habitation and work modules are centrally located. The initial design for the habitation and work modules was shaped as a large loop connected by hatches. This, too, was modified to eliminate the need for going all the way around the loop to reach a destination and save the space which would have been consumed by the hatches. The dual keel baseline design calls for a parallel clustering of the modules connected by nodes and tunnels which consume little of the working space. Four modules will comprise the initial configuration: the United States Laboratories, the European Space Agency Laboratory, the United States Habitation Module and the Japanese Experiment Module.

A stiff frame is the strong point of the dual-keel, baseline design. Living and working modules are clustered and connected by nodes and tunnels. International in scope, the first modules will be provided by the U.S., Europe and Japan.

Something New At Langley Research Center

A student inspects Space Station bay structure from the MRMS.

A new program has been introduced at Langley Research Center (LaRC) to acquaint students with aerospace. They present a seminar entitled "Aerospace — Gateway to the Future." Students attending receive information on the space shuttle, spacecraft design, crew selection and living in a microgravity environment. As part of the program students are shown how to use computers to design their own space station. They also take a ride on a full size Mobile Remote Manipulator System (MRMS) which takes them on a ride around a full scale space station truss. The MRMS will be the prime construction tool for assembling the space station structure in the 1990's. Some students don an astronauts spacesuit to experience the limits of flexibility imposed by the suit. This annual program and workshop provides students with first hand experiences in a variety of professions which use high technology.

WITHIN EARTH ORBIT

NASA has proven that a dimensionally stable composite exists and can be used in space to construct the frame for the space station.

Space Station Structure and Assembly

Space Station construction must be based on technology which has been proven by testing. On one of the Space Shuttle missions, a truss frame was assembled by astronauts in space. Truss frame construction has been used for both building and bridge construction on Earth. NASA has proven that a composite graphite material and aluminum can be used in space to build the truss frame for the Station. This material does not react to heat or cold, so it will not expand and contract as the Station encounters drastic temperature variations as it orbits the Earth. Composite materials are made by bonding two materials together. One material acts as a glue which surrounds the particles or fibers of the other material.

    Astronauts will work as a team to construct the huge dual keel frame. Each truss section will be a five meter cube. These cube trusses will be connected until a rectangle of 94.5 meters by 45.7 meters is completed. In the middle of this rectangle, a transverse beam will be placed for eventual attachment of the habitation and laboratory modules. All components for the Space Station will be transported by the Space Shuttle on a series of missions.

    The current schedule planned for assembling the Space Station involves

SPACE STATIONS

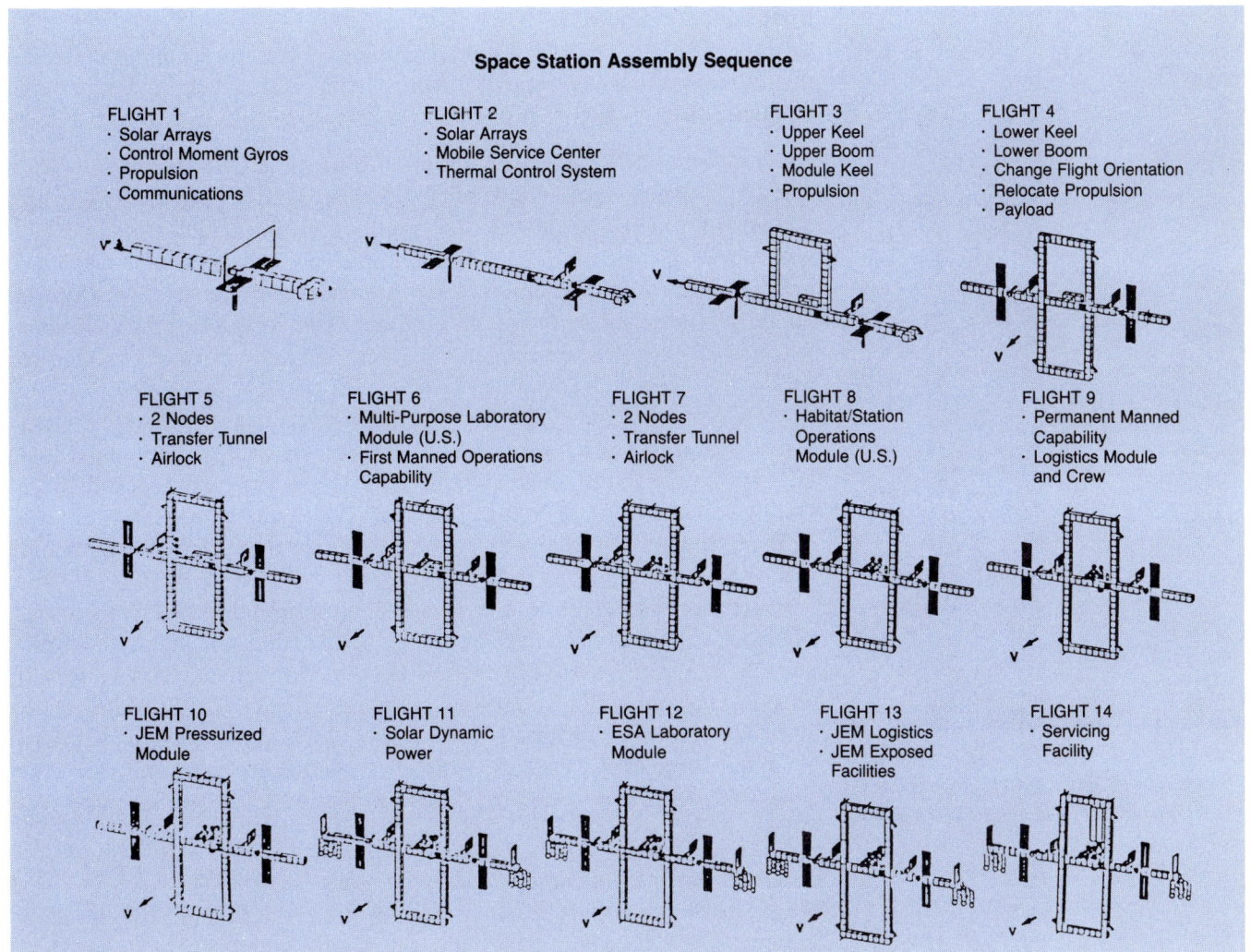

Fourteen Shuttle flights will be needed to assemble the space station.

fourteen Shuttle flights occurring approximately 45 days apart. Each of the segments will be assembled in the cargo bay and then swung out into space with the Canadian-built Remote Manipulator System (RMS). The early Shuttle flights will leave the partially assembled frame orbiting in space as the Shuttle crews return to Earth. Additional work on the frame will be accomplished by later Shuttle crews. Once the frame is complete, the three basic systems for electrical power, stabilization and data links to Earth can be installed. After the sixth assembly flight, the Space Station will have the capability of being manned. By the eighth assembly flight, the habitation module will be in place. The Station will be permanently manned by the ninth assembly flight.

WITHIN EARTH ORBIT

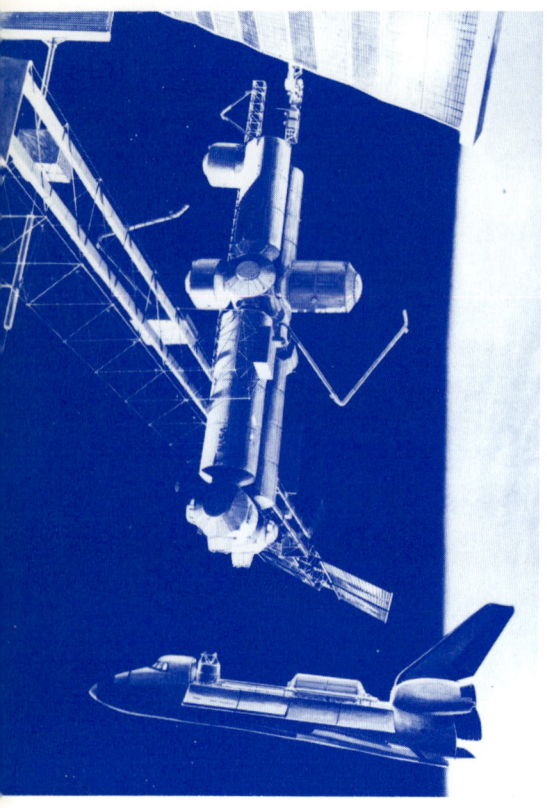

Design, construction and maintenance of the Space Station will foster a new era in space.

Space Station Systems

To build a Space Station is a giant technological feat. To maintain a permanently manned facility requires many systems using new and improved technologies.

Environmental Control and Life Support Systems (ECLSS)

The major elements of the environmental control and life support system are systems to control air conditioning, pressure in the modules, and air and water for sustaining life. The cabin atmosphere will be maintained at a sea level pressure of 101 kilopascals and have air with the same mixture of oxygen and nitrogen as we breathe on Earth. This will permit the astronauts to work in a shirt sleeve environment. When air locks are opened, some air will be lost. This air will have to be replaced, possibly using electrolysis of water to obtain oxygen which can be blended with nitrogen. The electrolysis of water produces both oxygen and hydrogen. The oxygen will be used for breathing while the hydrogen will be used to recover carbon dioxide from the air that the crew breathes. The hydrogen reacts with carbon to form methane and water. The methane will be vented into space and the water will be recycled.

Water, essential to life, will be obtained from a dehumidifier, from urine, and from waste water from experiments. Various filter and membrane technologies will purify water obtained from on-board systems. This water will be used for hand washing, showers and dish washing. The recycling of air and water requires advanced technologies and sophisticated equipment. Temperature control, humidity control, ventilation and waste management (solid wastes being returned to Earth) also require advanced technical systems.

Guidance, Navigation and Control

The Space Station must maintain the correct altitude and attitude. The Station orbits the Earth at an altitude of about 425 kilometers and a speed of 28,000 kilometers per hour. Each orbit will take 90 minutes. The Space Station must maintain the correct attitude in relation to the Sun so that the solar panels can provide ample power to the Station. The correct altitude must be maintained so that the position of the Station is known at all times for both experiments being conducted and arriving Shuttle flights.

Various factors will affect the orbit of the Space Station. Drag is a factor in low-earth orbit where the small amount of atmosphere causes the orbit of a spacecraft to slowly decay. Effects of solar wind as well as the small impacts of arriving spacecraft are also factors in maintaining orbit. Special berthing mechanisms and shock absorbers will counteract movement caused by the Shuttle, the Orbital Maneuvering Vehicle (OMV, see Chapter 4) or other spacecraft. The guidance, navigation and control system (GN&C) will control altitude as well as pitch, yaw and roll attitudes by obtaining the Station's attitude with respect to the stars. Its mechanisms will then maintain that fixed position. The pitch, yaw and roll deviations will be corrected by a control movement gyro. Pressure on a gimbal of the gyro will create a force equal to but in the opposite direction of the initial force. This follows Newton's third law of motion. This force will bring the gyro back to its original position. When that original position is obtained, attitude control thrusters will be fired to stabilize the position.

Altitude will be controlled by thrusters. As forces cause the orbit of the Station to decay, thrusters will be fired when the Station has dropped 48 kilometers from its original orbit. Resupply missions will take place when the Station is at its lowest orbit enabling the delivery of larger Shuttle payloads. After the resupply, the Space Station thrusters return it to its operational altitude.

Propulsion
The Space Station must be able to maintain operational orbit. Thrusters are positioned on each of the four corners of the dual keel frame. The thrusters are the same type as the main thruster engine used on the Space Shuttle, but they are smaller and less powerful. Less power is required for movement in space than for liftoff power needed to escape the Earth's gravity. The thrusters will use hydrazine and nitrous oxide or hydrogen and oxygen.

Power
The Space Station will require more power for its operation, 75 kilowatts, than any other spacecraft. The power will be used by both the spacecraft systems and some of the requirements of users, such as high temperature furnaces used for manufacturing and experimentation. Power for the Space Station will be generated by photovoltaic (solar) cells which convert sunlight directly into electricity. Since large solar arrays contribute to drag, which leads to orbital decay, NASA decided to generate only one third of needed power through solar energy. Small solar arrays, measuring 10.2 meters by 13.3 meters, will generate 25 kilowatts of power. This power will be used directly for Space Station operations. Excess power will be stored in nickel-hydrogen batteries.

The remaining power requirement of 50 kilowatts will be provided by heat engines known as dynamic generators. Parabolic mirror segments on the Space Station frame will be erected to collect heat from the sun's rays. These mirrors can collect heat at temperatures close to 1100° Celsius so that turbines can be driven to generate electricity. This form of energy conversion is more efficient than the solar arrays. Therefore, the mirrors can be smaller and not produce as much drag as the solar arrays. It is anticipated that either the Rankine or Brayton cycle engine will be used (see DeOld, 1986, p. 459-460).

Data Management
The data management system on board the Space Station is known as the Space Station Information System (SSIS). It consists of two global networks, interface units, mass storage devices and standard data and programs. One of the two networks will handle all Space Station engineering and housekeeping data. The second network will communicate commands and data between users and the payloads. Keeping these two systems separate precludes the data from interfering with each other. This is a much safer plan than using just one system.

Communications and Tracking
The communication system for the Space Station needs to be diverse to accomplish the many functions planned for the Space Station. There will be a need to communicate between: 1) ground and Space Station, 2) Space Station and space vehicle, 3) Space Station base and Station platforms, 4) Space Station and astronauts performing extra-vehicular activities, 5) astronauts performing extra-vehicular activity, and 6) astronaut and the ground.

The overall configuration must transmit both audio and video signals as well as large amounts of digital data. Therefore the communication and tracking system will actually consist of many subsystems. During the assembly and checkout stages, the Station will use radios at S-band frequencies (see Chapter 2). The main communication system will use Ku-band frequencies after the Space Station is completed. The S-band radio will then be the backup system. Once the Station is constructed, many antennas will be attached to the boom and directed at satellites such as TDRSS to maintain constant communications.

Fluids
The management of fluids aboard the Space Station will be divided into two categories. Those systems which are not hazardous to the crew will be piped inside the Space Station modules. Substances that are toxic or corrosive will be piped outside the modules as a safety measure in the event of a leak. The fluid system is integrated with the ECLSS, propulsion and thermal systems.

Thermal Management
The thermal management system (TMS) will incorporate new technology not used on previous spacecraft. The system must include radiators, a fault detection system, an isolation and control system, and thermal stage devices. The components must be repairable in orbit. The system must also be expandable as features are added to the Space Station.

The TMS will be divided into three processes: heat rejection, heat acquisition and system integration. When heat must be dissipated, the process of heat rejection will be used. A number of options are being considered, including heat pipe radiators, high efficiency radiator fins and radiator to

SPACE STATIONS

Telecommunications Via Space

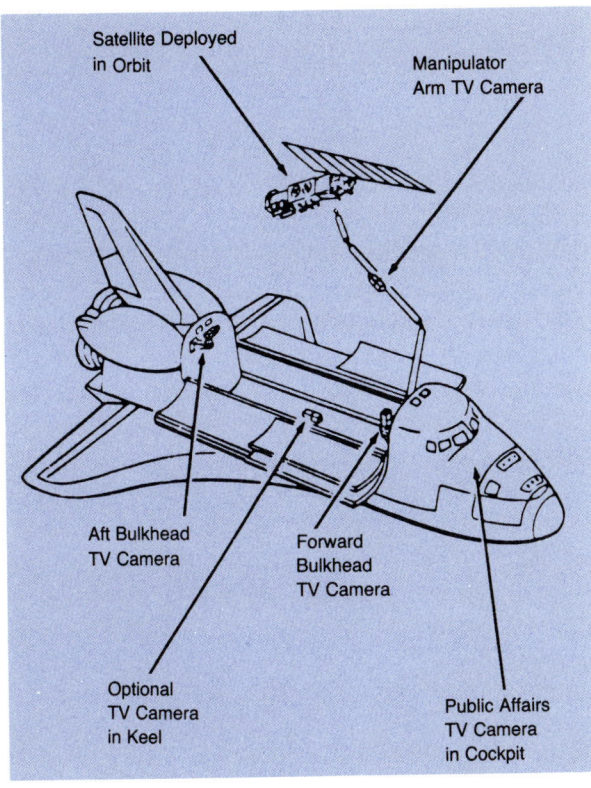

Just a few hundred years ago communication over long distances was accomplished by beating sticks on a hollow log. When wireless communications were developed about a hundred years ago, messages could be sent over longer distances but were limited by the distance to the horizon. Long distance cables soon permitted communications between countries across the Atlantic Ocean. With the advent of the space age, communication satellites in Earth orbit permitted a vast communications network to develop.

Today the Soviet Union and the United States have communication satellites in low Earth orbit, elliptical orbit and geosynchronous orbit. The latter rotate around the Earth at the same speed as the Earth's rotation and appear stationary. These satellites and their corresponding ground stations provide round the clock communication to almost every place on Earth. With the coming of the space station and OMV's, these satellites will be able to be serviced and redeployed without having to be returned to Earth.

heat transport loop interface devices. Radiator devices on gimbals are planned so that the radiators can be orientated to the coldest portion of space.

For heat acquisition, there will be a thermal bus which provides the functions of centralized heat acquisition and transport. It will be a two phase loop providing uniform thermal control for the Station and the users. It will interface with heat loads and heat rejection elements to pass excess heat produced by the heat sources to the heat rejection system.

WITHIN EARTH ORBIT

Space Station Module Configuration

In its initial configuration the Space Station will have four modules. Part of the plan to make the Station an international effort will be accomplished by utilizing modules and elements developed by other countries. Two of the modules will be supplied by the United States. One will be supplied by the European Space Agency and one will be supplied by Japan. These modules will be pressurized at sea level pressure of 101 kilopascals. The Space Station will also include space platforms and a module servicing Station supplied by Canada.

United States

The two United States modules are the logistics module and the servicing facility. The logistics module will handle four types of cargo: pressurized cargo, unpressurized cargo, propellants and fluids. As pressurized supplies arrive in the Shuttle, they are transferred directly into the pressurized logistics module where the astronauts live and work. This eliminates the need for extra-vehicular activity to access these supplies. Unpressurized

The United States will provide the logistics module and the servicing facility.

cargo consists of dry cargo and fluids used for resupply of the environmental control and life support system. It will be placed in a nonpressurized supply storage area until needed. A separate propellant pallet will contain propellants for the Space Station, OMV and free-flying platforms. As these various propellants are removed from the cargo bay of the Shuttle, they will be hooked up and tested before the propellant systems which have been in use are removed to be returned in the Shuttle cargo bay.

The second United States module will be a servicing facility. Its purpose is to permit the crew to service payloads and free-flying vehicles. An astronaut will use an in-bay manipulator system with hands called effectors to grasp the payload or free-flyer. It can then be positioned for refueling or standard maintenance with replacement components. If a payload needs repair, an extra-vehicular activity may be necessary.

European Space Agency (ESA)

A pressurized laboratory module will be supplied by the European Space Agency. This laboratory module will be used for studies in physics, life science research and materials research. Another planned use of the European module is to provide a safe haven for astronauts in case of a systems failure or other unexpected problem that might occur elsewhere in the Station. The module will be similar in size to the two United States modules.

Japan

The fourth module to be part of the Space Station is the Japanese Experiment Module (JEM). This module will be pressurized and have an airlock to an external facility. It will be equipped to handle general science and technology research activities including microgravity research. The airlock which links the pressurized module to the external facility will be used to transfer materials and experiments to the external environment.

In addition to JEM, plans call for an Experiment Logistics Module (ELM) which attaches to the JEM, but can be removed and returned to Earth to deliver experiments and products. It can then be refilled with new materials and experiments and brought back to the Station and reattached to the JEM.

Canada

Another element of the Space Station to be used by all of the modules is being built by Canada. It is a Mobile Servicing Center (MSC). Its design expands on techniques already developed for the Canadian-built manipulator arm on the Space Shuttle. The MSC will consist of a base for payloads, orbital replacement units, utilities and thermal control units. This portion of the Space Station will contain the Space Station Remote Manipulator System as well as special purpose dexterous manipulators, end effectors and servicing tools. It will have both internal and external control stations.

WITHIN EARTH ORBIT

Canada is coordinating its system with NASA since NASA is developing the transporter which will be used to move the MSC along the Station truss structure.

The initial function of the MSC will be to help assemble the Station. Afterwards, it will aid in maintaining the Station through external servicing of attached payloads, and moving equipment and supplies around the Station. It will also be capable of deploying and retrieving satellites and lending support to astronauts during extra-vehicular activity.

Other Platforms

The ESA and NASA are also studying polar orbiting platforms which will accommodate payloads for land, ocean, solar and atmospheric observations, plasma physics, remote measurements and environmental effects monitoring. The polar platforms are part of the initial configuration of the Space Station Program. Plans are for the ESA and NASA to each provide two platforms to accommodate various payloads in a low inclination orbit. These platforms will be self powered through solar panels but will be maintained and refueled by returning to the Space Station.

Working and Living at the Space Station

Astronauts will be very busy aboard the Space Station. Many users' payloads will be delivered by the Shuttle. Instead of docking, a concept known as berthing will be used to connect the vehicle to the Station. Docking involves the vehicle propelling itself to the Station, with a hard bump occurring to complete the docking action. This bumping can cause the Station to move and possibly interfere with on-going experiments. In berthing, a vehicle maneuvers to within a few centimeters of the docking port. Then a Space Station mechanism reaches out and grasps the vehicle and draws it slowly to the port, thus eliminating the bumping action. The payloads will be off-loaded by astronauts using the Canadian MSC. Other payloads may also arrive after being transported by expendable launch vehicles such as the European Ariane 5 or the Japanese H-2. These payloads will have to be retrieved and attached to the Space Station after which they will have to be moved to an external platform area or transferred through one of the hatches into the pressured modules. Other payloads will also arrive via the OMV (see Chapter 4), which will have retrieved a satellite or experiment from orbit and then returned it to the Station.

Once at or in the Station complex, the work of experimentation, manufacturing or research can be conducted. Some activities may include: pharmaceutic manufacturing, celestial observation, physics experimentation, low gravity experiments, weather reporting, communications, resource analysis, exotic alloy manufacturing, satellite repair, biomedical crystal formation, servicing of satellites and platforms, Earth sciences, life sciences, astrophysics and solar observation.

SPACE STATIONS

Berthing is one way of avoiding the transmitted jolt that goes with docking. Such a jolt could disrupt experiments going on in the station.

Space Stations and the Future

Space Stations are stepping stones to the future. While not yet on the drawing board, manned missions to the lunar surface or Mars would ideally be launched from a Space Station. It would require considerably less power to launch from a near zero gravity base for such expeditions. A Station could also serve as a base for a short term manned mission into geosynchronous orbit or a manned mission to examine meteors and asteroids. It could be used as a staging area for unmanned missions to the planets and a return site for samples to be analyzed.

Space exploration is sure to push the frontiers of many new technologies, including life support systems, materials processing, drug synthesis, Earth observations, computer programming and robotics. In the field of robotics, experimentation has already been done with a helmet that, when worn by a person, slaves a vehicle to move in response to the operators head. There may also be a need for a robot with arms which could be brought to a malfunctioning satellite by the OMV. One arm would hold the satellite in space while the other two replaced depleted or faulty units. The OMV could then return the repair robot to the Station or take it to another site for on-orbit repairs. Future Space Stations will be multifunctional bases for many activities, some of which we have yet to dream about.

WITHIN EARTH ORBIT

At Work on the Space Station

IMAGINE YOU ARE an astronaut on the space station. You have been in space for one month out of your scheduled four month assignment. As you wake up you find yourself floating in your sleeping bag, tethered to the wall. Two of the other astronauts have already risen. They can be heard in the kitchen, opening food bags. The fourth member of the crew is still sleeping. His arms are floating up near his shoulders. It is time to start work, so you unhook your tether and pull yourself along the handholds as you glide through the station to the kitchen area for breakfast.

After breakfast you clean yourself with premoistened towels. You would prefer a shower, but only one astronaut a day can take one. Partly because of this, the odors on the space station are offensive at first, even though the air is filtered. But after a few days you get used to it.

Outside the station the view is spectacular. The sun is setting again and brilliant colors light up the edge of the Earth. Since the station orbits the earth every hour and a half you work through about eleven sunrises and sunsets and sleep through about five sunrises and sunsets. Since humans are so accustomed to a 24-hour day, you and the other astronauts all keep on this schedule.

The first work for the day is to check the status of the most important space station systems. You and another astronaut go over many checklists on the computer. At the main console, the computer provides the status information that you ask for. Certain things, like air pressure and battery charge, are so important that one of you is responsible for checking instruments such as pressure gages and voltmeters in addition to checking their status on the computer. As you continue the computer checks, you see that the attitude control system shows a warning light on the computer console. After you select the proper menu on the touch-sensitive terminal screen, the computer program indicates that an orbit adjustment will be needed within 24 hours. Automatic checks with computers at the mission control center confirm that this is necessary. It should be initiated tomorrow, so you add it to the work schedule.

After many more checks of the systems on the station, it is time for the morning break. Years ago it was found that too much work with no time for relaxing affected astronauts' attitudes and performance. There had even been a work boycott on a Skylab mission in the 1970s. The astronauts were so exhausted from the work schedule imposed on them by ground controllers that they simply stopped work. Breaks for relaxing were quickly made an accepted part of the workday. Yesterday you took pictures of the Earth, but today you spend the half hour break star-gazing. Many more stars can be seen from outside the Earth's atmosphere than from the ground.

136

SPACE STATIONS

Life aboard the Skylab in the 1970s obviously had its happy moments.

Today you spot twelve constellations. Other crewmembers are reading books today. On occasion, one crewmember even practices his saxophone.

Before working again, the daily exercise session begins. Use of the exercise bicycle and isometric springs is very important. If muscle tone is not maintained, you would have a very difficult time readjusting to Earth's gravity after going home. To safeguard your health, when you first arrived at the station, medical checks were made every day during and after exercise. Now you only do these tests once a week.

After your long workout you have a quick lunch. Then you begin your work again. An extra-vehicular activity (EVA) is scheduled for you to repair a satellite. The orbital maneuvering vehicle (OMV) brought in a science satellite a few days ago. Yesterday you worked in the mobile servicing center (MSC) to berth the satellite with the space station. Now it is ready for refurbishing. You don a spacesuit with the help of your partner and then prebreathe oxygen while waiting for decompression in the airlock. After opening the hatch to the vacuum of space, you pull yourself out to the area where you don the manned maneuvering unit (MMU). You are soon floating free of the space station, surrounded by the still blackness of space. You slowly propel yourself to the other end of the station where spare fuel tanks are stored. Upon returning with the tank, you radio to your partner in the MSC that you are ready to begin work on the satellite. He looks out the window and controls manipulator arms and grips which assist you. The satellite is opened up and the old fuel tank is removed. You replace it with the new one. A battery and a radio must also be replaced, but today you only have time to remove the old ones from the satellite. You then return to the airlock, doff the MMU, enter the airlock and eventually take off the space suit.

Again you meet with the crewmembers for a meal in the kitchen area. This time you are all a little tired so you relax by being silly with floating food. An after-dinner break is spent listening to music on earphones while watching the Earth slowly spinning below.

Next you assist a crewmember in the experiments area. She is an expert on growing crystals in zero gravity, so you pay close attention to explanations of the experiments being monitored. Being an astronaut means that you must always be eager to learn new things.

At the end of the day, you all draw straws to see who will be first to phone home. Short calls are allowed each day to speak to families. After saying good night to your family, you do the same to your crewmates. Everyone glides into the tethered sleeping bags as the day ends. With three months to go, you fall asleep realizing that the adventure of living and working in space provides an exciting challenge every day.

WITHIN EARTH ORBIT

Summary

The Soviet Union was the first nation to have a Space Station. The development of their stations was in three phases: the first generation Salyut Stations with one docking port, the second generation Salyut Stations with two docking ports and the third generation Mir Station with six docking ports and improved computer systems. The Soviets have made a commitment to manned spaceflight and learning about long duration effects on humans living in space.

The United States has used one Space Station called Skylab. Currently plans are underway for a large dual keel Space Station. The Station is expected to be in place by the late 1990s. The United States Space Station will be launched through the use of a reusable Space Shuttle as opposed to using expendable launch vehicles. The Station will make use of advanced technological systems to maintain life aboard the Station. It is anticipated that Space Stations will serve as the base for many additional space activities in the future.

Terms

avionics
axial docking ports
berthing
composite material
deployed
dual keel
effectors
free-flyer
geosynchronous orbit
Kvant
Mir
modules
nodes
oscillate

parabolic mirror
photoreconnaissance
photovoltaic cells
power tower
Progress
Salyut
Skylab
slaving
solar wind
Soyuz
thrusters
trajectory
truss frame

Important People, Ideas and Events

- In 1971, the Soviet Union orbited the first Space Station.
- The United States launched Skylab in 1973.
- President Reagan initiated the United States Second Generation Space Station in a 1984 speech.
- The first crew transfer takes place in 1985 aboard Salyut 7.
- In 1986, international cooperation between the United States, the European Space Agency, Japan and Canada takes place in planning Space Station modules.

- Mir becomes the first Space Station complex of four modules through successive dockings in 1987.
- During the 1990's, the construction of the dual keel United States Space Station takes place.

Interesting Things to Do

1. Write to Canada, the European Space Agency and Japan for updates on module development.
2. Keep a notebook or scrapbook from newspapers and magazines following the construction progress of the United States Space Station.
3. Construct models of various types of truss frames that might be used for future Space Stations.
4. Decide how many rotations per orbit are needed for a Space Station to stay pointed down at Earth.
5. Construct models of Space Station modules.
6. All of the following are directly attributed to aeronautics and space exploration:

    1 Insulin Infusion Pump
    2 Reading Machine For The Blind
    3 Vehicle Controller For The Handicapped
    4 New Window Into The Human Body
    5 Weather Forecasting
    6 Voice Controlled Wheelchair And Manipulator
    7 Speech Autocuer
    8 Water Recycling
    9 Scratch Resistant Glasses
    10 Advanced Wheelchair
    11 Laser Heart Surgery
    12 New Flame Resistant Materials
    13 Dental Braces
    14 Search And Rescue
    15 Anti Corrosion Paint
    16 Advanced Turboprop
    17 Breathing System For Firefighters

For more detailed information on these spinoffs from space exploration write to:

Superintendent of Documents
United States Printing Office
Washington, D.C. 20402

Request the latest edition of *Spinoff*.

GLOSSARY

Accelerometer a device, usually consisting of a spring on a mass, which senses acceleration by measuring the movement of the spring when the mass moves.
Actuator a device that transforms an electronic signal into a mechanical motion using hydraulic or pneumatic power.
Attitude the direction an object is pointing on the pitch, roll, and yaw axes.
Avionics the application of electronics to systems and equipment used in aeronautics; a combination of the words aviation and electronics.
Axial docking port a port at one end of Mir which aligns an arriving vehicle with the axis of the Mir Station.
Berthing the use of a mechanical device to draw a space vehicle in for soft docking with the Space Station.
Bipropellant one of two propellants required for combustion.
Booster a rocket or launch vehicle.
Bulkhead a transverse dividing wall which provides access between internal sections of a vehicle.
CAD computer aided design; a computer tool for drawing and calculating design parameters.
Centi a prefix meaning 1/100.
Communication subsystem the part of a system which includes communication equipment, usually radios.
Control subsystem the part of a system which controls the motion of the system.
Conduction the transfer of heat through a solid object.
Controller a person who controls a space mission; a device which controls a subsystem.
Cryogenic super cold; often used in reference to fuels or oxidizers that liquify only at very low temperatures.
Data bus a communication path used for the transfer of information between the devices connected to it.
Deboost to reduce vehicle velocity to less than that required to remain in orbit; same as deorbit.
Deorbit to reduce vehicle velocity to less than that required to remain in orbit; same as deboost.
Deploy to place a satellite in its orbit; to activate a mechanism by turning it on and swinging it into place.
Doffing taking off clothing or a spacesuit.
Donning putting on clothing or a spacesuit.
Drogue a small anchor parachute which deploys to stabilize and slow a craft before the main chutes are released.
Dual-keel a rectangular framework which is structured into two main legs, to which the United States Space Station modules are attached.
Effector a mechanical device which responds to inputs by grasping objects, similar to the way a hand does.
Elevon a horizontal aerodynamic control surface which controls pitch.
ELV expendable launch vehicle; a rocket which is only used once.
ESA European Space Agency; an organization which manages space transportation for European countries.
EVA extra-vehicular activity; moving outside of a space vehicle.
External tank a large liquid-fuel tank to which the Space Shuttle is attached prior to and during launch.
Fail-safe a property of a system which keeps working after some parts fail because it has redundant parts to replace them.
Fairing a shell-like nose cone on top of a launch vehicle which protects the payload during launch.
Free-flyer an independent vehicle or platform that can be sent from a Space Station into its own orbit and can return under its own power.
Frustrum a truncated cone on top of a solid rocket booster which joins the nose cone to the booster.
FSS flight support system; an MMU subsystem.
Geosynchronous an orbit in which a satellite revolves around the Earth at the same rate at which the Earth rotates on its axis, thereby appearing stationary to people below it.
Gimbal a device which provides a point of rotation and allows an engine or thruster to point in different directions.
GPS global positioning system; a set of satellites used to aid navigation.
Grain the molded shape of solid propellants in a rocket.
Gram the metric unit of mass.
Grapple a mechanism that grabs and locks onto another object.
Guidance subsystem the part of a system which determines the course of the system.
Gyro a device which measures rotation or attitude.
Honeycomb a lightweight but strong structure based on the beehive honeycomb shape.
HOTOL horizontal take-off and land; the official name of an aerospace plane proposed by British Aerospace.
Hypersonic far above the speed of sound; typically above Mach 5.
ICBM intercontinental ballistic missile; a type of rocket originally used to launch bombs.
Jettison to release or discard.
Kilo a prefix meaning one thousand.
Kinetic energy the energy of a moving object.
Kvant a Soviet experimentation module which attaches to the Mir Space Station.
LEO low-Earth orbit; an orbit between 100 and 1000 kilometers altitude which is usually circular.
Life support subsystem the part of a system that maintains a livable environment for humans.
Liquid propellant a fluid fuel or oxidizer used to power a liquid-propellant rocket.
Longeron a main longitudinal framing member of a fuselage.
Mach number the speed of an object expressed in terms of the local speed of sound.
Mandrel a core placed in the casting segments of solid-propellant rockets to form a hollow interior.
Meter the metric unit of length.
Mir the third generation Soviet Space Station.
Mission kit extra equipment which can be attached to the OMV to allow it to perform new tasks.
MMU Manned Maneuvering Unit; a powered backpack which allows unteth-

ered human flight.
Modular design a design concept which uses parts which can be easily assembled and replaced.
Modules self-contained units which serve as building blocks for an overall structure.
Monopropellant a chemical that can provide propulsion by itself.
NASA National Aeronautics and Space Administration; an organization which manages the civilian use of space for the United States.
NASP National Aerospace Plane; an American aerospace plane development program.
Newton the metric unit of force.
Nodes connecting sections between two Space Station modules.
OMV Orbital Maneuvering Vehicle; a remote-control space tug.
ORU orbital replacement unit; an equipment module made to be replaced in orbit.
Orbit the path of an object as it travels around the Earth.
OTV orbital transfer vehicle; a proposed reusable vehicle used for placing satellites into geosynchronous orbit.
Orbital velocity the horizontal speed, which varies with altitude, that a satellite must have to stay in orbit.
Oscillate to move back and forth or vibrate.
Oxidizer a bipropellant used with fuel to cause combustion and produce thrust.
Parabolic mirror a curved mirror used to collect and concentrate sunlight for producing power.
Pacal the metric unit of pressure.
Payload a satellite or manned vehicle which is put into space by a launcher.
Photoreconnaissance the examination of territory from high altitudes using specialized cameras to gather information.
Photovoltaic cell a cell in which light causes the generation of electricity.
Pitch up and down rotation of an object.
PLSS primary life support system; an MMU subsystem.
Port the left side of a vehicle when facing forward.
Power subsystem the part of a system which supplies electric power to the rest of the system.
Power Tower one of the initial configurations suggested for the United States Space Station.

Progress an unmanned Soviet resupply vehicle for the Mir Space Station.
Propulsion subsystem the part of a system which causes motion.
Radar radio detecting and ranging; a radio that pulses on and off so that radio echoes bouncing off objects can be measured so that distance and direction can be estimated.
Radiation electromagnetic waves of different frequencies, such as radio waves, infrared, light, ultraviolet, x-rays, and gamma rays.
Ramjet an air-breathing device which can cause propulsion when it moves so fast that incoming air is rammed into it to a high enough pressure and temperature that fuel can be directly added and burned to produce thrust.
Reboost to deploy for a second time; same as redeploy.
Redundancy having extra or backup parts so that a system can keep operating after a part fails.
Re-entry entering the Earth's atmosphere from space.
Reefing a line or rope used to restrict the deployed area of a parachute.
Reference mission a specific mission for a space vehicle to perform, carefully described so that contractors can design the best vehicle.
Reliability the probability that a device will successfully perform its duty.
Remote-control the ability of a system to be controlled from a distant place.
Remote Manipulator System a Canadian built mechanical robot arm used in the Space Shuttle to assist in working in space.
Roll the rotation of an object around its centerline, or roll axis.
Rotation the turns or spins of an object around an axis.
RSR metals rapid solidification rate metals; metals which are cooled from a molten state to a solid state so quickly that they take on different properties than normal metals.
Sanger II an aerospace plane proposal by the German company MBB, named after the scientist Eugene Sanger.
Salyut first and second generation Soviet Space Stations.
Scramjet supersonic ramjet, which is actually a hypersonic ramjet, since it requires speeds far above the speed of sound to operate.

Six degrees of freedom a property of an attitude control system which means that it can cause translation in all three directions and rotation around all three axes.
Skylab the first United States Space Station.
Slaving movement of a device in direct response to the movements or commands of an operator.
Slosh baffles obstructions in a fuel tank which limit propellant movement to prevent oscillations.
Solar wind the flow of atomic particles and radiation outward from the sun.
Solid propellant a solid, chemical mixture containing both fuel and oxidizer, which powers solid-propellant rockets.
Solid rocket boosters a solid propellant rocket motor system which is used to augment the thrust of the Space Shuttle main engines.
Soyuz the Soviet manned spacecraft which is used to ferry cosomonauts to and from Space Stations.
Space Shuttle the American, manned, reusable space vehicle; the generic name for shuttle-type vehicles.
Spacelab a portable scientific laboratory built by the European Space Agency and used by astronauts to perform experiments when it is housed in the cargo bay of the Space Shuttle.
Sputnik the first satellite launched into Earth orbit.
Stage (noun) one of several rockets which makes up a launch vehicle; (verb) to break free from the prior stage and fire the next stage.
Starboard the right side of a vehicle as viewed when facing forward.
Stringer Panel a slender, lightweight structural member used lengthwise in rocket bodies to strengthen and shape the external skin.
Subsonic traveling below the speed of sound.
Subsystem a portion of a system which performs a specific function.
Supercomputer a computer which can make many calculations in a very short time.
Supersonic above the speed of sound; above Mach 1.
System a set of subsystems which work together to perform a mission.
TDRSS tracking and data relay satellite system; a NASA system which uses satellites in geosynchronous orbit to communicate with and track many other satellites in Earth orbit.

Tether   to fasten or connect one object to another by way of a rope or cord.
Thrust   the force acting on a rocket that is a reaction to the action of the hot gases blasting out of the rocket in the other direction.
Thruster   a small engine used for attitude control and precision movements.
Trajectory   the path of an object in flight.
Translation   the movement of an object in a straight line; movement forward, backward, sideways, up, or down.

Trunnion   a strong pin or pivot protruding from the side of an object, used for attaching other objects.
Truss frame   the structure of the United States Space Station which forms its rigid framework.
Turbine   a device which converts the kinetic energy of expanding gases into the rotational energy of a shaft.
Turbojet   a propulsion device which causes motion by compressing air with rotating blades, mixing it with fuel, and sending the hot combustion gases blasting out of the back for thrust, while saving some of the combustion energy with a turbine to power the compressor.
Turbopump   a device which uses the rotational energy of a turbine to push fluids with pumps.
Vortex   the formation of a whirlpool action.
Yaw   left and right rotation of an object in the horizontal plane

INDEX

accelerometer, 18, 19, 53, 95, 97
actuator, 40, 41, 42, 44, 47, 50
aerodynamic drag, 37
aerospace plane, 9, 67–78
    American, 67, 75
    British, 67, 75
    German, 67, 74
aft fuselage, 37, 42, 44
airlock, 38, 58, 104, 108, 109, 110, 112, 115, 117, 127, 128, 133, 137
America Bomber, 67–68
anti-vortex, 37
Apollo, 12, 23, 56, 57, 122, 123, 124
Ariane, 23, 61, 134
astronaut, 27, 58, 136
Atlas, 20
atmospheric drag, 128, 129
attitude control, 53, 107, 121, 128, 136
avionics, 44, 49, 52–55, 121
axial docking port, 115, 117, 119, 120, 121, 134, 135

base support, 84, 87, 88
berthing, 128, 134, 135, 137
biomedical, 116, 118, 134
bipropellant, 15–17
body flap, 42, 47, 52, 53, 55
booster, 12, 13, 14, 15–23, 35, 86, 122
Braun, Werhner von, 12
bulkhead, 109

CAD, 74
cargo bay, 27, 28, 40, 63, 64, 89, 100, 127
cathode ray tube, 55
Chinese Space Launcher, 22, 23
commode system, 48–49

communication subsystem:
    Mir, 121
    MMU, 112
    OMV, 95–96, 97
    Salyut, 117
    Space Shuttle, 53, 54, 55, 59–60
    United States Space Station, 127, 130, 131
computer, 18, 19, 32, 52, 53, 55, 58, 59, 95–96, 97, 99, 120, 121, 136
computer-aided design, 74
conduction, 98
control subsystem, 81
    Mir, 120–121
    MMU, 110
    OMV, 90, 96–97
    Salyut, 115, 116, 117
    Space Shuttle, 50, 52–53, 55
    United States Space Station, 128–129, 130
controller, 23, 32, 41, 95, 104
cosmonaut, 116
crawler transporter, 56
crew transfer, 38, 103, 118, 122
CRT, 55
cryogenic propellant, 15, 23, 32
CSL, 22, 23

data bus, 95, 96
deboost, 84, 86–87, 100
Delta, 16, 20, 23
deorbit, 30, 44, 47, 52, 120
deploy, 35, 117, 134
docking port:
    Mir, 120, 121
    Salyut, 115, 117, 119

    United States Space Station, 134, 135
doff, 109, 110, 137
don, 109, 110, 137
drogue parachute, 35
dual keel, 124, 125, 126, 129

ECLSS, 38, 44, 46, 48–49, 53, 109, 128, 130, 133
effector, 40, 41, 133
elevon, 43, 47, 52
ELM, 133
ELV, 9, 11–24, 68, 83, 134
EMU, 104, 108, 109, 110
Energia, 23, 122
environmental control and life support system, 38, 44, 46, 48–49, 53, 109, 128, 130, 133
ESA, 109, 124, 127, 132, 133, 134
European Space Agency, 109, 124, 127, 132, 133, 134
EVA, 29, 38, 40, 54, 58, 103, 104, 108, 110, 112, 122, 130, 132, 133, 134, 137
expendable launch vehicle, 9, 11–24, 68, 83, 134
experiment logistics module, 133
external tank, 29, 31, 32, 34, 36–37, 47, 52, 56, 68
extravehicular activity, 29, 38, 40, 54, 58, 103, 104, 108, 110, 112, 122, 130, 132, 133, 134, 137
extravehicular mobility unit, 104, 108, 109, 110

fail-safe, 105, 107
fairing, 24
flight deck, 37, 38, 40, 52, 58

flight support system, 104, 108, 109, 110, 112
forward fuselage, 37–38
free-flying platform, 133
Freon, 48, 49
frustrum, 35
FSS, 104, 108, 109, 110, 112
fuel cell hydraulic power system, 46–47, 53

Gemini, 103–104
geosynchronous, 14, 23, 24, 88, 131, 135
gimbal, 12, 18, 24, 34, 44, 52, 129, 131
global positioning system, 97
Goddard, Robert H., 12
GPS, 97
grain, 17
grapple, 41, 88, 92, 93, 96, 99
guidance, 15, 18, 19, 24, 52–53, 96–97, 117, 128–129
gyro, 18, 19, 53, 97, 105, 127, 129

H-2, 23, 134
heat shield, 31, 42, 98, 119
Hermes, 61
honeycomb structure, 42, 43
HOPE, 61
Horus, 61
HOTOL, 75
Hubble Space Telescope, 28, 85
hypersonic, 64, 70, 72, 74, 76, 77–78

ICBM, 11, 12, 20
Indian Ocean, 29, 36
intercontinental ballistic missile, 11, 12, 20

Japanese experiment module, 124, 127, 132, 133
JEM, 124, 127, 132, 133
jettison, 23–24, 29, 40, 62

Kennedy Space Center, 29, 56, 99
kinetic energy, 12–13
Korolev, Sergei P., 12
Ku-band, 54, 59, 130
Kvant, 120

LEO, 14, 24, 62, 70, 107, 115, 117, 128, 131
life support subsystem, 12, 119
  Mir, 121
  MMU, 104, 105, 108, 109, 110
  Salyut, 116
  Space Shuttle, 38, 44, 46, 48–49, 53
  United States Space Station, 128, 130, 133
lifting body, 60
liquid hydrogen, 15, 23, 31, 32, 33, 37, 57, 72
liquid oxygen, 15, 31, 32, 33, 37, 68
liquid propellant, 12, 15–17, 23, 60
logistics module, 127, 132
longeron, 39, 40

low-Earth orbit, 14, 24, 62, 70, 107, 115, 117, 128, 131

Mach number, 70, 71, 72
main engine, 31–33, 42, 44, 47, 52, 94
main parachute, 35
mandrel, 17, 34
manned maneuvering unit, 7, 81, 83, 103–112, 137
manufacturing, 115, 122, 129, 134
meteoroid shield, 122
mid deck, 38, 48, 58, 109
mid fuselage, 37, 39–40, 46
Mir, 115, 120–122
mission control center, 55, 59–60
mission kit, 88, 99, 100
MMU, 7, 81, 83, 103–112, 137
mobile servicing station, 127, 133–134, 137
modular design, 89, 90, 91, 121, 132–134
module, 37, 38
module exchange, 84, 87
monopropellant, 15
MSC, 133–134, 137
multiple payload mission, 84, 87

NASA, 12, 75
NASP, 75
National Aeronautics and Space Administration, 12, 75
National Aerospace Plane, 75
navigation, 52–53, 55, 96–97, 117, 128–129
Newton's Third Law of Motion, 12, 129
node, 124, 125, 127
nozzle, 16, 17, 29, 32, 33, 34, 44, 72
NSI, 34

OMS, 29, 31, 42, 44, 50
OMV, 7, 63, 64, 76–77, 78, 81, 82–100, 128, 131, 133, 134, 135, 137
orbit, 12–14, 44, 62, 81
orbital maneuvering system, 29, 31, 42, 44, 50
orbital maneuvering vehicle, 7, 63, 64, 76–77, 78, 81, 128, 131, 133, 134, 135, 137
orbital replacement unit, 89, 91, 93, 96, 97, 98, 99
orbital transfer vehicle, 88
orbital velocity, 13, 36, 70, 78
orbiter processing facility, 53, 56, 57
orient express, 76
ORU, 89, 91, 93, 96, 97, 98, 99
oscillate, 124
OTV, 88
oxidizer, 15, 17, 32, 33, 34, 37, 44, 45, 57, 68, 94, 119

parabolic mirror, 129
payload, 12, 14, 21, 23, 37, 38, 39, 40, 41, 58, 59, 74, 84, 85, 86, 87, 88, 94, 97, 98, 103, 110, 124, 127, 129, 130, 133, 134

payload door, 49, 50, 103, 109
payload operation control center, 53, 55
payload transfer, 84, 88, 103
payload viewing, 55, 84, 87
photoreconnaissance, 115
photovoltaic cell, 129
pilot parachute, 35
pitch, 40, 41, 44, 52, 106, 128–129
PLSS, 104, 105, 108, 109, 110
polar platform, 134
power subsystem:
  Mir, 120
  OMV, 97–98
  Salyut, 117
  Space Shuttle, 44, 46–47, 52, 53
  United States Space Station, 122, 127, 129
power tower, 124
primary life support system, 104, 105, 108, 109, 110
Progress, 117, 119–120, 121
propellant, 44, 119, 120, 132, 133
propulsion module, 89, 91, 93, 94, 99, 100
propulsion subsystem:
  aerospace plane, 68–74
  expendable launch vehicle, 15–17
  Mir, 120
  MMU, 106–107, 108, 109
  OMV, 94–95
  Salyut, 116, 117
  Space Shuttle, 31–37, 42, 44, 57
  United States Space Station, 123, 127, 129, 130
purge, vent and drain system, 44, 50

radar, 54, 97
radar beacon, 54
radiation, 107
radiator, 130–131
radio and telemetry communication system, 54, 55, 59, 62, 95, 97, 99
ramjet, 70, 72, 73, 77, 78
rapid solidification rate metals, 72
RCS, 44, 45, 94, 96, 100
reaction control system, 44, 52, 94, 96, 100
reboost, 84, 86
redeploy, 27
redundancy, 20, 32, 44, 48, 52, 95, 96, 98, 107
reefing line, 35
reentry, 30, 31, 42, 44, 50, 51, 84, 86–87, 119
reference mission, 83, 84
refueling, 118, 119, 133, 134
reliability, 18–20, 94
remote manipulator arm, 27
remote manipulator system, 40, 41, 55, 58, 62, 63, 64, 83, 89, 93, 99, 100, 127, 133
remote servicing, 84, 87
remote-control, 90, 95, 96, 97, 99, 100, 134
rendezvous, 29, 37, 44, 97, 104
research, 29, 115, 120, 134

143

RMS, 40, 41, 55, 58, 62, 63, 64, 83, 89, 93, 99, 100, 127, 133
roll, 40, 41, 44, 52, 106, 128–129
RSR metals, 72
rudder speed brake, 42, 47, 52

S-band, 54, 59, 130
Salyut, 115–118, 119, 120, 122
Sanger, 61, 74
Sanger, Eugene, 67, 68
satellite, 14, 20, 22, 23–24, 27, 28, 55, 62, 63–64, 68, 69, 75, 81, 83, 85, 86, 87, 88, 91, 94, 96, 99, 100, 110, 112, 115, 131, 134
Saturn IB, 122
Saturn V, 12, 23, 56, 122
Scout, 20
scramjet, 70, 72, 73, 77, 78
Shuttle data processing complex, 60
SISS, 130
six degrees of freedom, 41, 105, 106
Skylab, 103, 104, 122–123, 136
slaving, 135
slosh baffle, 37
solar panel, 117, 120, 128, 134
solar wind, 128
solar wing, 122
solid propellant, 15, 17, 23, 60
solid rocket boosters, 9, 31, 34–35, 36, 44, 52, 53, 56, 57, 62, 68
Soyuz, 116, 117, 118, 119, 120, 121, 122, 123
space debris, 76, 88, 100, 107
Space Shuttle, 9, 18, 27–64, 68, 69, 74, 75, 83, 86, 87, 89, 91, 96, 97, 99, 100, 103, 109, 110, 123, 126–127, 128, 129

space station, 7, 12, 28, 81, 83, 86, 87, 88, 96, 97, 100, 115–137
space station information system, 130
space tracking and data network, 55, 59
Space Transportation System, 27
Spacelab, 28, 38, 40, 109
Sputnik, 7, 11, 12
SRB, 9, 31, 34–35, 36, 44, 52, 53, 56, 57, 62, 68
stage, 74, 75, 122
staging, 29, 53, 135
STDN, 55, 59
strap-on booster, 61
stringer panel, 37
structures:
    OMV, 91, 93
    United States Space Station, 81, 125, 126–127, 134
STS, 27
subsatellite mission, 84, 87
supercomputer, 72, 74

TDRSS, 54, 55, 59–60, 95, 130
telemetry, 54, 60, 117
telephone communication system, 23, 117
television system, 23, 55, 58, 59, 60, 87, 96, 97, 99, 117, 131
tether, 103, 104, 107, 136, 137
thermal control, 44, 48, 50, 51, 98, 127, 130–131, 133
throttle, 53, 99
thrust, 12–13, 14, 15, 17, 31, 32, 34, 35, 36, 44

thruster, 24, 30, 31, 45, 81, 94–95, 96, 97, 98, 99, 100, 104, 105, 106–107, 112, 129
Titan, 20, 23
TMS, 130–131
Tracking and Data Relay Satellite System, 54, 55, 59–60, 95, 130
trajectory, 52, 60, 120
transfer compartment, 117, 127
transverse beam, 126
tripropellant, 15
trunnion, 39, 91
truss frame, 126, 134
Tsiolkovsky, Konstantin Eduardovich, 11–12
turbine, 16, 32, 47
turbojet, 70, 72, 73, 77, 78
turbopump, 16, 32, 33

United States Space Station, 115, 122–137

Vandenberg Air Force Base, 20, 29
vertical stabilizer, 37, 42
von Braun, Werhner, 12
vortex, 37

wing, 37, 39, 43, 50, 67, 68, 69

x-30, 75

yaw, 40, 41, 44, 52, 106, 128–129

zero gravity, 58, 81, 105, 121, 124, 135, 137